The Role of Behavior in Evolution

The Role of Behavior in Evolution

edited by H. C. Plotkin

A Bradford Book
The MIT Press
Cambridge, Massachusetts
London, England

This book was set in Palatino by Asco Trade Typesetting Ltd. in Hong Kong and printed and bound by Halliday Lithograph in the United States of America.

Library of Congress Cataloging-in-Publication Data

The Role of Behavior in Evolution.

Includes indexes.
1. Behavior evolution. 2. Evolution. I. Plotkin, H. C. (Henry C.)
QH371.R63 1988   575.01   87-29693
ISBN 0-262-16107-9

Contents

Preface

Biologists, by and large, have paid too little attention to the possible causal role of behavior in the process of evolution. What follows is intended as a remedy to this deficiency in the literature on evolutionary theory.

The idea that what a phenotype does may in some way be causal in the evolution of the population to which it belongs strikes a slightly heterodox chord among orthodox evolutionists. This is partly because many of the chief proponents of such an idea in the past (including Waddington, Piaget, and Lorenz), as important as they have all been to their own specialist areas of biology, have always been peripheral to mainstream evolutionary theory; and partly because some of the supporters of the position have been Lamarckians, or vitalists, or both. They make uncomfortable bedfellows when one is trying to convince colleagues whose theoretical views are usually somewhere to the center of center. Of course, it hasn't always been the case that elevating individual behavior to a cause rather than just an effect of evolution is something that has been pursued only by those peripheral to the development of evolutionary theory or by cranks, as the first chapter shows. One of the founders of "the synthesis" consistently, if rather thinly, expounded on the importance of behavior to evolution. Recently, an excellent general text on animal behavior—*The Study of Animal Behavior*, by F. Huntingford (London: Chapman and Hall, 1984)—devoted a whole chapter to "the role of behavior in the evolutionary process." And scattered through the literature there are attempts to redress the balance in behavioral biology, where "behavioral ecologists are usually concerned with the way the behavior of animals—as individuals or as groups—may have evolved, with little reference to the consequences such behavior may have for the population dynamics" (M. P. Hassell and R. M. May, "From Individual Behavior to Population Dynamics," in *Behavioral Ecology: Ecological Consequences of Adaptive Behavior*, ed. R. M. Sibley and R. H. Smith [Oxford: Blackwell, 1985]). But as far as I know, this is the first book to be devoted entirely to this matter. The aims, simply stated, are to explore the rudimentary theoretical requirements for such an approach to evolutionary theory and to consider a very limited number of its empirical implications. My concern has been to balance the emphasis on theory that is necessary at this stage with actual or potential empiricism.

The shape of the book is explained in chapter 1, which also outlines some of the conceptual minefields that we, and others before us, have tried to negotiate. What is an adequate theory of evolution? What is behavior, and is it possible to maintain a distinction between behavior and other attributes of the phenotype? Is all, or only some special subset, of behavior both a cause and a consequence of evolution? And what does it all mean in empirical terms? I urge the reader to begin with chapter 1—I have deliberately written it as an "easy read" rather than an exhaustive survey, but it does establish a context for the chapters that follow.

Each chapter was sent for review to independent authorities. I am grateful to Richard Burian, Morris Gosling, Timothy Johnston, Aubrey Manning, Stanley Salthe, Robert Seyfarth, L. B. Slobodkin, and Elliott Sober, who generously gave of their time in this matter. If the book has errors, they are certainly not the fault of these reviewers. Their comments served only to improve the chapters. Robin Dunbar and John Odling-Smee were kind enough to comment on chapter 1. My thanks also to an anonymous reviewer; to Robert Bolick of The MIT Press; and to Margaret Boden, who first put me in mind of The MIT Press as a suitable publisher for this work. Above all, I am grateful to my co-authors, who patiently endured a lengthy review process when they might have published their contributions elsewhere.

H. C. Plotkin

The Role of Behavior in Evolution

Chapter 1

Behavior and Evolution

H. C. Plotkin

Such is the scope for misunderstanding that it is important to say at the outset what this book is *not* about. It is not about the evolution *of* behavior, and nothing in it challenges the assumption that, like all other phenotypic attributes, the behavior of most animals is the product of a history of evolution. Darwin wrote a great deal on what this means for our understanding of behavior and on how behavior should be studied in this light. The classical ethologists, armed with Whitman's dictum that "instincts and organs are to be studied from the common viewpoint of phyletic descent," developed this position with considerable success; and what was essentially comparative field study some decades ago now finds expression in contemporary behavioral ecology, with a powerful analytical base in concepts centering around selfish genes and game theory. This book is not a criticism of behavioral ecology. Rather, it is an attempt to examine whether a case can be made for that same behavior which is the product of evolution, or some portion of it, also and at the same time being a part cause in the process of evolution.

I want to use this introductory chapter to achieve two goals. The first is to show the reader that whether behavior is also cause and not just consequence of evolution is a significant theoretical issue that has not received the attention it deserves from evolutionary biologists. The second is to prepare the reader to understand following chapters better and to see them as a coherent set of writings. That is, I want to outline the shape of the book, explain why it has that shape, and hence show how this book is one kind of approach to the problem of the role of behavior in evolution. As a convenient and optimistic form of shorthand, the first section will be called "the problem" and the second "a solution."

The Problem

I will not attempt here to write a complete history of the ideas relating behavior to evolution. Instead I will be highly selective, trying to extract the maximum on how best to go about examining the role of behavior in evolution by concentrating on the minimum number of writers necessary for that task. I will begin with a little history; then I will consider its lessons.

Some History

Ernst Mayr, who has surveyed 3,000 years of thought about biology (Mayr 1982), has written some interesting essays on behavior (e.g. Mayr 1974). This is important, because the originator of the founder principle cannot be held to be unmindful of behavior. Yet in *The Growth of Biological Thought* there are only three entries in the index under "behavior." True, Mayr specifically excludes ethology from his survey, but that simply helps to put the paucity of references to behavior into a context devoid of considerations of the evolution of behavior. That there are only three references itself speaks volumes. Clearly the thoughts of evolutionists have been elsewhere. However, it is when one examines those few entries that the real problem becomes apparent. One of them is trivial and need not concern us here. The other two, separated by almost 500 pages of text, are startling. Here is the first of them (the second is given in chapter 5 below):

> Since many ecological factors are ultimately behavioral characteristics, such as predator thwarting, feeding strategies, niche selection, niche recognition, all evaluations of aspects of the environment, and many others, one can perhaps even go so far as saying that, at least in animals, the greater part of ecological research is now concerned with behavioral problems. Furthermore, all work in plant as well as animal ecology ultimately deals with natural selection. (Mayr 1982, p. 122)

As it stands, the statement is ambiguous, since it is not certain whether behavior is being referred to as cause or effect. Reference to Mayr's earlier book *Animal Species and Evolution* makes the position clear:

> A shift into a new niche or adaptive zone is, almost without exception, initiated by a change in behavior. The other adaptations to the new niche, particularly the structural ones, are acquired secondarily. With habitat and food selection—behavioral phenomena—playing a major role in the shift into new adaptive zones, the importance of behavior in initiating new evolutionary events is self-evident. (Mayr 1963, p. 604)

Putting these two statements together makes it obvious that Mayr assigns a central role in evolution to behavior. Ecology is intimately connected, he claims, to both behavior and natural selection; and natural selection is one of the key evolutionary processes. The links are not spelled out, but that is the implication. What is astonishing is the incongruity between the magnitude of the claim made on page 122 of the 1982 book and the failure to mention it again for most of the rest of what is a very large book. (When

Mayr does return to it, he does so merely to iterate the point.) In the 1963 book, the role of behavior is referred to only near the end. This incongruity between the importance of the assertion and the lack of discussion of it, I suggest, expresses the absence of an adequate conceptual framework from which to examine the role of behavior in evolution. It is one thing to say that the importance of behavior is self-evident, and quite another formally to incorporate the behavior of phenotypes into a theory of evolution.

Bateson (1979), Hardy (1965), Lorenz (1966), Piaget (1979), Popper (1972), Waddington (1960), A. C. Wilson (1985), and Wolsky and Wolsky (1976) have made similar claims, usually of a similar degree of vagueness. (Wilson is an exception in a number of ways, not least in that he deals in data and suggests some form of mechanism. His work is discussed in some detail in chapter 5 below.) The most frequently stated conception is that behavior somehow drives evolution at a faster pace than would occur in the absence of such behavior, the term usually used to describe this role for behavior being "evolutionary pacemaker." At its broadest, the notion is that behavioral traits change more quickly, for whatever reason, than other kinds of phenotypic attributes, and that they may expose the phenotype to a wider range of selection pressures than would otherwise occur; the latter is thought to lead to general evolutionary change in a population, with the implication, again, that such evolutionary changes occur more rapidly than would be the case in the absence of such individual behavior. Evidence that behavior has the role of evolutionary pacemaker can be seen, it is claimed, in behavioral divergence in closely related species. That "sibling species, in spite of their morphological similarity, often show remarkable behavioral differences" (Mayr 1963, p. 604) is a typical claim of this kind.

Of all the above-mentioned writers, Piaget is the most specific. He invokes a mix of Baldwin's concept of organic selection (not itself a homogeneous notion, because of the length of time over which Baldwin wrote of the idea—so long that it straddled the discovery of Mendelian genetics, and changed its meaning accordingly) and recent work on reverse transcription. The result is that he arrives at an almost Lamarckian position. Piaget's argument is that during development, states of "disequilibria," partly resulting from behavior and partly resolved and compensated for by behavioral adjustments, act to modify the genome. The unstated assumption is that these genetic changes are passed on to offspring when the phenotype becomes reproductively competent. Since behavior may lead to these states of "disequilibria," and may also resolve them, it is behavior that is the "motor" of evolution.

This is no place to enter the debate about Piaget. Suffice it to say that as a philosopher and psychologist he may have been a creative genius. As an evolutionist, in my view, he was a Lamarckian. The need to avoid slipping into a Lamarckian position through negligence is a very important lesson to be learned from Piaget.

One other theorist who warrants singling out in any discussion of the role of behavior in evolution is Waddington (one of Piaget's principle evolutionary gurus), who explored the notion of what he termed an "exploitive system"—"the capacity of animals to select, out of the range open to them, the particular environments in which they will pass their life, and thus to have an influence on the type of natural selective pressure to which they will be subjected" (Waddington 1975, p. 273). The diagram that Waddington often used to depict the exploitive system is shown here (in a redrafted version) as figure 1. As can be seen, the exploitive system is explicitly presented as one of four systems that enter into the evolutionary process, and each seems to be accorded coequal causal status. "Cause" is used here in Mayr's (1961) sense that the crucial events relating to evolution are grouped together as "ultimate" causes, which must be distinguished from proximate physiological causes. Thus, in postulating an exploitive system, Waddington was claiming that the capacity for "choosing" is an ultimate cause in evolution in the same way that genetic replication and propagation is held to be a cause in the process of evolution, or in the same way as natural selection, sorting between variant phenotypes, is also held to have the special status of a cause (perhaps "a causal focus" might be a better term) in evolution.

Waddington was either unable or too cautious to spell out exactly how the exploitive system relates to his other three systems. The most that one can deduce from his explicitly anti-Lamarckian position is that the altered selection pressures caused by the exploitive system (which is some unstated subset of psychological and behavioral attributes) results in canalization of certain developmental trajectories. But although he was extremely vague about the relationships of his four systems, Waddington repeatedly rejected the Lamarckian assumption that changes can be directly written into the genome of gametes by any of his other systems.

Anyone wishing to undertake detailed reading in this area must include the writings of Hardy, Popper, and the others referenced earlier, but the approaches of Mayr, Waddington, and Piaget are representative of the approaches taken by all previous theorists concerned with the role of behavior in evolution. Mayr makes very strong claims without presenting any detailed findings or any substantial discussion, Waddington's explicit statements of causal status are devoid of any analytical or empirical content, and Piaget's attempt to explicate mechanisms is made within an essentially Lamarckian framework. If we are to do better than those who have previously attempted to insert behavior into evolutionary theory in a causally significant role, we must learn certain lessons from their attempts.

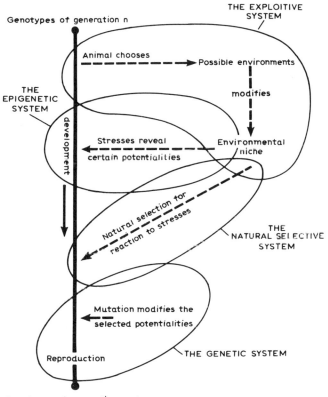

Figure 1
The causal structure of the evolutionary process. Changes in gene frequency between successive generations result from the operation of four subsystems: the exploitive, the epigenetic, the natural selective, and the genetic. After Waddington (1960).

The Lessons to Be Learned

Contemporary neo-Darwinism places great emphasis on events occurring at the genetic level and on the ability to measure evolution by changes in the frequencies of genes in the gene pools of breeding populations (G. C. Williams's [1986] bookkeeping metric of evolution). It is perhaps an overstatement to say that this emphasis on genetics sometimes makes those of us who are evolutionists but not geneticists feel like second-class evolutionists, but I think it is undeniable that many of the criticisms leveled at neo-Darwinism come from developmentalists, ecologists, cognitive scientists, and the like who feel that their access to evolutionary theory is by way of the theory as an explanatory device for their area of biology rather than by way of their subject matter entering in a causally significant way into the theory. It is one thing to say that X is a product of evolution and quite another to say that X is one of the component processes or mechanisms of evolution. In other words, a common complaint is that neo-Darwinism has too narrow a base to explain how evolution works.

If there is any truth in the observation that too much causal status in evolutionary theory is focused on genetics, then there is a very important lesson to be learned from the history of attempts to get behavior into evolutionary theory in a causal role. It is that to assert our claims we do *not* necessarily need to show direct causal links between genetics and the phenomena that constitute our specialist area of knowledge. In other words, we must separate the problem of relating behavior to genetics from that of relating behavior to evolution. These are quite different issues, and any attempt to fuse them by arguments that go something like "Genetics is central to evolution; behavior must therefore be related to genetics if behavior is to be related to evolution" are simply wrong—the mechanisms mediating the direct causal links between behavior and genetics just do not exist, and any attempt to create them results in a Piagetian form of Lamarckism.

That, then, is the first and obvious lesson to learn: One must not succumb to the prejudice that, because genetics is considered to be so important, the establishing of direct causal links with genetics is the only good answer to our problem. Waddington's exploitive system, as undeveloped a scheme as it was in his hands, was a quite different kind of approach. What Waddington claimed was that a causal explanation of evolution cast purely or even primarily in terms of genetics will be incomplete, that seeking direct links between behavior and genetics is wrong, and that a more complete theory of evolution entails complexity and subtlety that cannot be encompassed by a genetic reductionism. Simple and elegant as this may be, it isn't enough.

Complexity of explanation and theory for its own sake is not something that any scientist aims for. If genetic reductionism would suffice, then we would all feel content with such a theory of evolution. But certain biological phenomena do seem to require a more complex theoretical structure if they are to be meshed into a general theory of evolution. Development, it is being claimed with increasing frequency (Thomson 1986), is one such phenomenon. This book argues that behavior, or certain particular forms of behavior, is another. That, then, is the second lesson we learn from a brief glance at the literature in this area: We are going to need more complexity in the theory, but no more than is necessary.

It is important to be clear about what is meant by complexity in this context. Theories are causal explanations. Any attempt to consider the role of behavior in evolution is a specific examination of the causal role of a particular aspect of the phenotype in evolution. The question would not be asked, the issue would not have been raised, and this book would not have been written if it were felt that existing evolutionary theory already supplied an adequate causal explanation for evolution. It is doubt about the sufficiency of the "causal shape" of orthodox neo-Darwinism that is being questioned.

There is a third lesson to be learned from previous approaches to the role of behavior in evolution. *Behavior* is a word with very wide meaning. Its origin lies in the Latin *habere* (meaning "to have"), according to the Oxford English Dictionary. Its most general meaning is "having possession of" or "being characterized by." If the word is used in this broad sense, questions about the role of behavior in evolution are a curiously restricted phrasing of the much wider question about the role of the phenotype in evolution. But that is not the question being asked here, and it was not the question asked by previous writers. Behavioral biologists simply don't use the word *behavior* to refer to all aspects of the phenotype. They usually mean some interaction of the whole animal with its environment, such as occurs when a single-cell organism moves down some chemical gradient or when a bird migrates from one geographic region to another. It can also mean a more restricted form of interaction, for example the manual manipulation of a twig by a chimpanzee or a vocal warning signal of vervet monkey. The range is still enormous, but all forms are held together by the common notion of *behavior* as a word describing some kind of "doing" rather than "having."

This is not an easy distinction to make or hold to, but in general it does leave us with a good sense of what *behavior* is taken to mean by contemporary behavioral biologists. That, then, raises two immediate questions.

The first question is: Just how specific can one be about behavior as a property of the phenotype? For example, can tree climbing be distinguished from a morphological attribute—such as digit (metacarpal and phalange) length—that is going to be an important determiner of the form and the efficiency of the climbing behavior? The answer must be that the distinction can be made. More than that, it must be made. This is because if the answer were No, then, since every phenotypic attribute relates to every other, we would be back to the undifferentiated question of the role of the phenotype in evolution. But the intuition upon which this book is based is that it *is* important to distinguish behavior from other phenotypic attributes. Put more strongly, it is my intuition that it is precisely because behavior is at once cause and consequence of evolution, whereas most phenotypic attributes are just consequence, that makes behavior different from those other phenotypic attributes.

Such a line of argument may prompt the retort that, since natural selection always acts *on* the phenotype, every aspect of the phenotype is therefore both cause and consequence of evolution. But this misses the point that is being argued here as the reason why the whole issue of the role of behavior in evolution warrants close examination: that behavior is an active co-agent *along* with natural selection in causing evolution, rather than that evolution is caused by natural selection acting alone on passive phenotypes. It is behavior that transforms the phenotype into something that actively affects the natural selection to which it is subjected.

That still leaves us with the problem of how to make the distinction between behavior and other phenotypic attributes. One way of doing so is to be guided by Piaget's (1979, p. ix) definition: "By 'behavior' I refer to all action directed by organisms toward the outside world in order to change conditions therein or to change their own situation in relation to these surroundings." Sidestepping the spectre of intentionality that it raises, the definition is clearly a device by which one can distinguish between (on the one hand) "climbing" and (on the other hand) "metacarpal length" and all other phenotypic attributes that are essential supporting features of the behavior but are not the behavior itself. It also helps us to make another necessary distinction: that, for example, between micturition in a dog when that micturition is properly to be understood as a problem in renal physiology and micturition as behavior when the micturition is a part of the scent-marking of a territory. In human behavior, coughing can serve as the example: It is respiratory physiology when what causes a cough is a tickle in the throat, whereas it is behavior when a cough is used to attract attention or solicit sympathy.

Piaget's definition is entirely consonant with chapter 4 of this book, in which Odling-Smee treats behavior in an "unrestricted" way—that is, as if behavior should be seen and dealt with as a single subset of phenotypic attributes. That leads to the second question: Given that behavior can be demarcated from other phenotypic attributes, should it be subject to further subdivision—i.e., considered in a more "restricted" way?

Mayr paints with a very broad brush, seeming to lump "predator thwarting" and "feeding strategies" together with "habitat and food selection."

Waddington, however, employs a much more restricted usage insofar as the role of behavior in evolution is concerned. He quite clearly places some kind of semi-autonomous "choice" device as the controlling structure at the heart of the exploitive system. For Waddington, movement from A to B that does not involve choice is different from the same movement from A to B that does follow from a choice so to move.

Waddington's distinction can be better understood with the help of an analogy I have used elsewhere (Plotkin 1987): When American space scientists were preparing to send an unmanned space vehicle to explore the surface of Mars, they were faced with the problem that the radio transmission times between Mars and Earth made moment-to-moment control of Mars Rover's behavior from Earth impossible. Thus, they had to build some artificial intelligence ability into Mars Rover. If Mars Rover was to negotiate Martian holes and boulders successfully, and, surviving these hazards, to carry out experiments appropriate to its current circumstances, then it had to be able to make some of its own decisions on the basis of its own knowledge-gaining structures. This meant that part of its artificial-intelligence capacity had to allow Mars Rover to generate *its own causes* for its behavior, independent of its designers and controllers. Thus, a causal explanation of part of Mars Rover's behavior is vested in its intelligence and its immediate history and not just on the design boards of its earth bound engineers. Mars Rover had been given a capacity to choose—an exploitive system. The "causal shape" of an explanation of one or another feature of Mars Rover's behavior depends on whether that capacity for choice operated prior to the execution of that particular behavior. If it did not, then the "causal shape" need not extend beyond the design and construction of Mars Rover (which are roughly analogous to genetics and development in biological terms). But if choice did operate, the "causal shape" of the explanation of that behavior must be extended to include the cognitive or intelligence mechanisms inside Mars Rover's "head."

Now, whether behavior that is a consequence of a choosing intelligence has a role in evolution that is different from the role of behavior that is not a consequence of a choosing intelligence is a question that is left open in this book. As will be seen, we shamelessly face both ways at once. We consider both possibilities, and also the possible relationships between them. All that can be said in defense of this is that previous work has made us aware that the distinction may be important; and further work will show whether or not it is.

In summary, a reading of the literature leads me to conclude that any evaluation of the role of behavior in evolution, and any incorporation of behavior in a causal role into the theory of evolution, requires an expansion of orthodox neo-Darwinism into a more complex theoretical structure and a clarification as to how behavior can be seen as a distinctive subset of phenotypic attributes. In this regard, we need to consider both the possibility that the role of behavior in evolution is different from the general issue of the role of the phenotype in evolution and the possibility that only certain behaviors may have significant causal roles in evolution. Also, though it has barely been mentioned, there is a crucial need for data of some kind to back the theoretical claims.

A Solution

This book is an attempt to satisfy the theoretical needs discussed in the preceding section. It is an expression of the lessons learned from the writings of Mayr, Waddington, Piaget, and others on the role of behavior in evolution. In what follows, I will briefly outline the contents of each chapter and show how it fits into the set of requirements outlined above. The aim is not to summarize the book but to establish its coherence.

The modern synthesis was formed from the marriage of genetics and Darwinian natural selection. As Robert Brandon notes in chapter 3 below, evolution by natural selection has usually been seen as a two-step process. One step is selection acting upon phenotypic variation to result in differential reproduction; the second is the inheritance, by genetic transmission, of the genetic differences that lead to phenotypic differences. Thus, selection acts upon the phenotype, and that which is selected—the genes—provides for the continuity of selected characters in time. Genes, if selected, are able to replicate themselves with a high degree of fidelity, and so their structure, in the form of copies, is very long-lived; the phenotype, whatever its fate with regard to selection, has a relatively short-lived structure.

Over the last two decades or so, neo-Darwinism has taken on a strong reductionist flavor (Williams 1986). There has been a tendency to assume that the primary cause for evolution is vested in "the continuance of the dependent germ plasm" (Williams 1966, p. 44). Dawkins (1976, 1982) has developed these ideas into a conception of evolution as the differential survival of replicators. Replicators are any entities of which copies can be made, the paradigmatic form of a replicator being a gene. Replicators are conveyed through space and time by vehicles, the phenotype being the paradigmatic case of a vehicle. It is the vehicles upon which selection acts and whose differential survival results in the differential survival of replicators.

The power of the Dawkins formulation is that it is an abstract account of any evolutionary process anywhere in the universe where life is evolving. It need not be restricted to genes and phenotypes as we terrestrial biologists understand these things. But one of the disadvantages of the Dawkins formulation is that the word *vehicle* has passive connotations. A vehicle transports genes, and may shelter them, but the genes seem to be in command. An analogy is that of the "ducks" in a shooting gallery. For some, the Dawkins conception is that the ducks, as vehicles, are wheeled across the stage in a passive manner. Some are shot and some survive. Would it not be better if the ducks were less passive—if they jumped and dodged and dived, or even changed the environment by exuding clouds of smoke so that they would be harder to see and hit? Dawkins is happy with such active and clever vehicles, because, as I understand him, it would ultimately be genetic differences between the ducks that would cause the clever activity. But in this way "he would restrict the concept of fitness to the genes and not try to salvage its applicability to their interactors" (Williams 1986, p. 24). That is another way of saying that explanatory power in such a theory is always limited for the phenotype, and that has to be a shortcoming for any attempt to vest causal evolutionary significance in some aspect of the phenotype.

In chapter 2, David Hull presents an abstraction of the evolutionary process that serves as an alternative to Dawkins's (though in some respects it is very similar). Instead of vehicles, Hull talks about interactors. The change in terminology is of no importance, and neither, for that matter, are the connotations. But the way in which Hull's interactors shift some of the causal focus away from replicators to the entity upon which selection is acting is significant, and is essential to this book. For Hull, interactors are a part *cause* of differential replication. This is because selection is the process of differential extinction and proliferation of interactors, which in turn leads to differential perpetuation of replicators. Interactors are the causally significant entities upon which selection acts. Behavior, as the word is used and understood by behavioral biologists, is what paradigmatic interactors—phenotypes—do. If the behavior of phenotypes can alter the selection pressures to which they are subjected, there is no reason to believe that the role of phenotype behavior cannot be generalized to the behavior of other kinds of interactors. It should be possible to generalize the notion of the behavior as causally significant in evolution to the activities of any and all interactors.

Hull begins by pointing out in some detail just how insecure the conceptual basis of the modern synthesis is. He then develops a hierarchy of replicators, interactors, and lineages as an abstraction that will encompass any evolutionary process. That this is a much more general and powerful formulation than the traditional genes-organisms-species hierarchy is attested to by Hull's application of the notions of replicators and interactors to conceptual evolution.

Thus, what Hull does is provide a general account of evolution that applies not only to "biological" evolution, as traditionally understood, but also to other kinds of evolution, such as conceptual evolution (in Hull's case, that of science). This is a part of a tradition, going back at least as far as the writings of William James, that holds that human thought and creativity, and human culture itself, can be understood as evolutionary processes—that is, not just as *products* of biological evolution but as *working* by way of the same evolutionary processes that lead to adaptation and speciation. Campbell 1974 is the classic review of this school of thought; the most recent collections of essays are Callebaut and Pinxten 1987 and Riedl and Wuketits 1987. Now, culture, with its necessary conceptual components, is one form—possibly an extreme form—of the role of behavior in evolution. It certainly has influenced human evolution, and doubtless will continue to do so in the future. What is present in such a dominant form in one species may be present to a lesser degree in other species. It is so obvious and important a part of the role of behavior in evolution that it is considered in several other chapters as well. Hull lays the foundations for these discussions with his treatment of conceptual evolution in terms of replicators and interactors.

The application of the replicator-interactor formulation to conceptual evolution is in line with the view of modern cognitive psychologists in general, and of Piaget and his disciples in particular, that the gaining of knowledge is a dynamic and active process. It never occurs passively, and it never occurs in isolation from other knowledge already present in the system. So too with biological evolution. There is a beautiful symmetry in Hull's view of biological and conceptual evolution.

How, though, are biological and conceptual evolution to be related to one another? How, in general, does the conception of an interactor relate to that of its replicators? And if the complexity of a living system is such as to require the postulation of multiple replicators and interactors, how are *they* to be related to one another? What, to use Simon's (1962) phrase, is the appropriate "architecture" for the theoretical complexity that is needed to support an examination of the role of behavior in evolution? Robert Brandon considers this question in chapter 3. The answer is a hierarchy. In itself this is not a novel idea. Brandon and Burian 1984 and Salthe 1985 are recent accounts of this burgeoning area of theory. A previous generation's concern can be found in the series *Towards a Theoretical Biology* (Waddington 1968, 1969, 1970, 1972) and in Ayala and Dobzhansky 1974. What is important about Brandon's contribution here is, first, that some consideration of hierarchies is essential to the undertaking of this book. There is a consensus that hierarchy theory is the way to introduce complexity into biological theory, and no consideration of the role of behavior in evolution can be accomplished without some reference to hierarchy theory. Brandon provides us with that reference. Second, Brandon addresses an issue that, quite apart from its value to this specific task, is important to the application of hierarchy theory in general: How do we distinguish levels of a hierarchy from one another? Specifically, how is the notion of hierarchy to be applied to replicators and interactors? Brandon uses the statistical concept of "screening off" to establish a nonarbitrary basis for distinguishing between levels. Then, using that method, he develops a hierarchy of especial significance to our enterprise: a hierarchy of interactors. He also considers the possibility of a hierarchy of replicators. Thus, his chapter is closely related to Hull's.

Three further points must be made to get Brandon's chapter into perspective. The first is that, in principle, certain behaviors may be used to partially define a level of selection, i.e. an interactor, by the method of screening off. So not only does a hierarchical scheme do important work for an examination of the role of behavior in evolution, but behavior itself may be used to sort out some of Brandon's levels. Second, Brandon makes the point (emphasized above, but of particular significance to a hierarchical treatment of interactors) that behavior may alter both the patterns and the levels of selection. The third point is more general but no less important. As Richard Burian pointed out in a personal communication, Brandon "argues that considerations of parsimony (such as motivated by G. C. Williams in his arguments against group selection) impair the proper testing of evolutionary theories built on hierarchical levels of selection." This is going to be an issue of real importance over the coming years.

Brandon and Hull thus both address and develop general concepts and issues that are the essential theoretical underpinning for an understanding of the behavior of phenotypes in relation to evolution. Indeed, they do more than that. Through much of this chapter and much of this book, the word *behavior* is used to refer to what phenotypes do. But, as already noted, although phenotypes are paradigmatic interactors, they are not the only interactors. That being the case, it must be possible to extend the generality of the argument of the role of behavior of phenotypes in evolution to that of the role of the behavior of all interactors in evolution. Such generality is the ultimate goal of the kind of theory being developed here. But as a first step, the rest of this book is concerned with the role of the behavior of that paradigmatic interactor, the phenotype.

So what of phenotype behavior? What kind of theoretical structure is needed to encompass the behavior of phenotypes, given either the unrestricted definition (that behavior is everything an animal does) or the restricted definition (that behavior is the product of a "choosing intelligence")? This is the problem that F. J. Odling-Smee considers in chapter 4. His focus is an unrestricted definition of behavior; however, his treatment is entirely compatible with Piaget's definition given earlier, and hence is more than just a generalized account of how to get the phenotype into evolutionary theory. By drawing causal links between how individual behavior affects the environment and how the environment affects the selection pressures acting on the phenotype, Odling-Smee shows how behavior and evolution can be related without having to resort to unsupportable notions of intra-organism effects of behavior on genes. He provides, in other words, a Waddingtonian account of the role of behavior in evolution, but with a detail that Waddington never began to approach.

Odling-Smee's starting point is that parents can increase the viability of their offspring in one of *two* ways: by bequeathing better genes for anticipated environments or by bequeathing better environments for anticipated genes. That is, the environment may be altered by the behavior of the parents, and when such behavior increases the fitness of offspring it will be selected for. Within this general framework, Odling-Smee is also able to account for the evolution of learning and memory as devices that will increase the efficiency of niche construction.

For Odling-Smee, then, animals certainly are not passive vehicles for genes. They are interactors in Hull's sense, interactors that partly construct their own environments. Such niche construction, by which interactors alter their own selection pressures, is locked into changes in gene frequencies in populations by a co-evolutionary cycle that is supported by two kinds of inheritance: genetic and ecological. In order to discipline his approach and formalize the ways in which interactors may alter their environments, Odling-Smee offers a formidable taxonomy of interaction types. He also develops the concept of an organism-environment interface as the device that mediates the interaction of the phenotype with its environment. The complexity of Odling-Smee's conception presents the challenge of further refining and simplifying his theory, and, more important, considering how it will generate testable hypotheses. I am certain that it will be further refined, and that it can generate testable hypotheses, but such developments are for the future. One lesson that Odling-Smee teaches us is that determining the role of behavior in evolution is a complex problem, and one that requires a theory that can rise to that level of complexity.

Whereas chapters 2–4 explore the rudimentary theoretical requirements for resolving the problem of the role of behavior in evolution, chapters 5 and 6 share two rather different functions. The first of these is to concentrate on the restricted definition of *behavior* that is pointed to by Waddington's use of the word *choice* in his depiction of the exploitive system. As in the case of Mars Rover, the behavior of the animals discussed in chapters 5 and 6 is the result of the operation of a semi-autonomous cognitive or intelligent ability located inside each animal's head. By definition, behaviors caused by individual intelligence cannot be reductively explained by genetics and epigenetics. These two chapters are thus an examination of the exploitive system in action. And that is the second function of both of these chapters. The role of behavior in evolution is, in the first instance, a theoretical issue. But if the theory merely addresses an empirically empty area, then it ceases to be science. So what these final chapters do is address empirical matters explicitly, first in terms of what is already known about intelligent behavior as a determining factor in evolution and, second, by advancing ideas as to what are potential and feasible empirical undertakings for future studies.

My chapter (5) is devoted to learning and to learned behavior. The phenotypes of some species are able adaptively to alter their own behavior as a result of their own individual histories. This chapter reviews what is known empirically, or what might be possible empirical studies, about how such learning might influence the evolution of the populations to which the individuals belong. This influence may be indirect (e.g., a sharpening of the adaptiveness of behavior) or direct (as in cases where learning leads to assortative mating). Attention is also paid to learning from conspecifics, which, though phylogenetically rare, is one of the prerequisites for the evolution of culture. This book is not specifically about culture. The understanding of cultural evolution is growing rapidly (Boyd and Richerson 1985; Cavalli-Sforza and Feldman 1981), however, and this book does help to bridge the gap between more fundamental (i.e., phylogenetically more widespread) issues in the relationship between behavior and evolution and the study of culture and evolution. Finally, chapter 5 attempts a direct examination of the concept of the exploitive system, especially through the studies of A. C. Wilson: Can learning expand the niche of a species and hence alter, perhaps radically, the selection pressures acting on phenotypes?

In chapter 6, Robin Dunbar deals with how the social systems of vertebrates (primates, in particular)—consequent as they are upon ecological demands and the behavior of individuals—may give rise to their own complex dynamic by which a nesting of different kinds of social groupings is mediated by complex cognitive abilities of individuals as well as by ecological necessity. Dunbar writes as an informed field primatologist whose knowledge of what animals actually do is expressed in a theoretical stance that takes reductionist explanations to the point where the data cannot be contained. Only then does he raise the level of explanation.

Cost-benefit analysis, which helps to understand how inclusive fitness is maximized, has become a commonplace conceptual tool of behavioral ecology. The widely accepted assumption is that whereas humans have the individual intelligence to make the calculations in their heads (though usually rather inexactly and haphazardly), and possibly to adjust their social behavior accordingly, nonhumans generally do not (Maynard Smith 1984). The social behavior of nonhumans is the result of the dynamics of the population as a whole; the "calculations" are performed by natural selection adjusting genetic differences, which are expressed as specific behavioral predispositions. Dunbar, however, suggests that in some species the calculations may be carried out, as they are in humans, by individuals.

If he is correct—and recent studies in experimental psychology have revealed some unexpectedly complex cognitive facilities in apes and Old World monkeys—then the social behavior of individuals is much the more likely to enter, in a causal capacity, into their own species' evolution, just as it must have in man.

The data that Dunbar presents illustrate beautifully the need to extend the causal analysis of evolution in species that have complex social behaviors. Just as in the case of Mars Rover, it is necessary to take into account the "choosing intelligence" that resides in the heads of individual phenotypes. Such behavior cannot be reductively explained in terms only of genetics and epigenetics. The data also provide marvelous examples of how field studies of animal behavior are showing how learned behavior may increase the fitness of individual learners (as described in chapter 5), of the way in which individual manipulation of social relationships partly embodies Odling-Smee's ideas of niche construction (in this case, social niche construction), and of how such behavioral studies link up with the notions of interactors and hierarchies of interactors depicted in chapters 2 and 3. In other words, the findings that Dunbar describes are classic examples of how data can show that theory must be changed and expanded, and of how theory, in turn, can find support in empirical studies.

That, then, is the shape of what follows, that shape being dictated by the lessons learned from past attempts to incorporate the role of behavior into evolutionary theory. No claim is made for the completeness of the book. The data chapters are highly restricted. There is little on habitat selection (Cody 1985 provides wide coverage of this specific topic) or dietary choice, and almost nothing on migratory and predator-prey behaviors. Culture and culturally determined behavior are dealt with only sparsely and sporadically. What is attempted is a specific and limited attack on a large problem that covers extensive areas. If the book is successful in stimulating thinking about the role of other forms of behavior in evolution, then subsequent writings can address the many issues not treated in these pages.

References

Ayala, F. J., and T. Dobzhansky. 1974. *Studies in the Philosophy of Biology*. London: Macmillan.

Bateson, G. 1979. *Mind and Nature*. London: Fontana.

Boyd, R., and P. J. Richerson. 1985. *Culture and the Evolutionary Process*. University of Chicago Press.

Brandon, R. N., and R. M. Burian. *Genes, Organisms, Populations: Controversies over the Units of Selection*. Cambridge, Mass.: MIT Press. A Bradford Book.

Callebaut, W., and R. Pinxten. 1987. *Evolutionary Epistemology: A Multiparadigm Approach*. Dordrecht: Reidel.

Campbell, D. T. 1974. "Evolutionary Epistemology." In *The Philosophy of Karl Popper*, volume 1, ed. P. A. Schilpp. La Salle, Ill.: Open Court.

Cavalli-Sforza, L. L., and M. W. Feldman. 1981. *Cultural Transmission and Evolution*. Princeton University Press.

Cody, M. L. 1985. *Habitat Selection in Birds*. Orlando: Academic.

Dawkins, R. 1976. *The Selfish Gene*. Oxford University Press.

Dawkins, R. 1982. *The Extended Phenotype*. San Francisco: Freeman.

Hardy, A. C. 1965. *The Living Stream*. London: Collins.

Lorenz, K. Z. 1966. "Evolution of Ritualization in the Biological and Cultural Spheres." *Philosophical Transactions of the Royal Society* B 251: 273–284.

Maynard Smith, J. 1984. "The Evolution of Animal Intelligence." In *Minds, Machines and Evolution*, ed. C. Hookway. Cambridge University Press.

Mayr, E. 1961. "Cause and Effect in Biology." *Science* 134: 1501–1506.

Mayr, E. 1963. *Animal Species and Evolution*. Cambridge, Mass.: Harvard University Press.

Mayr, E. 1974. "Behavior Programs and Evolutionary Strategies." *American Scientist* 62: 650–659.

Mayr, E. 1982. *The Growth of Biological Thought: Diversity, Evolution, and Inheritance*. Cambridge, Mass.: Harvard University Press.

Piaget, J. 1979. *Behavior and Evolution*. London: Routledge and Kegan Paul.

Plotkin, H. C. 1987. "Evolutionary Epistemology as Science. *Biology and Philosophy* 2: 295–313.

Popper, K. R. 1972. *Objective Knowledge*. Oxford University Press.

Riedl, R., and F. M. Wuketits. 1987. *Die evolutionare Erkenntnistheorie*. Berlin: Verlag Paul Parey.

Salthe, S. N. 1985. *Evolving Hierarchical Systems*. New York: Columbia University Press.

Simon, H. A. 1962. "The Architecture of Complexity." *Proceedings of the American Philosophical Society* 106: 467–482.

Thomson, K. S. 1986. "The Relationship between Development and Evolution." *Oxford Surveys in Evolutionary Biology* 2: 220–233.

Waddington, C. H. 1960. "Evolutionary Adaptation." In *The Evolution of Life*, ed. S. Tax. University of Chicago Press.

Waddington, C. H., ed. 1968, 1969, 1970, 1972. *Towards a Theoretical Biology*, vols. 1–4. Edinburgh University Press.

Waddington, C. H. 1975. *The Evolution of an Evolutionist*. Edinburgh University Press.

Williams, G. C. 1966. *Adaptation and Natural Selection*. Princeton University Press.

Williams, G. C. 1986. "A Defence of Reductionism in Evolutionary Biology." *Oxford Surveys in Evolutionary Biology* 2: 1–27.

Wilson, A. C. 1985. "The Molecular Basis of Evolution." *Scientific American* 253: 148–157.

Wolsky, M. de I., and A. Wolsky. 1976. *The Mechanism of Evolution: A New Look at Old Ideas*. New York: Karger.

Chapter 2

Interactors versus Vehicles

David L. Hull

The distinction between organisms and species is as old as Western thought. Organisms are discrete, well-organized bodies that go through life cycles and die, while species are groups of similar organisms that mate and produce equally similar offspring. In 1859 Darwin added an evolutionary dimension to both concepts. According to Darwin, organisms are the things that possess the adaptations that allow some of them to cope better with their environments than do other organisms. Some organisms live long enough to reproduce; others do not. Through the culling action of selection, later generations can depart significantly in their characteristics from earlier generations. As a result, species evolve. In this century, genes joined organisms and species to form the basis for our common conceptions of biological phenomena. Genes are discrete bodies arranged linearly on chromosomes. They code for the structure of organisms and are passed on in reproduction. All that is needed to fit genes into an evolutionary framework is to note that on occasion they mutate.

As neat and intuitively appealing as the preceding characterization may be, biologists are challenging every part of it. Some biologists insist that the only entities that need to be referred to explicitly in evolutionary theory are genes. At bottom, evolution is a function of alternative alleles gradually replacing one another. Evolution is nothing but changes in gene frequencies. Other biologists insist that organisms are the primary focus of selection, and that individual genes cannot be selected in isolation from the effects of the entire genome in the production of organisms. Still others maintain that entities more inclusive than single organisms can be selected— possibly even species themselves. Others insist that selection is not as important to evolutionary change as advocates of the synthetic theory think, and that other factors are responsible for many if not most of the changes that occur.

Many of the issues that divide present-day evolutionary biologists are largely empirical, e.g., the prevalence of more gradualistic versus more saltative forms of evolution, the amount of genetic material that plays no role in the production of phenomes, and the extent of genetic disequilibrium. Others stem from the way in which biological phenomena are conceptualized. In this chapter I concentrate on conceptual issues, in particular the way that the traditional gene-organism-species hierarchy has influenced how evolutionary biologists conceive of the evolutionary process. Throughout the history of science, the ways in which scientists have conceived of natural phenomena have influenced the results of empirical research in ways that could not have been anticipated. The story of the tortoise and the hare is only one example. On some very common-sense notions of space and time, the hare should never be able to catch the tortoise; however, it does. Organisms and species are no less common-sense conceptions, conceptions that continue to bias how we all view biological evolution. These biases, in turn, bias how we view conceptual evolution when it is interpreted as an evolutionary process. Behavior evolved as surely as any other phenotypic characteristics of organisms and should be explicable in the same general terms—if they are general enough. Organisms can learn about their environments from interacting with them. What is more interesting, they can pass on this knowledge. They can learn from one another. Social learning has been developed to its greatest degree in science. Might not social learning in general and science in particular be explicable in these same terms? Might not biological evolution and conceptual change both be selection processes? If so, then we are aware of three different sorts of selection processes: biological evolution, the reaction of the immune system to antigens, and learning.

Although the source of a view is irrelevant to its ultimate validity, certain perspectives in the history of science have such bad track records that the presence of one of them in a conceptual system should at least raise doubts about the system. Anthropocentrism has long been recognized as an evil in science, a bias that supposedly was shed centuries ago. Yet it continues to influence the way we conceptualize the evolutionary process.

As organisms go, human beings are quite large, well organized, and discrete in space and time. We also reproduce sexually and give rise to our young in such a way that parents and offspring are easily distinguishable. Our reproduction and our growth are quite different processes. Similar observations hold for nearly all the organisms that immediately spring to mind when we think of organisms. The paradigm of an organism is an adult vertebrate, preferably a mammal. Unfortunately, these paradigmatic organisms are at the tail end of several important distributions. The vast majority of organisms that have ever lived have been small, unicellular, and asexual. According to recent estimates, systematists have described nearly 1.7 million species of organisms. Of these, about 751,000 are insects, 250,000 are flowering plants, and only 47,000 are vertebrates. But nearly all vertebrate species have been described, while most species of insects remain undescribed. According to one estimate, 30 million insect species are probably extant. But even that number shows a bias, because it includes only extant organisms when easily 99 percent of the species that have ever lived are extinct. Roughly 3.5 billion years ago, life evolved here on Earth. Not until 1.3 billion years ago did eukaryotes evolve. None of these were large, multicellular organisms, nor did they reproduce sexually. Multicellularity and sexuality evolved only 650 million years ago, during the Precambrian era. Hence, it seems strange to pick even insects as the paradigmatic organism, let alone vertebrates. The most common organisms that ever existed are blue-green algae.

None of this would matter to science if similar biases did not influence how evolutionary biologists think of biological evolution. When we think of evolution, we tend to think of fruit flies, flour beetles, deer, and humans. We do not think of slime molds, corals, dandelions, and blue-green algae, but if evolutionary theory is to be truly adequate it must apply to all sorts of organisms, not just to those organisms most like us. Multicellularity and sexuality are rare, peculiar, aberrant, deviant, yet nearly all the literature of evolutionary biology concerns large, multicellular organisms that reproduce sexually, and almost none of it deals with the vast majority of organisms. Critics complain of those biologists who want to generalize from the evolution of ordinary phenotypic traits to the evolution of behavior, but we have yet to generalize our understanding of the evolutionary process to the ordinary phenotypic traits of most of the organisms that have lived. If we are not sure whether our current understanding of biological evolution applies unproblematically to reproduction in blue-green algae, perhaps we should be a bit cautious about generalizing to the social organization of African hunting dogs or Yãnomamö Indians. To put this cautionary note differently: One should not dismiss cultural or conceptual evolution as aberrant on the basis of such peculiar phenomena as the transmission of eye color in fruit flies. Perhaps a theory of evolution that would be adequate to handle the entire range of organisms that have functioned in this process might also be adequate to handle cultural and conceptual evolution.

Only a very few biologists have protested the biases so inherent in the literature of evolutionary biology (e.g., Bonner [1974], Thomas [1974], Janzen [1977], Dawkins [1982a, b], Jackson et al. [1986]). They complain that many organisms lack *all* the characteristics usually attributed to organisms. Some organisms are not very well organized, at least not throughout their entire life cycle. For example, organisms that undergo considerable metamorphosis become dedifferentiated between stages, losing all their internal organization. In such circumstances, the parts of an organism can be rearranged quite extensively without doing much damage. Nor are the spatiotemporal boundaries of all organisms especially sharp. Some organisms go through stages during which they dissolve into separate cells. It becomes all but impossible in such circumstances to decide where one organism begins and another ends, whether one organism is present or hundreds. Zoocentrism notwithstanding, plants are organisms too. Furthermore, though a strawberry patch may look like a series of separate plants, below the surface of the earth the separate plants merge into a single network connected by runners.

As foreign as these conceptions are to zoologists, botanists recognize tillers and tussocks, ramets and genets. For example, grasses frequently grow in tufts (tussocks) composed of numerous sprouts (tillers) all growing from the same root system. Which is the plant: each tiller, or the entire tussock? More generally, botanists term each physiological unit a ramet, and all the ramets resulting from a single zygote a genet. According to Harper (1977), natural selection acts on the genet, not on the ephemeral ramets. As Cook (1980, pp. 90–91) remarks: "Through the eyes of a higher vertebrate unaccustomed to asexual reproduction, the plant of significance is the single stem that lives and dies, the discrete, physiologically integrated organism that we harvest for food and fiber. From an evolutionary perspective, however, the entire clone is a single individual that, like you or me, had a unique time of conception and will have a final day of death when its last remaining stem succumbs to age or accident."

None of this would matter much if the organismic level of organization did not exercise such a disproportionately strong influence over the way in which evolutionary biologists tend to conceptualize the evolutionary process. If selection is a process of differential perpetuation of the units of selection, and if organisms are the primary focus of selection, then we had better know which entities we are to count—e.g., whether to count each little tuft of crabgrass in a field or the entire field. In cases of sexual reproduction, the distinction between reproduction and growth is usually quite clear and can be used to distinguish organisms. Offspring tend to be genetically quite different from their parents and siblings, and the genetic differences can aid in distinguishing separate organisms. But in cases of asexual "reproduction," our common-sense conceptions begin to break down once again. If the two cells that result from mitosis stay in physical contact with each other, we tend to think of them as parts of a single organism and to count the instance of mitotic division as growth. However, if the daughter cells float away from each other we treat them as separate organisms and count the instance of mitotic division as reproduction. Thus, the distinction between growth and reproduction that makes so much sense for "higher" organisms makes little sense in such cases. Why is continued physical contact so important? As long as runners continue to connect all the various strawberry plants in a patch into a single network, is it to count as a single organism? If one of these runners is severed, are there suddenly two organisms? As always, common sense is not good enough for the needs of science. (For one set of answers to the preceding questions, see Dawkins 1982a.)

Precisely the same sorts of problems arise at the genetic level. Early geneticists extrapolated from conceptions of macroscopic entities to genes. Genes, they thought, were like beads on a string. As genetics continued to develop and was eventually joined by molecular biology, we discovered that genes are not in the least like beads on a string. Only in very special circumstances can we treat single genes as if they controlled discrete characters. Epistatic effects are too common. Nor is the genome a crystalline lattice. Instead it seethes with activity: genes turning on and off, introns being snipped out, other segments moving from place to place in the genome, and so on. Even though all this turmoil at the genic level may have very little to do with adaptive phenotypic change (King 1984), it cannot be ignored in the individuation of genes. Although evolutionary biologists disagree about the sufficiency of genes for an adequate characterization of the evolutionary process, they all agree about their necessity. If changes in gene frequencies play an essential role in evolution, then we had better be able to count genes.

Williams's (1966, p. 25) solution to the aforementioned complexities is to individuate genes in terms of selection. An evolutionary gene is "any hereditary information for which there is a favorable or unfavorable selection bias equal to several or many times its rate of endogenous change." Just as the limits of organisms are highly variable once one acknowledges the existence of such "nonstandard" organisms as dandelions and slime molds, the limits of evolutionary genes are also highly variable, depending on several contingent factors such as frequency of crossover. In organisms that reproduce sexually, the evolutionary gene tends to be quite small. In cases of asexual reproduction, it can be the entire genome. On the definition urged by Williams (1966) and adopted by Dawkins (1976), the genomes of some organisms consists in hundreds of thousands of genes; those of others in only one. Thus, from the perspective of either Mendelian or molecular genes, evolutionary genes are highly variable in size. Conversely, from the evolutionary perspective, Mendelian and molecular genes are no less artificial chimeras.

The most frequently voiced objection to Williams's evolutionary definition of *gene* is that it precludes neutral genes by definitional fiat. But this objection is no objection at all, because comparable implications follow from any definition in terms of activity. For example, Mendelian genes are defined in terms of patterns of phenotypic transmission. The only genes that count as Mendelian genes are those that exhibit phenotypic variation. If there are no alleles, there are no Mendelian genes. Of course, there are segments of the genetic material that do not have any differential effect on the phenotype. They are no less a part of the genetic material even though they do not function as Mendelian genes. Only if one thinks that a particular gene concept must subdivide all the genetic material into units of some sort or other do the preceding observations count as objections. If Williams's evolutionary gene concept must be rejected because it distinguishes only those genes that enter differentially into the evolutionary process, then the concept of the Mendelian gene must be rejected as well because it distinguishes only those genes that enter differentially into intergenerational character transmission.

Parallel problems arise at the third level of our common-sense biological conceptions, the species level. Given our relative size, duration, and perceptual acuity, organisms seem to be highly structured, discrete individuals; species do not. On the contrary, species appear to be little more than aggregates of organisms. Through the years biologists have chipped away at this bit of common sense as well (Dobzhansky 1951, pp. 576–580; Mayr 1963, p. 21; Hennig 1966, p. 6). However, it was Ghiselin (1966, 1974, 1981) who finally forced biologists to recognize that species as units of evolution are not "mere classes" or "just sets" but are more like individuals. Species certainly do not exhibit anything like the structure presented by the most highly organized organisms; however, they do possess spatiotemporal characteristics, and some even exhibit what is commonly termed "population structure." According to Michod (1982, p. 25), "population structure" refers traditionally to "any deviation from panmixia resulting in nonrandom association between genotypes during mating." But Michod sees no reason not to extend this term to include nonrandom associations during any part of a life cycle. I agree with Kitcher (1984) and Williams (1985) that removing or rearranging parts is likely to have a more serious effect on most organisms than on kinship groups, populations, or species, but the differences are in degree rather than in kind. The distinction that is commonly drawn between well-organized, discrete organisms and these more inclusive entities is not as absolute as one might think.

From these and other considerations, numerous authors have argued that species are the same sort of thing as genes and organisms—spatiotemporally localized individuals. Certainly species do not *seem* to be the same sort of thing as genes and organisms when one thinks of genes as beads on a string and vertebrates as typical organisms; however, once one surveys the wide variety of entities that count as genes and organisms, the suggestion begins to look more plausible. More important, this shift in our conception of species matters. It influences in fundamental ways the manner in which we understand the evolutionary process (Hull 1976, 1978a; Eldredge and Salthe 1984; Vrba and Eldredge 1984; Eldredge 1985). For instance, if species are conceived of as the same sort of thing as genes and organisms, it is at least *possible* for them to perform the same functions in the evolutionary process. For instance, if species are conceptualized as individuals, it is at least possible for them to be selected. It does not follow, of course, that they are (Sober 1984). Ghiselin (1985, p. 141) presents this point as follows: "It would seem that species do very few things, and most of these are not particularly relevant to ecology. The speciate, they evolve, they provide their component organisms with genetical resources, and they become extinct. They compete, but probably competition between organisms of the same and different species is more important than competition between one species and another species. Otherwise, they do very little. Above the level of the species, genera and higher taxa never do anything. Clusters of related clones in this respect are the same as genera. They don't do anything either." Eldredge agrees and notes the irony in the fact that the very people who argued most forcefully for the real existence of species went on to deny them any significant role in the evolutionary process. Once species selection is properly understood, Eldredge (1985, p. 160) is forced to conclude that species result from the evolutionary process but do not function in it: "Species, then, do exist. They are real. They have beginnings, histories, and endings. They are not merely morphological abstractions, classes, or at best classlike entities. Species are profoundly real in a genealogical sense, arising as they do as a straightforward effect of sexual reproduction. Yet they play no direct, special role in the economy of nature."

The point of the preceding is to jar those who are complacently satisfied with traditional, common-sense conceptions. Anyone who thinks that the preceding pages are excessive has never urged a nonstandard view on an intellectual community. The most common response is furious frustration. The world *must* be the way that it *seems*. The certainty with which such observations are proclaimed is historically quite contingent. No longer do ordinary people stamp their feet in frustration as they insist that the Earth must be in the middle of the universe or that space cannot possibly be curved. Many do continue to insist that species cannot possibly evolve. But such responses are not limited to ordinary people. Scientists (not to mention philosophers) are just as prone to such responses when their current common-sense perceptions are challenged. It is one thing to claim that over great stretches of space and time "straight" is "curved." Such expanses are not part of common sense, but organisms and species are. Hence, any attempt to alter how we view these entities is as threatening as any conceptual alteration can be.

As if treating genes, organisms, and species as the same sort of thing were not sufficiently counterintuitive, I have argued elsewhere that stratifying the organizational hierarchy in biology into genes, organisms, and species is "unnatural" (Hull 1980). I am not objecting to a hierarchical view of evolution (Arnold and Fristrup 1981; Eldredge 1985; Eldrege and Salthe 1984; Plotkin and Odling-Smee 1981). To the contrary, I think that evolution must be viewed hierarchically. Instead I am arguing that the traditional gene-organism-species hierarchy is seriously misleading. Common sense notwithstanding, it is "unnatural," and it is unnatural in just those respects that make the evolution of behavioral and conceptual evolution look so nonstandard. Ojecting to *one* particular hierarchical ordering is not quite equivalent to objecting to all such orderings.

For me, a way of dividing the world is "natural" if it produces entities that function as such in general processes. If "genes" are a natural level of organization distinct from organisms and species, then there must be some function that genes and only genes perform in some natural process. As genes are commonly conceived, I think that there are no general processes in which genes and only genes function. The same can be said for organisms and species. There is nothing that all and only organisms do; nothing that all and only species do. To state the obvious: When I claim that there is no function performed by all and only genes, or organisms, or species, it does not follow that these entities perform no functions in any natural process; only that these are not natural subdivisions. Given a particular function, most genes and some organisms might perform it; given another function, most genes and organisms plus some species might perform it; and so on.

At one time, the division of plants into trees, bushes, and plants (herbs) seemed quite natural. Biologists now find it to be of no significance whatsoever. Currently, most people, including most biologists, find the distinction between genes, organisms, and species to be just as natural. It is not. One reason why evolutionary biologists have been unable to discover universal regularities in the evolutionary process is that they are not comparing like with like. They are dividing up the organizational hierarchy inappropriately. The appropriate levels are not genes, organisms, and species as they are traditionally conceived, but replicators, interactors, and lineages. Evolution needs to be viewed as a hierarchical process. The issue is the character of this hierarchy. My claim is that the regularities that elude characterization in terms of genes, organisms, and species can be captured if natural phenomena are subdivided differently: into replicators, interactors, and lineages. If not, this reworking of biological common sense serves no purpose whatsoever.

Previously I have set out the distinction between replicators, interactors, and lineages with respect to biological evolution (Hull 1980) and have shown how they might be extended to social learning and conceptual change (Hull 1982), but my emphasis in those papers is on replication. Here I expand on the notion of interaction with respect to both biological and conceptual evolution. Neither biological evolution nor social learning can be understood adequately entirely in terms of replication. The process that I term *interaction* plays too central a role to be omitted. The sort of social learning with which I am most concerned occurs in science. The account I set out is intended to apply to conceptual change in general, but the sort of conceptual change I emphasize is the sort that takes place in science.

Replicators and Interactors

In his classic work, Williams (1966) redefined *gene* so that the extent of the genetic material that counts as a single gene depends upon the effects of selection. Dawkins (1976, p. 69) introduced the more general notion of a *replicator* to take the place of Williams's *gene*. Replicators include genetic replicators but "do not exclude any entity in the universe which qualifies under the criteria listed." According to Dawkins, replicators are those entities that pass on their structure intact through successive replications. Identity of structure is not good enough for selection processes. Identity by descent is required. However, identity seems a bit stringent for the individuation of replicators. Mutations with varying degrees of effect do occur. Allowing variations that have minimal effect on the functioning of a stretch of the genetic material to count as replicates of the "same" gene would not do excessive damage to the spirit of Williams and Dawkins' notion. Abandoning the requirement of descent would.

In his early writings, Dawkins (1976) emphasized replication so strongly that many of his readers interpreted him as arguing that replication is not just necessary for selection but also sufficient. In the interim Dawkins has "clarified" his position or, as his critics claim, "changed" it (Sober 1984). In any case, according to Dawkins's (1982a, b) current views, replication is necessary but not sufficient for selection. A second process, which I term *interaction*, is also necessary (Hull 1980). Interactors are those entities that interact as cohesive wholes with their environments in such a way as to make replication differential. Thus, selection can be characterized generally as any process in which differential extinction and proliferation of interactors causes the differential perpetuation of the replicators that produced them. Vrba (1984, p. 319) phrases this same definition of selection as follows: "Selection is that interaction between heritable, emergent character variation and the environment which causes differences in birth and/or death rates among variant individuals within a higher individual."

The most important feature of the preceding definitions of selection is that selection involves more than just correlations. As Sober (1981, 1984) and Brandon (1982) emphasize, selection is a *causal* process. In my terminology, replicators produce interactors, and the survival of these interactors is causally responsible for the differential perpetuation of replicators.[1] Brandon and Burian (1984) and G. C. Williams (personal correspondence) have complained that my definition of selection mistakenly includes drift as a form of selection. However, when the notion of *interactor* included in this characterization of selection is unpacked, drift is excluded. An entity counts as an interactor only if it is functioning as one in the process in question. It is not enough that in past interactions it functioned as an interactor. Thus, if changes in replicator frequencies are not being caused by the interactions between the interactors they produced and their environments, then these changes are not the result of selection. In instances of drift, there may be genes and organisms, but there are no interactors, only replicators.

Like Dawkins's notion of replicator, *interactor* is defined with sufficient generality that it is not necessarily limited to one common-sense level of organization. Certainly organisms are paradigm interactors, but entities at other levels of the traditional organizational hierarchy can also function as interactors. Genes, chromosomes, and gametes interact with their environments just as surely as do organisms, and these interactions can influence replication frequencies. Entities more inclusive than organisms can also function as interactors—e.g., colonies, hives, and other forms of kinship groups. If the traditional organizational hierarchy is retained, then both replication and interaction wander from level to level. The obvious solution to this state of affairs is to replace the traditional organizational hierarchy with a hierarchy whose levels are delimited in terms of the evolutionary process itself.

The distinction between replication and interaction is important because it helps to disambiguate the phrase "unit of selection." When gene selectionists say that genes are the primary units of selection, they mean that genes are the primary units of replication. They do not mean to assert that they are the only or even primary units of interaction. For example, Williams (1966) emphasizes the role of genes in replication without proposing that evolution is nothing but changes in gene frequencies. Organisms play as large a role in his discussion as in the writings of his critics, in some cases more so. Conversely, when organism selectionists insist that organisms are the primary units of selection, they mean that organisms are the primary focus of interaction, not of replication. Similar remarks hold with respect to group selection. When Wilson (1975) insists that colonies can function as units of selection, he does not mean that they are replicators; he means that they form higher-level interactors. Some species selectionists seem to maintain that species can sometimes function as replicators, others that they might well function as interactors (Dawkins 1982a; Eldredge 1985; Williams 1985).

Although distinguishing replicators from interactors helps to clarify the disagreements between advocates of various sorts of selection, it does not eliminate them completely. Proponents of group selection insist that close kin form groups and that these groups function as interactors in the evolutionary process. Organism selectionists counter that everything that needs to be said about kin selection can be said in terms of the inclusive fitness of individual organisms. The difference is between kin-group selection and kin selection. Gene selectionists dismiss inclusive fitness as a sop that Hamilton (1964a, b) threw to organism selectionists. Gene selectionists acknowledge that both replication and interaction function in the evolutionary process, but they maintain that evolutionary theory can, at bottom, be couched entirely in terms of replication, and that any causal processes that do not eventuate in changes in replicator frequencies (usually gene frequencies) simply do not matter. Opponents of genic selectionism, including Wimsatt (1980) and Sober and Lewontin (1982), admit that reference to changes in gene frequencies is adequate for the "bookkeeping" aspect of selection but insist that the bookkeeping aspect by itself leaves out too much of the causal story. They want to expand the axioms of evolutionary theory to include reference to the causal relations responsible for evolution's taking place the way that it does. Williams (1985, p. 2) is content with evolutionary theories limited to the bookkeeping aspect and finds the criticisms of such theories by Wimsatt (1980) and Sober and Lewontin (1982) to be based on "unrealistic expectations." Genic selectionists also seem to fear that including explicit reference to the causal interface between interactors and their environments will complicate evolutionary theory prohibitively, possibly even challenging the Weismann barrier.

Strangely enough, the most vocal defenders of the necessary role of organisms (or, more generally, interactors) in the evolutionary process—in opposition to what they see as an overemphasis on genes (or, more generally, replicators)—are also among those who are most skeptical about evolutionary "just so stories" (e.g., Gould and Lewontin [1979]), while several of the strongest advocates of genic selectionism see nothing wrong with evolutionary scenarios (Dawkins [1982b], Ridley [1983], Williams [1985]). Defenders of the role of organisms in evolution warn that many of the characteristics that evolutionary biologists claim are adaptations might well be nothing but effects. In addition, the ease with which adaptationist scenarios can be constructed to explain particular adaptations casts considerable doubt on the entire program. Hence, they conclude that we cannot leave organisms and their adaptations out of the evolutionary story, but we must include reference to them only with great care. Defenders of the adequacy of genes in setting out the basic axioms of evolutionary theory do not think that discerning organismic adaptations is all that problematic. Although organisms and their adaptations do not play a central role in the fundamental axioms of evolutionary theory, secondary reference to them is nevertheless scientifically reputable. At the risk of putting too fine a point on the dispute, Williams (1985, pp. 2, 15) thinks that his critics are too optimistic about the potentialities of evolutionary theory and too pessimistic about the legitimacy of adaptive scenarios.

I find myself in partial agreement with both sides of this dispute. I think that any adequate theory of evolution must include reference to the interactor-environment interface (Odling-Smee and Plotkin 1984), but that the inclusion of such reference need not complicate evolutionary theory any more than including reference to replication does. It is certainly true that interactions are as varied as the myriad causal situations that give rise to the incredible array of adaptations that makes the study of biology so endlessly fascinating, but the information contained in the genetic makeup of organisms for these adaptations is just as multifarious. The introduction of either sort of complexity into the general characterization of the evolutionary process would be lethal, but no such introduction is necessary. In both cases, all that must actually be included in formal statements of evolutionary theory are the general characteristics of replicators and interactors and how they are interrelated. Only when this general theory is applied to particular cases is the actual informational content of the replicators and the causal situations that produced the particular adaptations relevant. Scientific theories are general. Their applications are contingent and often idiosyncratic.[2]

With respect to applications, I see no reason to shy away from claiming that a particular characteristic arose as an adaptation to a putative past environment, even though such claims may often be false. In most cases, little rides on the correctness of particular adaptationist scenarios. Showing that processes other than replication and interaction are actually responsible for biological evolution would be of prime importance. It would bring into question our basic conception of the evolutionary process. Detailing difficulties in applying evolutionary theory is of secondary importance. All scientific theories are difficult to apply. Inferences to particular cases must be possible if evolutionary theory is to be testable, but such testing need not be easy or automatic. Critics of evolutionary theory are not content with its being falsifiable. They insist that it must be easily falsifiable, when no scientific theory is easily falsifiable.

However, adaptationist scenarios are so fascinating that they often seduce biologists into ignoring even more fundamental aspects of the evolutionary process. Also, there is a tendency to think that adaptationist scenarios have greater warrant than they actually have. For most species, such misplaced confidence is unlikely to do must harm. However, similar mistakes in the context of the human species can do considerable damage. We may be innately territorial or sexually dimorphic in socially relevant ways. We *may* be, but the substantiation available for such claims is not all that impressive. Social policies based on such shaky ground are likely to be misconceived and the results deleterious. But to repeat my general point: The general notion of adaptation is central to a selectionist view of evolution. Questions about which particular structures arose as adaptations to which particular environmental changes are relevant only to the testing of selectionist versions of evolutionary theory.

Although Dawkins has come to accept the distinction between replicators and interactors, he prefers a somewhat different terminology: "My main concern has been to emphasize that, whatever the outcome of the debate about organism versus group as *vehicle*, neither the organism nor the group is a *replicator*. Controversy may exist about rival candidates for replicators and about rival candidates for vehicles, but there should be no controversy over replicators *versus* vehicles. Replicator survival and vehicle selection are two aspects of the same process." (Dawkins 1982a, p. 60)

Once the distinction between replicators (on the one hand) and vehicles or interactors (on the other hand) is made, the issues that divide present-day evolutionary biologists can be stated more clearly. Of course, this distinction does not decide these issues. Slight differences in how the distinction is drawn can influence the resulting resolutions. As Kawata (1987) points out, Dawkins's vehicles and my interactors are not precisely equivalent concepts. According to Dawkins, genes are replicators, not vehicles. They ride around in vehicles, directing their behavior. On my account, genes are both replicators and interactors. If genes are anything, they are entities that interact with their environments in such a way as to bias their own replication. In one place, Dawkins (1982a, p. 45) notes that the wings of birds are for flying and then asks, "What are DNA molecules for?" He answers that "DNA is not 'for' anything. If we wish to speak teleologically, all adaptations are for the preservation of DNA; DNA itself just *is*." Yes and no. Organisms are characterized by adaptations. So are molecules of DNA. They are extremely well adapted to replicate. The major effect of this replication is, as Dawkins insists, the preservation of the structure of DNA. Once it is recognized that one and the same entity can function both as a replicator and as an interactor, the image of genes riding around in vehicles becomes less persuasive.

Sober (1984, pp. 253–255) also complains that Dawkins defines his terms in ways to guarantee that organisms cannot possibly function as replicators. One reason that Dawkins has for rejecting organisms as replicators is meiosis. At meiosis, parental genomes are dismembered; then new genomes are reassembled at fertilization. If retention of structure largely (or totally) intact is necessary for replicators, then only small sections of the genome can function as replicators in cases of sexual reproduction in genetically heterogeneous populations. Both restrictions should be noted. Dawkins's central argument for genes being the only replicators applies only to organisms when they reproduce sexually. If genes are the only replicators in cases of asexual reproduction, he needs an additional argument. His central argument also does not apply to sexual reproduction in genetically homogeneous populations. Although crossover can occur in such populations, it makes no difference to the structure of the resulting genomes. However, as Williams (1985, p. 5) notes, even in such cases, phenotypes "can play no role in bookkeeping because, even in a clone, the successive generations of phenotypes may be markedly different because of environmental variables that affect development."

The best example of an organism functioning as a replicator is the direct transmission of a phenotypic change to successive generations through fission. For example, if a portion of the cortex of a paramecium is surgically removed and reinserted with the cilia facing the opposite direction, this phenotypic change is transmitted to subsequent generations. In light of this example, Dawkins (1982b, p. 177) responds as follows:

> If, on the other hand, we look at underlying replicators, in this case perhaps the basal bodies of cilia, the phenomenon falls under the general heading of replicator propagation. Given that macromolecular structures in the cortex are true replicators, surgically rotating a portion of cortex is analogous to cutting out a portion of chromosome, inverting it, and putting it back. Naturally the inversion is inherited, because it is part of the germ-line. It appears that elements of the cortex of *Paramecium* have a germ-line of their own, although a particularly remarkable one in that the information transmitted does not seem to be encoded in nucleic acid.

When Dawkins (1976) introduced the term *replicator*, he intended it to be more general than *gene*. Although genes, as they are currently understood, may not be limited to the nucleus, they are limited to nucleic acids—DNA and RNA. The basal bodies of cilia do not count as genes, but they might well count as replicators and form a "germ-line" of their own. Even so, in the paramecium example, the inverted cortex is not being transmitted indirectly via the basal bodies but directly. Obviously something must be going on at lower levels of analysis when a paramecium splits down the middle to form two new organisms, but I fail to see why this fact counts against treating organisms in this situation as replicators. After all, even though entities less inclusive than genes are involved in genetic replication, it does not follow that genes are not replicators. Standards should not be invoked for organisms more stringent than those applied to genes. Organisms behave in ways that make them candidates for replicators seldom enough without ruling them out by definition. As it turns out, in the most common situation in which one might want to view organisms as replicators—asexual reproduction via fission—it makes no difference. In asexual reproduction, usually the entire genome functions as a single replicator, and there is a one-to-one correlation between genomes and phenomes. Hence, the numbers will always turn out to be the same.

A second reason that organisms are not very good candidates for replicators concerns the different senses in which genes and organisms can be said to "contain information" in their structure. Genes do not code in a one-to-one fashion for phenotypic traits. Given a particular genome, numerous alternative phenomes are possible depending on differences in the environment. Given any one gene, numerous different alternative traits are possible depending on difference in the environment as well as elsewhere in the genome. The net effect is that both individual genes and entire genomes code for reaction norms, not for specific traits or phenomes. In this sense, the information in a genome is largely "potential." In any one instance of translation, these reaction norms are narrowed to one eventuality, to a single phenome. All other possibilities, equally "programmed" into the genetic material, are not realized. To use Wimsatt's felicitous terminology, each genotoken gets to produce a single phenotoken. The net effect is the loss of nearly all the potential information in the genome. The only information that an organism as a replicator can pass on is the information realized in its structure. (For an exhaustive treatment of the role of "information" in evolution, see Brooks and Wiley 1986.)

Both Dawkins (1982b) and I (Hull 1976, 1978a) have been concerned to break the hold that a fairly narrow conception of organisms has on the minds of many evolutionary biologists, but toward different ends. According to Dawkins, nests and mating calls are as much a part of a bird's phenotype as are its beak and webbed feet. In response to Gould's (1977) claim that selection cannot see genes and pick among them directly but must use bodies as an intermediary, Dawkins (1982a, p. 58) retorts: "Well, it must use *phenotypic effects* as intermediaries, but do they have to be bodies? Do they have to be discrete vehicles at all?" In answering No to both questions, Dawkins plays down the role in evolution of organisms as discrete bodies or even as vehicles. I have argued at some length that organisms are not as discrete, unitary, and well organized as we tend to assume in order to urge a role for entities more inclusive than single organisms as interactors, not in order to question the role of organisms as paradigmatic interactors. Dawkins (1982b) and Williams (1985) argue that organisms can never function as replicators in the evolutionary process. Although I am not willing to go this far, I agree that when organisms do function as replicators, the effects of organismal replication are likely not to be extensive.

The point of the preceding discussion has been to show why traditional conceptions are not adequate for biological evolution strictly construed. If simplistic notions of genes, organisms, and species are not adequate for ordinary biological evolution, then they are surely not adequate for construing social learning as a selection process. But before turning to this topic, I need to present at least one particular example of the improved understanding that my revised conceptual apparatus brings to biological phenomena. One of the major topics in recent literature in population biology has been explanations of the prevalence of sexual reproduction. The problem can be stated quite simply. If the name of the game in biological evolution is to pass on one's genes, then sexual reproduction is a very inefficient way of accomplishing this end, because sexual reproduction has a 50 percent cost. At any locus where the male and the female differ, each has only a 50-50 chance of passing on its alleles rather than those of its mate. Conversion from sexual reproduction to parthenogenesis would double the contribution of a female to future generations. So, though in theory sexual reproduction should be quite rare, in fact it is "almost universal" (Maynard Smith 1971, p. 165).

The problem is so acute that evolutionary biologists who are strongly inclined to dismiss group selection in other contexts are forced back on this mechanism for the evolution of sex. For example, Williams (1971, p. 161) concludes: "Sexual reproduction must stand as a powerful argument in favor of group selection, unless someone can come up with a plausible theory as to how it could be favored in individual selection. And if group selection can produce the machinery of sexual reproduction, it ought to be able to do many other things as well."

Among the many things that group selection has been introduced to explain is the evolution of sociality and, with it, the rise in importance of social learning. Hence, sex and society are intimately connected in theorizing about the evolutionary process. But in the preceding discussion, the most important premise gets slipped in when no one is noticing, i.e., that sexual forms of reproduction are prevalent. As my earlier discussion indicates, sexual reproduction is a relatively recent innovation. For three-quarters of the existence of life on Earth, the sole form of reproduction was asexual. If one looks at every measure save one, it is still extremely common. If one looks at number of organisms, amount of energy transduced, biomass, etc., asexual reproduction remains extremely prevalent. Only if one compares numbers of species do sexual forms of reproduction turn out to be "nearly universal," But asexual organisms do not form species of the sort that exist among sexual organisms. To be sure, systematists group all organisms in species (taxospecies); however, as far as real groupings in nature are concerned, asexual organisms do not form *genealogical* units of the sort formed by sexual organisms.

The difference between asexual and sexual reproduction is fundamental. As Maynard Smith (1971, p. 163) notes, "At the cellular level, sex is the opposite of reproduction; in reproduction one cell divides into two, whereas it is the essence of the sexual process that two cells should fuse to form one." In fact, the differences are so fundamental that many authors argue that the same term should not be applied to both. Either sexual or asexual reproduction is not really "reproduction." Hence, one solution to the problem of the prevalence of sex when meiosis exacts a 50 percent cost is that it is not prevalent. It is as rare as it should be given its cost. The reason why it took as long for sex to evolve is that it is advantageous in only very special circumstances. In fact, it took only a little over a billion years for the first living creatures to evolve. It took almost 3 billion years more for sexuality to make an appearance. If the time it takes for something to evolve is any measure of its evolutionary advantage, sexual reproduction may not be all that advantageous. Hence, from this perspective, Williams's (1985, p. 103) explanation of sexuality in vertebrates begins to sound more plausible. According to Williams, sexual reproduction in derived low-fecundity organisms such as vertebrates is "a maladaptive feature, dating from a piscine or even protochordate ancestor, for which they lack the preadaptations for ridding themselves."

The usual response to the preceding observations is that something has gone wrong. Sexual reproduction evolved quite early and has been widespread throughout the history of life on Earth. After all, forms of parasexual reproduction exist among extant blue-green algae. There is no reason to assume that such forms of gene exchange were any less prevalent in the past. In the first place, mere gene exchange does not pose the same problem as meiosis. The issue is the cost of meiosis. And by all indications gene exchange among prokaryotes is extremely rare, ranging from one cell in 240,000 replications to one in 20 million. If such rare occurrences of gene exchange are sufficient to label an entire higher taxon "sexual," then Jackson et al. (1986) are just as warranted in labeling an entire group "clonal" just because a few forms exhibit clonality. One need not argue that sexual reproduction evolved quite early and is nearly universal in order to recognize it as an important innovation in biological evolution. Even though it is a relatively recent innovation and still quite rare, it served as an "evolutionary trigger" to give rise to species and, through them, to much of the diversity of life that we see all around us.

On the view that I am urging, replicators should be compared with replicators, interactors with interactors, and lineages with lineages. When one makes such comparisons, the results are quite different than when one compares genes with genes, organisms with organisms, or species with species. For one thing, sexual reproduction becomes "rare." Although their terminology is different, those authors who have looked at clonal organisms have been forced to make very similar distinctions. When the authors in Jackson et al. 1986 look at evolution in clonal organisms, they are forced to distinguish between ramets and genets. They compare ramets with ramets and genets with genets in estimating such things as fitness and the speed of evolutionary change. The effects of this change in perspective are dramatic in biological evolution. They should be no less pervasive when one turns one's attention to social learning as a selection process.

Conceptual Evolution: Replication

Dawkins introduced the notions of replicator and vehicle because of their generality and because of the common associations of such terms as *gene* and *organism*. However, *replicator* and *vehicle* also have their connotations. As far as I can see, the connotations of the term *replicator* are entirely appropriate whereas those of *vehicle* are not. Vehicles are the sort of thing that agents ride around in. More than this, the agents are in control. The agents steer and the vehicles follow dumbly. The picture that Dawkins's terminology elicits is that of genes controlling helpless and hapless organisms. Although Dawkins explicitly assigns an evolutionary role to both replicators and vehicles, his terminology is likely to mislead one into treating vehicles as passive tools in the hands of all-powerful replicators. As Sober (1984, p. 255) repeatedly emphasizes, "The units of selection controversy began as a question about causation." For this reason, I prefer *interactor* to *vehicle* (see also Williams 1985).

Dawkins intends *replicator* to apply to any entity that happens to possess the appropriate characteristics. In biological evolution, he insists that only genes function as replicators (the paramecium example notwithstanding). However, Dawkins (1976, p. 68) recognizes that in other sorts of selection processes other entities might function as replicators—for example, in "cultural analogues of evolution." He terms the cultural analogues of genes *memes* (See also Semon 1904). According to Dawkins, genes and memes are equally replicators. If memes are to function as replicators, then they must have structure and be able to pass on this structure through successive replications. If conceptual change is to occur by means of selection processes, memes cannot exist in some other "world" (Popper 1972) but must exist in the material world—in brains, computers, books, etc. A second reason for preferring *interactor* to *vehicle* is that the father of evolutionary epistemology, Donald Campbell (1979), uses *vehicle* to refer to replication in both biological and conceptual evolution. Genes are the vehicles that transmit the information in biological evolution, whereas everything from stone tablets and papyrus to magnetic tapes and electronic chips can serve as the physical vehicles in conceptual evolution. Using *vehicle* to refer both to interactors and to the physical basis of replication begs for misunderstanding, and misunderstanding comes along easily enough on its own. One need not beg for it.

Thus far, the burgeoning literature on conceptual change as a selection process has concentrated primarily on conceptual replication and how it differs (or does not differ) from replication in biological evolution. The most common alleged disanalogies between the two processes are that conceptual evolution is Lamarckian whereas biological evolution is not, that conceptual evolution is not biparental the way that biological evolution is, that cross-lineage borrowing is common in conceptual evolution but rare or nonexistent in biological evolution, and that conceptual evolution can be and often is insightful and intentional whereas biological evolution is blind and mechanical. Elsewhere I have argued that these alleged disanalogies are exaggerated, and that they stem from the failure to distinguish adequately between gene-based biological evolution and meme-based conceptual change (Hull 1982).

Though proponents and opponents of treating conceptual change as a selection process have often claimed that conceptual evolution is somehow "Lamarckian," no one has explained at much length what this term means in connection with conceptual change. In biological evolution, inheritance counts as "Lamarckian" if adaptive changes in the phenotype of an organism were transmitted to the genetic material and thereafter inherited by the organism's progeny. Acquired characteristics must be *inherited*, not just transmitted. The above example of alterations in the cortex of a *paramecium* is not an example of Lamarckian inheritance because the genetic material is bypassed. Social learning would be literally Lamarckian if the knowledge that an organism acquired about its environment somehow came to be encoded in its genetic material and thereafter was inherited by its progeny. As far as I know, none of the advocates of an evolutionary analysis of conceptual change view social learning in such a literal fashion. The whole point of social learning is that information is transmitted independently of genes. If social learning is Lamarckian, it must be so only in a metaphorical sense of this term. Such conceptual entities as memes must be substituted for genes, but it should be noted that memes are analogous to genes, not to characteristics. Hence, their transmission does not count as an instance of the inheritance of acquired characteristics precisely because they are not the analogues of characteristics. In sum, on a literal interpretation, social learning is not an example of the inheritances of acquired characteristics because inheritance is not involved (just transmission). On a metaphorical interpretation, social learning does not count as an instance of the inheritance of acquired characteristics because the things being passed on are analogues of genes, not of characteristics. Social learning is, if anything, an instance of the inheritance of acquired memes. One organism can certainly give another fleas, but this is hardly an instance of the inheritance of acquired characteristics. Social learning is to some extent "guided" (Boyd and Richerson 1985), but to call it on that account "Lamarckian" is to use this term in its most caricatured form, as if giraffes got such long necks by striving to reach the leaves at the tops of trees.

In this connection, commentators often state that biological evolution is always "vertical" whereas conceptual evolution is likely to be "horizontal." By this they mean that the transmission of characteristics in biological evolution is always from parent to offspring (i.e., inheritance). Characteristics always follow genes. In point of fact, biological evolution is not always vertical, even when characteristics follow genes. For example, it is horizontal when bacteria, paramecia, etc. exchange genetic material. Horizontal transmission can even be cross-lineage, as when viruses pick up genes from an organism belonging to one species and transmit them to an organism belonging to a different species. In conceptual contexts, parents can instruct their offspring, but they can also teach things to their elders, to others of their own biological generation, or to younger organisms to which they are not closely related. From the perspective of gene lineages, considerable cross-lineage borrowing occurs in conceptual evolution, but all this shows is that the relevant lineages for conceptual evolution are not gene lineages. The transmission of memes is what determines conceptual lineages. Hence, by definition, if a significant amount of cross-lineage borrowing is taking place between two conceptual lineages, these are not two conceptual lineages but one. The situation is exactly analogous to the situation in biological evolution. If a significant amount of gene exchange is taking place between two putative lineages, these lineages count not as two lineages but one (Hull 1982, 1984, 1985a).

Sometimes conceptual change is "biparental"—that is, ideas are obtained from two different sources and combined—but quite obviously information can be transmitted from a single source to another or combined from several sources. If the transmission of genes were actually always biparental, this would be an important difference between biological and conceptual evolution, but of course it is not. Both asexual reproduction and polyploidy are common. In general, those who oppose treating conceptual change as evolutionary reason from an extremely impoverished view of biological evolution to the context of conceptual evolution. Their view of biological evolution is so narrow that most biological evolution does not fit.

In this same connection, commentators on an evolutionary analysis of conceptual change are nearly unanimous in noting that conceptual change can occur much more rapidly than biological evolution (for an exception see Boyd and Richerson 1985). For example, under the most extreme selection pressures, a mutation that arose in the time of Julius Caesar would only now be becoming widely distributed in the human species. In this same time interval, conceptual systems have undergone great changes several times over. But the preceding contrast depends on taking calendar time as the appropriate time frame for both biological and conceptual evolution, when it is adequate for neither. Biological evolution is phylogenetic; it occurs only through a succession of biological generations. Individual learning is ontogenetic. It takes place within the confines of a single biological generation. In this respect it is like the immune system. Social learning is both ontogenetic and phylogenetic. It can occur both within and between biological generations. However, neither calendar time nor biological generations is the univocal time frame appropriate for either biological or conceptual selection processes.

With respect to calendar time, bacteria reproduce much more quickly than elephants; from the perspective of generations, they reproduce at the same speed. One reason why claims about molecular clocks caused such consternation among evolutionary biologists is that they were supposed to be constant with respect to calendar time, regardless of the generation time of the organisms in which these changes were occurring. With respect to the evolutionary process, a variety of time frames are relevant. For example, for mutation, cell cycle time is more appropriate than the generation time of the entire organism (Lewin 1985); however, for the evolutionary process as such, calendar time enters in only with respect to ecological interactions. For example, because of differences in generation time, new strains of bacteria and viruses pose dangers for organisms with slower generation times. They themselves cannot evolve fast enough to keep up with the bacteria and viruses, but their immune systems can. As a result of the preceding considerations, the appropriate time frame for replication in conceptual evolution is generational. Each time a meme is replicated, that is a generation. Thus, in the course of his biological lifetime, a geometry teacher may replicate the Pythagorean theorem hundreds of times. From the perspective of physical time, conceptual generations are much shorter than certain biological generations and longer than others; but from the perspective of generations *per se*, biological and conceptual evolution take place at the same speed—by definition.

The only frequently alleged difference between biological and conceptual evolution that does not arise from a straightforward misunderstanding concerns intentionality. Intentionality certainly plays a role in biological evolution. Both human and nonhuman organisms strive to elude predators, find mates, etc. However, a small number of the organisms belonging to the human species are aware that species evolve. As a result, they are in a position to influence that evolution consciously. Members of all species influence the evolution of their own and other species *un*intentionally, but the few people who acknowledge the existence of biological evolution and understand it sufficiently are in a position to direct it intentionally. We already do so in the case of domesticated plants and animals. Most of the changes that we have wrought in these creatures have been unintentional, but some have been consciously brought about. In the past, we have had to wait around until a particular variation happened to crop up. We are now in the position to introduce specific variations and to select the resulting variants. It would seem that we have always been in this position in cases of conceptual change. For instance, scientists often strive to solve problems and in doing so intentionally direct the course of conceptual evolution. In conceptual evolution both the introduction of variations and their selection can be done consciously toward certain ends.

Whether or not intentionality presents a significant disanalogy between biological and conceptual evolution depends upon how we distinguish between the two. Two criteria have been suggested: the sort of entity that functions as the relevant replicators (genes versus memes) and the source of new variants and/or their subsequent selection (intentional or not). Given these two criteria, four combinations are possible. Two combinations pose no problems. Most biological change is gene-based and non-intentional. Neither the introduction of new variants nor their selection is in any sense intentional. Some conceptual change, (probably not much) is meme-based and intentional. A conscious agent either generated the conceptual variant intentionally, or subsequently selected this variant, or both. But the other two combinations raise some difficulties. Some change is gene-based and intentional—selective breeding. The things being changed are genes, and the traits that are being selected are being transmitted via genes. However, the agent involved is conscious of what he or she is doing and is doing it intentionally. In Darwin's day the presence of a conscious agent in artificial selection and the absence of such an agent in natural selection was considered extremely important. In reasoning from artificial selection to natural selection, Darwin took himself to be reasoning by analogy. Just as breeders could select wisely, so could nature (Young 1971; Ruse 1975; Waters 1986). However, today artificial selection is considered to be a special case of natural selection and part of the legitimate subject matter of evolutionary biology—the presence of an intentional agent notwithstanding (Rosenberg 1985, p. 171).

The final combination is unintentional meme-based change. If Freud is right, understanding, inference, conscious choice, and the like play much less of a role in human behavior than his more rationalistic contemporaries thought. Although I am hardly a fan of Freud, I have a fairly skeptical attitude toward the role of these factors in human affairs. The rule that human beings seem to follow is to engage the brain only when all else fails—and usually not even then. However, the relevant issue is not the frequency of the relevant behavior but its classification as biological or conceptual. If the presence of intentionality is the crucial difference between biological and conceptual evolution, then artificial selection belongs in the province of conceptual evolution and all the unintentional conceptual changes produced by humankind belong to neither. I am not sure what choices the critics of an evolutionary analysis of conceptual change are likely to make in these matters. However, further discussion requires the introduction of the second aspect of selection processes, interaction. (For a more extensive discussion of the place of intentionality in nature, see Searle 1984.)

Conceptual Evolution: Interaction

In biological evolution, entities at numerous levels of organization interact with their respective environments as cohesive wholes in such a way that replication is differential. Some sperm can swim faster than others, some antibodies are more effective than others, some kidneys are better able to eliminate wastes, some organisms can withstand dessication for longer periods of time, some beehives can keep their internal temperature more constant than others, and sexual reproduction may have arisen as a species-level adaptation to increase speciation rates (Lewontin 1970). Any characterization of biological evolution that leaves out reference to interactors and their adaptations is leaving out half the causal story. The same observation holds for conceptual change. If the notion of conceptual replication makes sense, the task of identifying conceptual interactors remains. To put the issue in more restricted terms: Analogues to the genome-phenome distinction must be specified in conceptual evolution. In conceptual change, memes physically embody information in their structure. This structure is differentially perpetuated. But what is responsible for certain information proliferating while other information is lost?

One sure sign in biological contexts that autocatalysis (the transmission of information in replication sequences) is being replaced by heterocatalysis (the translation of information contained in the structure of the replicators) is a precipitous loss of "potential" information. In sexual reproduction, each genotype is almost always instantiated by a single genotoken, and this single genotoken usually gets to produce only a single phenotoken. Hence, in such circumstances, each genotype is selected via a single phenotoken. In cases of cloning, particular genotypes are represented by several genotokens. Hence, they can be tested by means of several phenotokens. But even in such cases, numerous alternative representations are never realized. Biological evolution seems "unfair" on a host of counts. One of them is that neither single genes nor entire genomes ever get to show their "real stuff." They succeed or fail in replicating themselves, depending on a relatively small number of actual exemplifications of all possible exemplifications permitted by the information they contain.

The same is true of conceptual replicators. Natural languages serve many functions. One of them is communication. Another is description, and part of what is communicated are these descriptions. Communication is the analogue to replication, whereas the testing of descriptive statements is the analogue to interaction—the translation of the information contained in a descriptive statement in such a way that it can be tested. A single gene corresponds roughly to a single concept, an entire genome to a more inclusive conceptual entity such as a scientific theory. Just as single genes never confront their environments in isolation, single concepts are never tested in isolation.

Philosophers have argued at great length that the meaning of a theoretical term is never exhausted by the various operational "definitions" used to apply it. A particular experiment or observation bears on only one small part of the meaning of the theoretical claim. For descriptive statements, the analogue to the interactor-environment interface is testing. Any minimally sophisticated conceptual system implies a huge array of observational consequences. Only a very few are ever likely to be tested, but the system will be accepted, rejected, ignored, or modified on the basis of these few tests. Conceptual change is hardly less unfair than biological evolution. Sometimes just the right test is run in just the right way; at other times an unfortunate choice results in the rejection of a theory. Mendel's work on garden peas is an example of the first sort; his choice of a particular species of *Hieracium* to extend his theory is an instance of the second sort. Garden peas could not have been a better choice. They exemplify what has come to be known as Mendel's laws with admirable clarity. His second choice could not have been worse. Inheritance in *Hieracium* is near chaos.

Thus, the translation of a particular genome (genotoken) into a particular phenome that either does or does not survive to reproduce is equivalent to the testing of a particular descriptive statement (a conceptual token) in a particular context. Either it survives the test or it does not. In biological evolution, each genome is an instance of a genotype. Indirectly, then, the genotype has been tested, albeit inadequately. However, especially in cases of sexual reproduction, each genotype is instantiated only by a single genotoken. One reason for narrowing one's focus in studying evolution to small segments of the genetic material is that they are more likely to have numerous copies. The same genotype is likely to have numerous genotokens to be tested in a variety of contexts. Thus, some estimation of the relative "worth" of this genotype can be gathered. Similarly, conceptual systems of considerable scope are extremely complex. It is very unlikely that more than one scientist adheres to precisely the same global conceptual system. In fact, a given scientist is unlikely to retain allegiance to the same global conceptual system for very long. Scientists change their minds. Global systems are tested only in the form of "versions." What makes something a "version" is not just similarity in structure. Descent is also required. Theories are best interpreted as families of models (Giere 1984), but these "families" have a necessary genealogical dimension. That the comparison just outlined is appropriate is indicated by the massive loss of information in both contexts and the messiness at the relevant interfaces. Only one small aspect of a scientific theory can be tested in a particular experimental setup, and the results can always be accommodated in a host of ways (in part because in any test too many concessions must be made to experimental contingencies). There are no absolutely crucial experiments.

In my discussion of both biological and conceptual evolution I have emphasized the essential role of tokens ordered in lineages. The primary replicators in biological evolution are genotokens ordered into gene lineages. The primary replicators in conceptual evolution are conceptual tokens ordered in conceptual lineages. Is there no role for types—similar tokens regardless of descent? In biological evolution, there might well be. For example, albinism, eusociality, and photosynthesis apparently have each evolved numerous times. They are all tokens of the same type. From the point of view of phylogenetic descent, they are convergences—homoplasies rather than homologies. As such, their use in reconstructing phylogeny is likely to produce error. But there is more to evolutionary biology than phylogeny reconstruction. There is, for instance, the formulation of general statements concerning the evolutionary process, and one thing that is certain about the concepts incorporated in such general statements is that they must refer to types of phenomena. In this connection I do not think that either albinism or the ability to photosynthesize is a likely candidate for a type to function in general statements about the evolutionary process; eusociality and sexuality may be. If the concepts that function in statements of purported laws of nature are termed "natural kinds," then evolutionary biologists have not been tremendously successful in identifying natural kinds in the evolutionary process. One purpose of introducing such terms as *replicator*, *interactor*, and *lineage* is to specify class terms (types) more general than the traditional terms *gene*, *organism*, and *species*.

In the preceding discussion of the evolutionary process, terms such as *replicator* refer to types of entities. Anything anywhere that has the right characteristics counts as a replicator. It just so happens that included among these characteristics is temporal continuity. The entities themselves are historical entities; the type is not. However, when one moves to the level of conceptual evolution, *replicator* itself must be interpreted as a historical entity—a conceptual historical entity. As do all concepts, the term *replicator* has a history. Anyone who wants to understand the development of this concept must trace its history, and all the problems in distinguishing "homoplasies" and "homologies" arise. For example, Dawkins (1976) coined the term *meme* independent of Semon's (1904) earlier neologism. However, is there no role for type terms in our understanding of conceptual change? I think there is, just so long as one realizes that the instances of these type terms are themselves historical entities. To understand conceptual evolution, one must have a basic framework of conceptual historical entities. Periodically, a particular agent elaborates a set of conceptual entities in ways he or she takes to be genuinely general. These concepts will be evaluated as genuinely general (types with similar tokens), but in transmission this generality is lost once again. Only a few tokens actually get transmitted. The image that comes to mind is successive bursts of skyrockets. In each inflorescence, most of the rockets fizzle out; but a few explode into additional inflorescences, and so on (Hennig 1969, p. 43; Sneath and Sokal 1973, p. 321). Instead of treating the historically unrestricted types as constituting the general framework in which conceptual change is investigated, as is usually done, an evolutionary analysis takes a phylogenetic framework as basic; then conceptual types are periodically fitted into the interstices of this tree.

Numerous problems have been raised in connection with the testing of such conceptual systems as scientific theories that have nothing special to do with an evolutionary analysis as distinct from other analyses of conceptual change. However, one recurring problem that is particularly relevant concerns the social dimension of conceptual systems. Words do not confront the world in all their nakedness. Words do not mean anything. Instead, people mean things by the words that they use. In many semantic theories, people drop out and are replaced by an abstract relation between word and object or statement and state of affairs, a relation that ignores all characteristics of the actual meaning situation save the proposed isomorphisms. Omitting reference to the interaction in conceptual change leaves out not only the testing part of conceptual change but also the tester—in cases of science, the scientist.

As I have noted, both gene selectionists and organism selectionists find replication adequate to handle the bookkeeping aspect of biological evolution. If there is a "bookkeeping" aspect of conceptual change, it is embodied in simple changes in meme frequencies. Internalist historians of science are frequently chastised for leaving too much out of their histories of science, but even the most internalist historians include references to scientists in their histories. Scientists are the ones who devise and evaluate scientific theories. The relevant weakness of internalist histories is not that they omit reference to scientists but that they omit what is commonly termed the "social context" of science. However, one reason why many philosophers of science—among them Collins (1975), Bloor (1976), and Barnes (1977)—feel uneasy about reference to "social context" is that they fear that it signals a relativist view of truth, and in many cases they are right. However, such references can also signal a relativist view of meaning. For example, Kitcher (1978) proposes to avoid some common semantic problems by postulating a community-based reference potential for each expression type. The reference potential of an expression type for a particular community is the "set of events such that production of tokens of that type by members of the community are normally instituted by an event in the associated set" (Kitcher 1978, p. 540).

Analyzing meaning in the context of communities of language users is certainly a step in the right direction for an evolutionary analysis of conceptual change, but several points must be emphasized. First, the communities must be defined by the appropriate relations, including such social relations as communicating with one another. If "reference potential" is to be of any use, communities cannot be defined in terms of their members' meaning the same things by the terms that they use. If communities are defined by the appropriate social relations, such as writes-to, reads-the-papers-of, and uses-the-work-of, one thing becomes clear: that plenty of conceptual heterogeneity exists in such communities (Hull 1984, 1985a). Instead of being a weakness, such heterogeneity is a strength. If biological evolution is to occur by selection, variability is necessary—both intra- and interspecific variability. If conceptual evolution is to occur by means of selection, both intra- and intercommunity variability must exist, and it does. One of the chief strengths of Kuhn's (1970) analysis of scientific change is that he views it as a community-based activity. One of its chief weaknesses is that he thinks that all scientists belonging to the same scientific community share the same "paradigm." As Kuhn (1970, p. 176) puts his position, "A paradigm is what the members of a scientific community share, and, conversely, a scientific community consists of men who share a paradigm."

Whether Kuhn intends for his "paradigms" in the preceding statement to be entire disciplinary matrices or particular exemplars (his two primary uses of the term *paradigm*), his position simply will not do. Because Kuhn portrays communities as monolithic entities, the transition from one paradigm to another seems a highly problematic affair—so problematic that some of Kuhn's readers have interpreted him as claiming that it is arational. Actually, all Kuhn has claimed is that simplistic analyses of rationality cannot explain such transitions. A community-based notion of rationality is more appropriate (Sarkar 1982). However, once one acknowledges that considerable differences of opinion can exist within any socially defined community, the radical differences in kind between intragroup and intergroup communication disappear. There is often as much intragroup dissonance (incommensurability) as intergroup dissonance. To the extent that incommensurability is a genuine problem at all, it is as much of a problem within scientific communities as between them (Hull 1985a). In the life of a community, cooperation is more important than agreement. It is a contingent truth that the scientists who make up the small, ephemeral research groups that are so operative in science can disagree with one another without ceasing to cooperate.

The crucial feature of an evolutionary analysis of conceptual change is that conceptual tokens be ordered into conceptual lineages. Because human beings are among the chief vehicles for conceptual replicators, there will be a significant, though not perfect, correlation between communities and such lineages. In order to understand conceptual change, in science as elsewhere, both social groups (such as the Darwinians) and conceptual systems (such as Darwinism) must be interpreted as historical entities (Hull 1985a).

Marjorie Grene, in an unpublished manuscript, has objected to certain hierarchical treatments of behavior because in them the "actor" in "inter-actor" drops out altogether. But if conceptual change is construed as community-based, actors play several crucial roles in it. Not only are the brains of human beings important vehicles (in Campbell's sense) in conceptual replication series, but human beings are equally important inter-actors (vehicles in Dawkins's sense). They are among the chief vehicles for conceptual replicators. They are also the entities that juxtapose scien-tific hypotheses and natural phenomena in experiments and observations. Conceptual replication and interaction intersect in human agents.

Human beings also participate in the social relations that integrate individual people into communities. Science is inherently and necessarily a community affair. Certainly isolated hermits can learn about the world, but if science had been constituted in its early years by such hermits it never would have gotten off the ground (Hull 1985b). In order for science to be cumulative (to the extent that it is), transmission is required. Similarly, the sort of objectivity and rationality that gives science the peculiar features that it has are characteristics not of isolated individuals but of individuals cooperating and competing in peculiarly organized social groups (Hull 1978b, 1985b).

Biologists commonly note that entities at different levels persist for different lengths of time. One constraining factor on group selection is that the organisms that compose groups come into being and pass away so much more rapidly than the groups of which they are temporarily part. With respect to calendar time, species speciate much more slowly than organisms reproduce themselves. Plotkin and Odling-Smee (1981) have extended this same observation to conceptual change. At each level in the relevant hierarchy, selection operates on a different time base. In this connection, the career lengths of particular scientists place some constraints on the speed of conceptual change. If we actually had to wait for aging scientists to die off before radically new ideas could become prevalent, this constraint would be prohibitive; however, no strong correlation seems to exist between age and the alacrity with which scientists adopt new ideas (Hull et al. 1978). Scientists change their minds on numerous issues during the course of their careers, but one thing is surely true: Whatever a scientist is going to accomplish, he or she must accomplish in the space of a very few decades. Just when scientists get really good at doing what they are doing, they die. Individual scientists exist for a long time relative to the speed of conceptual change, but not long enough to encompass certain sorts of conceptual change. This is but another reason why scientific communities are important. In a more global sense, it is the continuity of scientific communities through time that allows for continued scientific change.

I once entitled a paper on sociocultural evolution "The Naked Meme." I ended that paper with the following cryptic observation: "If conceptual systems and their elements are interpreted as historical entities, actual transmission is essential, either directly from agent to agent in conversations or more indirectly through such means as the printed page. On the view being advocated by evolutionary epistemologists, conceptual evolution in the absence of social evolution leaves memes as naked as the apes who are their chief authors." (Hull 1982, p. 322) The main purpose of the present chapter has been to unpack this allusion by sketching the key role that actors play in section processes by emphasizing how important interaction is. Omitting interaction in characterizing biological evolution leaves out the causal relations that make replication differential. Including reference to such relations but terming the entities involved *vehicles* makes them sound much too passive. Perhaps replication alone is adequate to capture the "bookkeeping" aspect of biological and conceptual evolution; however, in the context of scientific change, omitting reference to interaction leaves out not only reference to testing but also reference to the entities keeping the books—scientists.

Acknowledgments

I would like to thank John Odling-Smee, Henry Plotkin, Elliott Sober, and G. C. Williams for reading and commenting on an earlier draft of this paper. Research for this paper was supported in part by NSF Grant SES-8508505.

Notes

1. Although Brandon (1982) and Sober (1984) agree that selection is a causal process, they disagree about which general analysis of causation can best handle selection adequately.
2. As much as Sober (1984) and Rosenberg (1985) disagree on other points, they agree that fitness is supervenient on the properties of individual organisms.

References

Arnold, A. J., and K. Fristrup. 1981. "The Theory of Evolution by Natural Selection: A Hierarchical Expansion." *Paleontology* 8: 113–129.

Barnes, B. 1977. *Interests and the Growth of Knowledge.* London: Routledge and Kegan Paul.

Bloor, D. 1976. *Knowledge and Social Imagery.* London: Routledge and Kegan Paul.

Bonner, J. T. 1974. *On Development.* Cambridge, Mass.: Harvard University Press.

Boyd, R., and P. J. Richerson. 1985. *Culture and the Evolutionary Process.* University of Chicago Press.

Brandon, R. N. 1982. "The Levels of Selection." In *PSA 1982*, volume 1, ed. P. Asquith and T. Nickles. East Lansing, Mich.: Philosophy of Science Association.

Brandon, R. N., and R. M. Burian, eds. 1984. *Genes, Organisms, Populations.* Cambridge, Mass.: MIT Press.

Brooks, D. R., and E. O. Wiley. 1986. *Evolution and Entropy.* University of Chicago Press.

Campbell, D. T. 1979. "A Tribal Model of the Social System Vehicle Carrying Scientific Knowledge." *Knowledge: Creation, Diffusion, Utilization* 1: 181–201.

Collins, H. M. 1975. "The Seven Sexes: A Study in the Sociology of a Phenomenon, or the Replication of Experiments in Physics." *Sociology* 9: 205–224.

Cook, R. E. 1980. "Asexual Reproduction: A Further Consideration." *American Naturalist* 113: 769–772.

Dawkins, R. 1976. *The Selfish Gene.* Oxford University Press.

Dawkins, R. 1982a. "Replicators and Vehicles." In *Current Problems in Sociobiology.* Cambridge University Press.

Dawkins, R. 1982b. *The Extended Phenotype.* San Francisco: Freeman.

Dobzhansky, T. 1951. *Genetics and the Origin of Species.* Third edition. New York: Columbia University Press.

Eldredge, N. 1985. *Unfinished Synthesis.* Oxford University Press.

Eldredge, N., and S. N. Salthe. 1984. "Hierarchy and Evolution." *Oxford Surveys in Evolutionary Biology* 1: 182–206.

Ghiselin, M. T. 1966. "On Psychologism in the Logic of Taxonomic Principles." *Systematic Zoology* 15: 207–215.

Ghiselin, M. T. 1974. "A Radical Solution to the Species Problem." *Systematic Zoology* 23: 536–544.

Ghiselin, M. T. 1981. "Categories, Life, and Thinking." *Behavioral and Brain Sciences* 4: 269–313.

Ghiselin, M. T. 1985. "Species Concepts, Individuality, and Objectivity." *Biology and Philosophy* 2: 127–145.

Giere, R. 1984. *Understanding Science.* Second edition. New York: Holt, Rinehart, and Winston.

Gould, S. J. 1977. "Caring Groups and Selfish Genes." *Natural History* 86: 20–24.

Gould, S. J., and R. C. Lewontin. 1979. "The Spandrels of San Marco and the Panglossian Paradigm: A Critique of the Adaptational Programme." *Proceedings of the Royal Society of London* B 205: 581–598.

Grene, M. Hierarchy and Evolution. Unpublished.

Hamilton, W. D. 1964a. "The Genetical Evolution of Social Behavior, I." *Journal of Theoretical Biology* 7: 1–16.

Hamilton, W. D. 1964b. "The Genetical Evolution of Social Behavior, II." *Journal of Theoretical Biology* 7: 17–32.

Harper, J. L. 1977. *Population Biology of Plants.* London: Academic.

Hennig, W. 1966. *Phylogenetic Systematics.* Champaign: University of Illinois Press.

Hennig, W. 1969. *Die Stammesgeschichte der Insectin.* English edition: *Insect Phylogeny* (New York: Wiley, 1981).

Hull, D. L. 1976. "Are Species Really Individuals?" *Systematic Zoology* 25: 174–191.

Hull, D. L. 1978a. "A Matter of Individuality." *Philosophy of Science* 45: 335–360.

Hull, D. L. 1978b. "Altruism in Science: A Sociobiological Model of Cooperative Behavior among Scientists." *Animal Behavior* 26: 685–697.

Hull, D. L. 1980. "Individuality and Selection." *Annual Review of Ecology and Systematics* 11: 311–332.

Hull, D. L. 1982. "The Naked Meme." In *Learning, Development, and Culture,* ed. H. C. Plotkin. New York: Wiley.

Hull, D. L. 1984. "Cladistic Theory: Hypotheses that Blur and Grow." In *Cladistic Perspectives on the Reconstruction of Evolutionary History,* ed. T. Duncan and T. Stuessy. New York: Columbia University Press.

Hull, D. L. 1985a. "Darwinism as a Historical Entity: A Historiographic Proposal." In *The Darwinian Heritage,* ed. D. Kohn. Princeton University Press.

Hull, D. L. 1985b. "Openness and Secrecy in Science: Their Origins and Limitations." *Science, Technology, and Human Values* 10: 4–13.

Hull, D. L., P. Tessner, and A. Diamond. 1978. "Planck's Principle." *Science* 202: 717–723.

Jackson, J. B. C., L. W. Buss, and R. E. Cook, eds. 1986. *Population Biology and Evolution of Clonal Organisms*. New Haven: Yale University Press.

Janzen, D. W. 1977. "What Are Dandelions and Aphids?" *American Naturalist* 111: 586–589.

Kawata, M. 1987. "Units and Passages: A View for Evolutionary Biology." *Biology and Philosophy* 2: 415–434.

King, J. L. 1984. "Selectively Neutral Alleles with Significant Phenotypic Effects: A Steady-State Model." *Evolutionary Theory* 7: 73–79.

Kitcher, P. 1978. "Theories, Theorists and Theoretical Change." *Philosophical Review* 87: 519–547.

Kitcher, P. 1984. "Against the Monism of the Moment: A Reply to Elliott Sober." *Philosophy of Science* 51: 616–630.

Kuhn, T. 1970. *The Structure of Scientific Revolutions*. Second edition. University of Chicago Press.

Lewin, R. 1985. "Molecular Clocks Scrutinized." *Science* 228: 571.

Lewontin, R. C. 1970. "The Units of Selection." *Annual Review of Ecology and Systematics* 1: 1–18.

Maynard Smith, J. 1971. "The Origin and Maintenance of Sex." In *Group Selection*, ed. G. C. Williams. New York: Aldine-Atherton.

Mayr, E. 1963. *Animal Species and Evolution*. Cambridge, Mass.: Harvard University Press.

Michod, R. E. 1982. "The Theory of Kin Selection." *Annual Review of Ecology and Systematics* 13: 23–55.

Odling-Smee, F. J., and H. C. Plotkin. 1984. "Evolution: Its Levels and Its Units." *Behavioral and Brain Sciences* 7: 318–320.

Plotkin, H. C., and F. J. Odling-Smee. 1981. "A Multiple-Level Model of Evolution and Its Implications for Sociobiology." *Behavioral and Brain Sciences* 4: 225–235.

Popper, K. R. 1972. *Objective Knowledge*. Oxford: Clarendon.

Ridley, M. 1983. *The Explanation of Organic Diversity: The Comparative Method and Adaptations for Mating*. Cambridge, Mass.: Harvard University Press.

Rosenberg, A. 1985. *The Structure of Biological Science*. Cambridge University Press.

Ruse, M. 1975. "Charles Darwin and Artificial Selection." *Journal of the History of Ideas* 36: 339–350.

Sarkar, H. 1982. "A Theory of Group Rationality." *Studies in the History and Philosophy of Science* 13: 55–72.

Searle, J. R. 1984. "Intentionality and Its Place in Nature." *Dialectica* 38: 86–99.

Semon, R. 1904. *Die Mneme als erhaltendes Prinzip in Wechsel des organischen Geschehens*. Leipzig: Engelmann.

Sneath, P. H. A., and R. R. Sokal. 1973. *Numerical Taxonomy: The Principles and Practice of Numerical Classification*. San Francisco: Freeman.

Sober, E. 1981. "Holism, Individualism, and the Units of Selection." In *PSA 1980*, volume 2, ed. P. Asquith and R. Giere. East Lansing, Mich.: Philosophy of Science Association.

Sober, E. 1984. *The Nature of Selection*. Cambridge, Mass.: MIT Press.

Sober, E., and R. C. Lewontin. 1982. "Artifact, Causes, and Genic Selection." *Philosophy of Science* 49: 147–176.

Thomas, L. 1974. "Survival by Self-Sacrifice." *Harper's Magazine* 251: 96–104.

Vrba, E. S. 1984. "What Is Species Selection?" *Systematic Zoology* 33: 318–328.

Vrba, E. S., and N. Eldredge. 1984. "Individuals, Hierarchies, and Processes: Towards a More Complete Evolutionary Theory." *Paleobiology* 10: 146–171.

Waters, C. K. 1986. "Taking Analogical Inferences Seriously: Darwin's Argument from Artificial Selection." In *PSA 1986,* volume 1, ed. A. Fine and P. Machamer. East Lansing, Mich.: Philosophy of Science Association.

Williams, G. C. 1966. *Adaptation and Natural Selection.* Princeton University Press.

Williams, G. C. (ed.). 1971. *Group Selection.* New York: Aldine-Atherton.

Williams, G. C. 1975. *Sex and Evolution.* Princeton University Press.

Williams, G. C. 1985. "A Defence of Reductionism in Evolutionary Biology." *Oxford Series in Evolutionary Biology* 2: 1–27.

Wilson, E. O. 1975. *Sociobiology: The New Synthesis.* Cambridge, Mass.: Harvard University Press.

Wimsatt, W. 1980. "Reductionistic Research Strategies and Their Biases in the Units of Selection Controversy." *Scientific Discovery* 2: 213–259.

Young, R. M. 1971. "Darwin's Metaphor: Does Nature Select?" *Monist* 55: 442–503.

Chapter 3

The Levels of Selection: A Hierarchy of Interactors

Robert N. Brandon

Biologists have long recognized that the biosphere is hierarchically arranged. And at least since 1970 we have recognized that the abstract theory of evolution by natural selection can be applied to a number of elements within the biological hierarchy (Lewontin 1970). But what is it for selection to occur at a given level of biological organization? What is a "unit of selection"? Is there one privileged level at which selection always, or almost always, occurs? In this chapter I shall try to clarify and partially answer these questions.

Genotypes and Phenotypes

As Mayr (1978) has emphasized, evolution by natural selection is a two-step process. According to the received neo-Darwinian view, one step involves the selective discrimination of phenotypes. For instance, suppose there is directional selection for increased height in a population. That means that taller organisms tend to have greater reproductive success than shorter organisms. The reasons for this difference depend on the particular selective environment in which the organisms live. In one population it may be that taller plants receive more sunlight and so have more energy available for seed production; in another, taller animals may be more resistant to predation. Whatever the reason, natural selection requires that there be phenotypic variation (in this case, variation in height). Selection can be thought of as an interaction between phenotype and environment that results in differential reproduction.

But natural selection in the above sense (what quantitative geneticists call phenotypic selection) is not sufficient to produce evolutionary change. In the case of directional selection for increased height, selection may change the phenotypic distribution in the parental generation (it will do so if selection is by differential mortality); but whether or not that results in evolutionary changes, (i.e., changes in the next generation) depends on the heritability of height. That is, it depends on whether or not taller-than-average parents tend to produce taller-than-average offspring and shorter-than-average parents tend to produce shorter-than-average offspring. This is the second step in the two-step process. Of course, height is not directly transmitted from parent to offspring; rather, genes are.[1] Thus, offspring of taller-than-average parents will tend to have genotypes different from those of offspring of shorter-than-average parents. In the process of ontogeny, these genotypic differences manifest themselves as phenotypic differences. And so the phenotypic distribution of the offspring generation has been altered; evolution by natural selection has occurred.

Thus, evolution by natural selection requires both phenotypic variation and the underlying genetic variation. In one step, phenotypes interact with their environment in a way that causes differential reproduction. This leads to the next step, the differential replication of genes. Through ontogeny, this new genotypic distribution leads to a new phenotypic distribution and the process starts anew.

Replicators and Interactors

The above description of evolution by natural selection seems perfectly adequate for cases of selection occurring at the level of organismic phenotypes. But during the last 25 years there has been increasing interest in the idea that selection may occur at other levels of biological organization. This interest was sparked by V. C. Wynne-Edwards's book *Animal Dispersion in Relation to Social Behavior* (1962). Wynne-Edwards argued that a major biological phenomenon, the regulation of population size and density, evolves by group selection. In reaction to this thesis, Williams (1966) and Dawkins (1976), argued that selection occurs primarily at the level of genes. The recent flurry of theoretical investigations into kin and group selection has produced some explicitly hierarchical models.[2] It is not obvious how we should apply the genotype-phenotype distinction to describe cases of gametic selection, group selection, or species selection. Thus, Hull (1980, 1981) and Dawkins (1982a,b) have introduced a distinction between replicators and interactors which is best seen as a generalization of the traditional genotype-phenotype distinction.

Dawkins defines a replicator as "anything in the universe of which copies are made" (1982a, p. 83). Genes are paradigm examples of replicators, but this definition does not preclude other things' being replicators. For instance, in asexual organisms the entire genome would be a replicator, and in cultural evolution ideas—or what Dawkins (1976) calls memes—may be replicators.

The qualities that make for good replicators are longevity, fecundity, and fidelity (Dawkins 1978). Here longevity means longevity in the form of copies. It is highly unlikely that any particular DNA molecule will live longer than the organism in which it is housed. What is of evolutionary importance is that it produce copies of itself so that it is potentially immortal in the form of copies. Of course, everything else being equal, the more copies a replicator produces (fecundity) and the more accurately it produces them (fidelity), the greater its longevity and evolutionary success.

In explicating Dawkins's notion of replicators, Hull stresses the importance of directness of replication. Although according to Dawkins organisms are not replicators, they may be said to produce copies of themselves. This replication process may not be as accurate as that of DNA replication, but nonetheless there is a commonality of structure produced through descent from parent to offspring. However, there is an important difference in the directness of replication between these two processes. The height of a parent is not directly transmitted to its offspring. As discussed above, that transmission proceeds indirectly through genic transmission and ontogeny. In contrast, genes replicate themselves less circuitously. Both germ-line replication (meiosis) and soma-line replication (mitosis) are physically quite direct. The importance of this is made explicit in Hull's definition of replicators as "entities which pass on their structure directly in replication" (1981, p. 33).

As discussed above, evolution by natural selection is a two-step process. One step involves the direct replication of structure. The other involves some interaction with the environment so that replication is differential. The entities functioning in the latter step have traditionally been called *phenotypes*. But if we want to allow that biological entities other than organisms can interact with their environment in ways that lead to differential replication, then we need to generalize the notion of phenotype. To this end, Hull (1980, 1981) suggests the term *interactor*, which he defines as "an entity that directly interacts as a cohesive whole with its environment in such a way that replication is differential" (1980, p. 318).

Although Hull and Dawkins are largely in agreement concerning the replicator-interactor distinction, there are two differences worth noting. The first is purely terminological. Dawkins has not adopted Hull's term *interactor*; instead he uses the term *vehicle*. According to Dawkins, a vehicle is "any relatively discrete entity, such as an individual organism, which houses replicators ... and which can be regarded as a machine programmed to preserve and propagate the replicators that ride inside it" (1982b, p. 295). I prefer Hull's term and his definition of it, and so I will use it here.

The second difference is more substantive. Dawkins holds that any change in replicator structure is passed on in the process of replication (1982b, p. 85; 1982a, p. 51). Thus, given the truth of Weismannism (the doctrine that there is a one-way causal influence from germ line to body), replicators are supposedly different from most interactors (e.g., organisms). But DNA is capable of self-repair, and so not all changes in DNA structure are passed on in the process of replication. Thus, the property of transmitting changes in structure in the process of replication does not sharply demarcate replicators from interactors. What seems to be important is that replication be direct and accurate. But both directness and accuracy are terms of degree, and if we allow some play in both, then under certain circumstances an organism could be a replicator (which would not preclude its being an interactor as well). For example, Hull (1981, p. 34) argues that a paramecium dividing into two can be considered a replicator since its structure is transmitted in a relatively direct and accurate manner.

An important point to note is that the definitions of interactors and replicators are given in functional terms, that is, in terms of the roles these entities play in the process of evolution by natural selection. Nothing in the definitions precludes one and the same entity from being both an interactor and a replicator. For instance, it is likely that the self-replicating entities involved in the earliest evolution of life on this planet were both interactors and replicators (see Eigen et al. 1981). Likewise, in cases of meiotic drive, parts of chromosomes or perhaps entire chromosomes can be considered interactors as well as replicators. Hull has suggested, as was mentioned above, that in some cases organisms can be considered replicators as well as interactors. (See chapter 2 of the present volume for a more detailed discussion of these issues.)

Levels of Selection

Having developed the notions of replicator and interactor, which are generalizations of the notions of genotype and phenotype, we may ask whether the process of evolution by natural selection occurs at other levels of biological organization. This seemingly simple question, however, is ambiguous.[3] Are we asking whether there are replicators other than single genes, or are we asking whether there are interactors other than organismic phenotypes? Both are interesting questions, but many who have addressed the units-of-selection question have failed to see that there are two separate questions and thus have confused the two. I shall discuss this in the next section; in this section I shall concentrate on the latter question, that is, the question concerning interactors.

What is it about standard cases of organismic selection that makes them cases of organismic selection?[4] Put another way, what features of standard cases of organismic selection make organisms the interactors? Put still another way, what justifies our claim that in such cases "natural selection favors (or discriminates against) phenotypes, not genes or genotypes" (Mayr 1963, p. 184)? Consider again our example of directional selection for increased height. Recall that taller organisms have a higher fitness on average that shorter organisms. Thus there is a positive association between height and fitness. But there is genetic variation in height, so there is also a positive association between certain genes and/or genotypes and fitness. So why not say that natural selection favors phenotypes and genes (or genotypes) equally? Where is the asymmetry between phenotype and genotype?

The asymmetry lies here: Reproductive success is determined by phenotype irrespective of genotype. Intuitively, selection "sees" a 4-foot-tall plant as a 4-foot-tall plant, not as a 4-foot-tall plant with genotype g. This idea can be made precise by using the probabilistically defined notion of *screening off* (Salmon 1971). The basic idea behind the notion of screening off is this: If A renders B statistically irrelevant with respect to outcome E but not vice versa, then A is a better causal explainer of E than is B. In symbols, A screens off B from E if and only if

$$P(E, A \cdot B) = P(E, A) \neq P(E, B).$$

(Read $P(E, A \cdot B)$ as the probability of E given A and B.) If A screens off B from E, then, in the presence of A, B is statistically irrelevant to E, i.e.,

$$P(E, A) = P(E, A \cdot B).$$

But this relation between A and B is not symmetric. Given B, A is still statistically relevant to E, i.e.,

$$P(E, B) \neq P(E, A \cdot B).$$

Thus, where A and B are causally relevant to E, it follows that A's effect on the probability of E acts irrespective of the presence of B, but the same cannot be said of B. The effect B has on the probability of E depends on the presence or absence of A. For our purposes the important point is that proximate causes screen off remote causes from their effects.

Let us return to our case of directional selection for increased height. In that case there is differential reproduction of interactors (organisms) and replicators (genes). But it is obvious that the means through which genes replicate differentially in this case is the differential reproduction of organisms. (In other words, in this case there would be no differential replication of genes without the differential reproduction of organisms.) So the fact to be explained is that taller organisms tend to leave more offspring than shorter organisms. Using the notion of screening off, we can see that this is best explained in terms of differences in height rather than in terms of differences in genotype.

What we need to show is that for any level of reproductive success n, phenotype p, and genotype g,

$$P(n, p \cdot g) = P(n, p) \neq P(n, g).$$

Gedanken experiments should suffice to show the correctness of both the equality and the inequality. Basically the idea is that manipulating the phenotype without changing the genotype can effect reproductive success. (Castration is the most obvious example.) On the other hand, tampering with the genotype without changing any aspect of the phenotype cannot affect reproductive success. Admittedly, the latter claim is not straight-forwardly empirical. One could tamper with germ-line DNA, say by irradiation, and negatively affect reproductive success without obviously affecting the phenotype. But I would argue that in every such case one could find some aspect of an interactor that had been affected. For example, in many cases of the irradiation of a male, sperm morphology and behavior are changed. The claim is that a change in the informational content of the genome alone will not make for a change in reproductive success.[5] Thus, the fact that phenotype screens off genotype from reproductive success shows that there is an asymmetry between phenotype and genotype and that in cases of organismic selection reproductive success is best explained in terms of properties of the phenotype. What is true of this relation between phenotype and genotype obviously holds for the relation between phenotype and gene.

One might worry that our conclusion is a product of our choosing to look at differential reproduction of interactors (organisms) rather than replicators.[6] In our case, taller organisms outreproduce shorter organisms, and it should be clear that this is the mechanism by which some genes outreproduce others. But let us change our focus. Let n stand for the realized fitness of a given germ-line gene, let p stand for the phenotype of the organism in which it is housed, and let g stand for some property of the gene (its selection coefficient or whatever else one might think is relevant). Still the phenotype of the organism screens off the genic property from its own reproductive success; i.e.,

$$P(n, p \cdot g) = P(n, p) = P(n, g).$$

Thus, in our case a particular gene's reproductive success is best explained in terms of the height of the organism in which it is housed.

I have argued that in standard cases of organismic selection the mech-anism of selection, the differential reproduction of organisms, is best explained in terms of differences in organismic phenotypes, because pheno-types screen off both genotypes and genes from the reproductive success of organisms. Thus, in such cases the interaction between interactor and environment that leads to differential reproduction occurs at the level of the organismic phenotype.

We can now return to the question with which we began this section: Do such interactions occur at other levels of biological organization; are there other levels of interactors besides that of the organismic phenotype? This is ultimately an empirical question. I do not intend to answer it definitively; rather, I shall try to offer the conceptual tools necessary for answering it. But before I offer a general definition of levels of selection, let us consider selection at the group level.

Intuitively, group selection is natural selection acting at the level of biological groups. And natural selection is the differential reproduction of biological entities that is *due to* the differential adaptedness of those entities to a common environment. I have defended this definition elsewhere (Brandon 1978, 1981b), but two points are worth reemphasizing. First, the definition is explicitly causal; thus, it does not include all cases of differential reproduction. For instance, it does not apply to cases where, by chance, a less-well-adapted organism has greater reproductive success than a better-adapted one (who, let us say, was struck by lightning). Second, it applies only to those cases where differences in reproductive success are due to differences in adaptedness to a *common* environment (for further discussion of this point see Damuth 1985, Antonvics et al. 1988, and Brandon (forthcoming). This is implicit in the above discussion where I moved from saying that the organism's phenotype best explains its level of reproductive success to saying that *differences* in phenotypes best explain *differences* in reproductive success. This move is valid only if we restrict our attention to organisms, or more generally interactors, within a common environment. This point can be illustrated by a simple example. Suppose we plant two seeds, one in good soil and the other in mildly toxic soil. The first will probably survive longer and produce more seeds than the second; i.e., the first will be "fitter" than the second. But to explain this difference we must refer to differences in their environments, not to differences in their phenotypes.

In biology we can distinguish at least three different notions of environment. The first I call the *external environment*. The external environment consists of all elements, both abiotic and biotic, that are external to the evolving population of interest. This is what ecologists typically refer to when they speak of *the* environment. The second notion I call the *ecological environment*. The ecological environment reflects those features of the external environment that affect the demographic performance of the organisms of interest. It is measured by using the organisms of interest as measuring instruments. Finally, the *selective environment* reflects those elements of the external environment or of population structure that affect the differential contribution of different types to subsequent generations (i.e., affect differential fitness). Again the selective environment is measured by using the organisms as measuring instruments, and changes in selective environments are indicated empirically by a genotype-environment (e.g. spatial position) interaction in fitness. In other words, a common selective environment is a population or an area of space or time within which the relative fitnesses of the varying types remain constant. The selective environment is what is most directly relevant to the theory of natural selection; natural selection occurs within common selective environments. A given selective environment may be quite heterogeneous in terms of its abiotic or its biotic components.[7]

As we have seen above, organismic selection is the differential reproduction of organisms that is due to the differential adaptedness of those interactors to a common environment. Group selection, then, is the differential reproduction of biological groups that is due to the differential adaptedness of those groups to a common environment. Thus, a necessary condition for the occurrence of group selection is that there be differential reproduction (propagation) among groups. But this necessary condition is not sufficient. In order for the differential reproduction of groups to be group selection (i.e., selection at the group level), there must be some group property (the group phenotype) that screens off all other properties from group reproductive success.[8]

It is by no means necessary that such a property exist. For instance, suppose that group productivity or group fitness depends simply on the number of organisms within the group at the end of a certain time period.[9] Suppose further that the adaptedness values of these organisms do not depend in any way on the group's composition. In that case the group "phenotype" (the distribution of individual phenotypes within the group) would not screen off all nongroup properties from group reproductive success. In particular it would not screen off the aggregate of the individuals's phenotypes; that is, the following relation would not hold:

$$P(n, G \cdot [p_1 \cdot p_2 \cdots p_k]) = P(n, p_1 \cdot p_2 \cdots p_k),$$

where n is the number of propagule groups, G is the group phenotype, and p_i is the phenotype of the ith member of the group. The equality would hold, but the inequality would not since the phenotype of each individual within the group would determine that individual's adaptedness and the adaptedness values of each member of the group would determine the adaptedness value of the group.

In summary, group selection occurs if and only if (1) there is differential reproduction of groups and (2) the group phenotype screens off all other properties (of entities at any level) from group reproductive success. One way to restate (2) is this: Differential group reproduction is best explained in terms of differences in group-level properties (differences in group adaptedness to a common selective environment). Still another way to restate (2)—a way that would have seemed question-begging prior to what has been said concerning screening off—is this: The causal process of interaction occurs at the level of the group phenotype.[10]

What has been said about group selection is easily generalizable into the following definition: Selection occurs at a given level (within a common selective environment) if and only if (1) there is differential reproduction among the entities at that level and (2) the "phenotypes" of the entities at that level screen off properties of entities at every other level from reproductive values at the given level.

A Hierarchy of Interactors

What sorts of biological entities fall under the above definition? Organisms certainly do; for ample documentation, see Endler 1986. What about entities at lower levels of biological organization? Eigen et al. (1981) have presented a plausible scenario concerning the origin of life. In this scenario, lengths of RNA interact with proteins in a "primordial soup" and by this selection process the genetic code develops. Thus, in this scenario, there is selection at the level of lengths of RNA. Clearly these bits of RNA qualify as replicators; they replicate their structure directly and accurately. But they are interactors as well. It is their physical structure, their "phenotype," that determines their adaptedness to given conditions. For instance, in one experimental treatment RNAs were selected under conditions of high concentrations of ribonuclease, an enzyme that cleaves RNA into pieces. In this treatment, variants developed that were resistant to cleavage. "Apparently the variant that is resistant to this degradation folds in a way that protects the sites at which cleavage would take place." (Eigen et al. 1981, p. 97).

Doolittle and Sapienza (1980) and Orgel and Crick (1980) have argued that intragenomic selection results in the spread of "selfish genes," i.e., genes that increase their representation in the genome not through their effects on the phenotype of the organisms in which they are housed but rather through their superior replication efficiency within the genome. Such genes may or may not be transcribed, but in general one expects them to have a negative impact on the fitness of organisms because of the energetic costs of excess DNA. Doolittle and Sapienza (1980) describe the selection process by which "selfish genes" spread as "non-phenotypic selection." In the terminology of the present chapter, what they mean is that the level of this selection process is not the organismic phenotype. But "selfish genes" are interactors. They interact within the cellular environment in a way that leads to differential replication. It is their "phenotype" (i.e. their physical structure) that matters, not the phenotype of the organism in which they are housed. Similar remarks apply to chromosomes or parts of chromosomes in cases of meiotic drive (Crow 1979).

I have already discussed the possibility of selection at the level of groups. Wade (1977) has created group selection in a laboratory setting. Group selection in nature is more controversial; see Wilson 1983b for an illuminating discussion of this controversy and Wilson 1983a for a plausible case of group selection in nature. I have not attempted here to answer the empirical question of how prevalent group selection is in nature; rather, I have tried to shed light on the conceptual question of what should count as group selection. For present purposes, however, the important point is that when there is selection at the level of groups, these groups are interactors.

The groups that are relevant to discussions of group selection are relatively small and relatively short lived. Can selection occur at higher levels of organization, for example at the species level? There have been many recent discussions of species selection (Stanley 1975, 1979; Gould and Eldredge 1977; Eldredge and Cracraft 1980), but most of these have not clearly distinguished between mere differential replication of species and true species selection. In the useful terminology of Vrba and Gould (1986), they have not distinguished between sorting and selection. Clearly there is sorting at the species level, i.e., there is differential replication of species. But is there species selection? Damuth (1985) argues that, in general, a species is not the right sort of entity to participate in a selection process. In cases of organismic selection, selection occurs among organisms inhabiting a common selective environment. Notice that the population consisting of these organisms (the organisms inhabiting a common selective environment) is not necessarily a population united by gene flow (a deme). According to most proponents of species selection (e.g. Stanley [1975]), species selection occurs among species within a clade. But a clade is a genealogical unit rather than an ecological unit, and it is implausible that, in general, the constituents of a clade share a common selective environment.[11] Likewise, different local populations of a species will often-times not share a common selective environment. Thus, species in clades are not analogous in the relevant way to organisms within a population of organisms inhabiting a common selective environment. In the first case we have a unit united by gene flow (a species) within a larger genealogically characterized unit (a clade). In the second case we have an interactor (an organism) within a population of interactors united by common selective forces. To have an explanatory hierarchical theory of selection, we need a hierarchy of the right sort of units. Units of selection need not, and usually do not, correspond to units of a genealogical nexus. Damuth argues that local populations of a species within an ecological community are the sort of thing that could be a unit of higher-level selection, and that the community (not the clade) would be the unit within which selection would occur. Again, it should be clear that these higher-level entities (which Damuth calls *avatars*) are interactors.

Nothing in Damuth's argument precludes species selection; his argument is that species qua units of gene exchange are not necessarily the sort of entities that participate in the selection process (i.e., interactors). But in some cases there may be differences in species-level properties that do lead to differences in speciation and extinction rates. For instance, among marine gastropods, species whose larvae are planktotrophic have greater larval dispersal than those whose larvae are not, and so have greater gene flow. This leads to lower levels of speciation and extinction (see Jablonski 1986 and references therein). This may represent a genuine case of species selection. Indeed, Jablonski (1986) presents persuasive evidence that during the end-Cretaceous mass extinction-selection occurred at even higher levels of organization. Clades with more extensive geographic ranges showed higher survivorship than clades with smaller geographic ranges. That this was an emergent property of clades was indicated by the fact that individual species' ranges had no effect on clade survivorship.

(I have argued that selection requires common selective environments. Selection at higher levels, e.g. species and clades, requires much more spatio-temporally extensive selective environments. If mass extinctions are indeed caused by catastrophic events, such as the impact of large meteors, then this may have the effect of homogenizing vast parts of the Earth with respect to certain selective pressures. If this is so, one would expect increased higher-level selection during such periods.)

I have offered a definition of levels of selection, and in this section we have discussed various levels at which selection may occur. Selection may occur among bare lengths of RNA within a "primordial soup," among lengths of DNA within cells, among chromosomes within cells, among organisms within (selectively homogeneous) populations, among groups of organisms within local populations, among local populations within communities, among species within groups of competing species (which may or may not correspond to clades), and among clades. I have argued in each case that when there is selection at a given level, the entities at that level are interactors. This should not be surprising, since my definition of levels of selection is designed to pick out levels of interaction. Thus, we have a hierarchy of interactors ranging from bare lengths of RNA through organisms to clades. Let me reemphasize that some of these interactors may also be replicators. The point is that when selection occurs at a given level, the entities at that level must be interactors.

The hierarchy presented here apparently differs from that presented by Lewontin (1970), Hamilton (1975), Wimsatt (1980, 1981), Arnold and Fristrup (1982), and Wade (1984),[12] all of whom agree that in cases of organismic selection the "unit" of selection is some genetic unit—a gene, an entire chromosome, or even the entire genome, depending on the amount of epistasis and gene linkage. For illustration I shall present Wimsatt's definition of units of selection, but I believe that what is said about it applies to all the aforementioned works. Wimsatt (1981, p. 144) defines a unit of selection as "any entity for which there is heritable context-independent variance in fitness among entities at that level which does not appear as heritable context-independent variance in fitness (and thus, for which the variance in fitness is context-dependent) at any lower level of organization." Wimsatt, following Mayr (1963) and Lewontin (1974), argued against those (e.g. Williams [1966]) who claimed that in standard cases of selection—cases we would classify as organismic selection—genes are the units of selection. Wimsatt's argument is based on certain general facts about genetic systems. Most important among them is the fact that, in general, genes interact in the way they affect the phenotype. In particular, a given gene's effect on fitness depends on its genetic context. Thus, the variance in fitness at the level of genes is, in general, not context-independent. Wimsatt concludes, again in agreement with Mayr and Lewontin, that the unit of selection in standard cases is a much larger genetic unit: the entire genome. But at other levels of selection Wimsatt's definition coincides with mine. Thus, when I would conclude that there is group-level selection, Wimsatt would say that groups are the units of selection, and when my approach implies that there is selection at the level of lengths of DNA, Wimsatt would say that these lengths of DNA are units of selection. Recall that such "selfish DNA" acts as an interactor. In fact, Wimsatt's analysis agrees with mine when and only when his units are interactors.

The hierarchy that results from approaches such as Wimsatt's is incoherent. It includes replicators qua replicators and interactors qua interactors. Interactors and replicators play different roles in the process of evolution by natural selection. In order to resolve the "units-of-selection controversy" we need to ask coherent questions. One coherent question is this: At what levels do the interactions between biological entity and environment that lead to differential replication occur? That is, what are the levels of interactors? This is the question my analysis is designed to answer. Using this analysis, I have argued for the plausibility of a hierarchy of interactors ranging from bare lengths of RNA to entire clades. I should point out that this hierarchy may not be exhaustive; there may be other levels of selection than those we have considered.

A Hierarchy of Replicators?

There is a second question one might ask. It has to do with levels of replicators. Is there is an interesting hierarchy of replicators corresponding to the hierarchy of interactors? Let us examine the selection scenarios discussed above to see what the replicators are in each case. In the case of the model of Eigen et al. (1981), bare lengths of RNA interacted within a "primordial soup." Differences in their physical structure resulted in differences in survivorship and rates of replication. Thus, they are interactors. But it is obvious that they are replicators as well—indeed, they are paradigm cases of entities that replicate their structure directly and accurately. In the case of "selfish genes" (sensu Doolittle and Sapienza 1980 and Orgel and Crick 1980), lengths of germ-line DNA interact within a cellular environment in a way that leads to some such lengths' dramatically increasing their representation within the genome. Again, these lengths of DNA are clearly interactors; it is equally clear that they are replicators as well. Cases of meiotic drive are similar. There, lengths of chromosomes or whole chromosomes are both interactors and replicators.

The next step in the hierarchy of interactors I have discussed is the level of organismic selection. Here organisms are interactors, but what are the replicators? The answer depends on the mode of reproduction. In sexual reproduction, the genomes of organisms are broken up by segregation and recombination. Thus, only parts of the genome reproduce their structure directly and accurately. What do we call these parts of genomes? Williams defines a gene as "that which segregates and recombines with appreciable frequency" (1966, p. 24). (The strength of selection determines what counts as an appreciable frequency.) So the replicators in cases of organismic selection with sexual reproduction are genes (sensu Williams). In cases of asexual reproduction, the entire genome is passed on directly from parent to offspring. In such cases we could say that the entire genome was the replicator. Notice that in asexual organisms the genome is a "gene" in Williams's sense. One could argue, as has Hull (1981), that in asexual reproduction the organism itself is a replicator. It replicates its structure in a fairly direct and accurate manner. In this case, the difference between whole organisms and their genomes is one of degree, and the vagueness of the notion of replicator allows us to say that either is a replicator.

The replicators in cases of group selection also depend on the nature of the reproductive process. At the risk of oversimplification, we can distinguish two basic types of group selection: *intrademic* and *interdemic*. In cases of intrademic group selection, groups are formed during part of the organismic life cycle (e.g. the larval stage) and fitness-affecting interactions occur within these groups. Then the group members disperse into a common mating pool. The process of group selection occurs by differential group dispersal caused by differences in group structure (usually represented in formal models by different relative frequencies of alleles or genotypes). But group structure is not passed on directly to the next generation of groups. Rather, individuals from all the different groups unite in a common mating pool and reproduce sexually. New groups are formed in the next organismic generation at the appropriate stage in the life cycle. The replicators here are simply the replicators in normal sexual reproduction, namely genes (sensu Williams). In cases of interdemic group selection, groups are more or less reproductively isolated. Organismic selection occurs within groups, and group selection occurs between groups by processes of differential group extinction and propagation. Here the replicators are the groups themselves (which is not to say that genes are not also concurrently replicators with respect to the process of organismic reproduction). Group reproduction is a splitting process more similar to ameboid or bacterial reproduction than to sexual reproduction in higher plants and animals.[13]

Cases of what Damuth calls avatar selection (selection among local populations of species within an ecological community) and other selection processes at even higher levels (species selection, clade selection?) are similar to interdemic group selection in that the group itself (avatar, species, clade) is the replicator, because the reproductive process is a splitting process of these higher-level entities. Thus we have the dual hierarchy of interactors and replicators shown in the table.

Selection scenario	Interactor	Replicator
Eigen's model for origins of life	Lengths of RNA	Lengths of RNA
"Selfish genes" (Orgel and Crick; Doolittle and Sapienza)	Lengths of DNA	Lengths of DNA
Meiotic drive	Chromosome (or a part thereof)	Chromosome (or a part thereof)
Organismic selection		
asexual reproduction	Organism	Genome (or organism?)
sexual reproduction	Organism	Genes
Intrademic group	Group	Genes
Interdemic group	Group	Group
Avatar selection	Avatar	Avatar
Species selection	Species	Species
Clade selection	Clade	Clade

I want to make three points concerning this dual hierarchy. The first is that the hierarchy in the "interactor" column of the table is a fairly neat hierarchy of inclusion whereas the "replicator" hierarchy is less neat.[14] The hierarchy of replicators could be made to look neater if we were to adopt Williams's abstract notion of gene (mentioned above). In that sense of gene, all the replicators up to the case of interdemic group selection are genes. But that neatness is illusory if we think of the hierarchy as one of *physical* inclusion. The second point I want to make is that the replicator hierarchy is derivative from the interactor hierarchy in the sense that we need to determine the level of interaction in order to determine the level of replication but not vice versa. For instance, if we know that group selection is occurring, then we can determine the appropriate replicators depending on the group reproductive process (intrademic versus interdemic selection). Because of this, the first point is of little import. Given a hierarchy of interactors, we simply let the replicators fall where they may.[15] My final point is that single hierarchies (such as that presented by Wimsatt) that mix interactors and replicators serve to answer neither the question about interactors nor that about replicators. Their incoherence clouds the real issues.

Behavior and Selection

A pervasive metaphor in evolutionary biology is that natural selection is like the process of fitting a key to a lock. The physical structure of the lock is fixed, and the key must be shaped to fit it. Likewise, the features of the external environment are fixed, and natural selection shapes organisms to fit it (Lewontin 1978, 1983). This metaphor founders on the assumption that it is the external environment that determines selection pressures. But, as mentioned above, it is the selective environment, rather than the external environment, that is directly related to natural selection. (For detailed arguments to this effect see Antonovics et al. 1988 and Brandon (forthcoming). Recall that a selective environment is an area or a population within which the relative fitnesses of the competing types within the evolving population are constant. In other words, an area or a population is *selectively homogeneous* if the relative fitnesses do not vary in a significant way within it. Thus, the patterns of selective homogeneity and heterogeneity depend on the organisms in at least two ways. First, differing sensitivities to factors of the external environment will affect the pattern of selective heterogeneity. For instance, some organisms may, while others may not, perceive a given pattern of changes in nitrogen concentrations in the soil as selectively relevant. Thus, the pattern of selective environmental heterogeneity depends on the organisms present and their sensitivity to nitrogen concentrations. Second, by behavior organisms can effectively damp out heterogeneity in the physical environment. For instance, egg-laying females within a population of phytophagus insects may choose from many available plant species one particular species on which to lay their eggs. These plants may differ in many ways that would affect the fitness of the insects (e.g., differential nutritional quality, differential protection from predators), but by behavioral choice this potential heterogeneity is damped out. Indeed this damping of external environmental heterogeneity seems to be one of the major trends of evolution. (The damping need not be behavioral; it can be morphological or physiological as well—consider blubber in sea mammals and warm-bloodedness as examples.)

Not only can behavior affect the patterns of selection; it can affect the level of selection as well. This is obvious from a consideration of group selection. Group selection requires some grouping of organisms. This grouping may result from external processes acting on passive organisms, but it is more likely to result from active behavior. Furthermore, some have argued that nonrandom grouping is a necessary condition for group selection (Hamilton 1975; Maynard Smith 1982; Nunney 1985). Whether or not one accepts this argument, it is widely recognized that nonrandom group formation is a condition that would increase the evolutionary effectiveness of group selection. Clearly, nonrandom group formation is most likely to result from specific behaviors among the relevant organisms.

If the selective environment is to be compared to a lock, it must be a malleable lock, one that can be changed to fit the key. By behavior organisms can change their selective environment. If these changes are selectively advantageous and if the behaviors are heritable, then we can expect the coevolution of organism and environment. (See chapter 4 below.) This can affect both the patterns of selection at a given level and the level (or levels) at which selection occurs.

Concluding Remarks

The theory of evolution by natural selection is the only theory we have that can explain the origins and the maintenance of adaptations. If these explanations are to be scientific rather than mere exercises in story telling, then adaptations must be carefully related to the selection processes that produce them (see Brandon 1981a and 1985). For instance, early- to mid-twentieth-century ecology and ethology are notorious for their explanations of organic features in terms of the features' being "for the good of the species." Nowadays we understand that benefit to the species is irrelevant to a selection process occurring at the level of organisms. But if there is a hierarchy of interactors, if selection occurs at different levels, then we cannot axiomatically assume that all adaptations are for the good of organisms. That is, we cannot assume that all adaptations are to be explained in terms of their benefits to organisms. Indeed it is just this assumption that Doolittle and Sapienza (1980) criticize as the "phenotype paradigm" (by "phenotype" they mean organismic phenotype). As they point out, it is futile to search for the organismic benefit of the repetitive sequences of DNA that they call "selfish genes." It is futile not because the organismic benefit does not exist (in this case it doesn't), but rather because of the irrelevance of any such benefit to the intracellular selection processes that produce these repetitive sequences. Similarly, the organismic benefit of any product of a higher-level selection process (e.g. group selection) is irrelevant to the explanation of its origin and/or maintenance. Of course, selection processes at different levels may interact (see Arnold and Fristrup 1982 or Vrba and Gould 1986 for discussion). This further complicates our theory of adaptation.

In this chapter I have presented a hierarchy of interactors, or rather a hierarchy of plausible interactors. I have not claimed that the importance of selection at any level other than the organismic has been conclusively demonstrated. Lacking such demonstrations, could one not argue that we should ignore considerations of hierarchical levels in applying the theory of natural selection to the biological world? I can think of only two such arguments, and both are seriously flawed. One is based on the assumption that we can know *a priori* that the only important level of selection is the organismic. In light of the conceptual and empirical work during the last ten years, that argument cannot be taken seriously (see Brandon and Burian 1984 and Wilson 1983b). The other argument, which is that considerations of parsimony lead us to try to explain all adaptations as products of organismic selection (as suggested in Williams 1966), is based on bad methodology. Once we see that other levels of selection are theoretically possible, we should not adopt a methodology that blinds us to their existence. Ultimately it may be that the only important level of selection is the organismic and so the major adaptations in nature are organismic adaptations. However, at least for the moment, we need a hierarchical theory of interactors, if only to test the claim that organisms are the only important interactors in evolution.[16]

Acknowledgments

My thanks to Richard Burian and Stanley Salthe, who provided helpful comments on an earlier version of this chapter.

Notes

1. Nuclear genes are not the only means of transmitting traits from parent to offspring. Among other means, cytoplasmic DNA and culture are prominent.
2. See Brandon and Burian 1984 for a collection of some of the more important papers on questions concerning the levels of selection. The papers of Hamilton, Wimsatt, and Arnold and Fristrup offer hierarchical models of selection.
3. I believe that Hull (1981), Dawkins (1982a), and I (Brandon 1982) arrived at this conclusion independently.
4. In this context I prefer the term *organismic selection* to the more common *individual selection* because, as Hull has pointed out, interactors at other levels (e.g. groups) must be individuals.
5. As we saw above, the notions of interactor and replicator are not mutually exclusive; one and the same entity can be both interactor and replicator. Similarly, the notions of genotype and phenotype are not mutually exclusive. The genotype of an organism is a part of its phenotype. Thus, my claim commits me to the position that any change in

genotype that does lead to a change in reproductive success must also be a change in the organism's phenotype. This should not be seen as counterintuitive so long as one realizes that genes (lengths of DNA) have a physical structure.

6. Sober (1984, pp. 229–230) has raised this objection. He writes: "Brandon chose an organism's reproductive success. But suppose we choose change in gene frequencies. Then the screening-off relation is inverted. Gene frequencies and genic selection coefficients determine change in gene frequencies, if the population is infinitely large, and confer a probability distribution on future gene frequencies, if drift is taken into account." This objection is based on a simple equivocation. In the first instance we are concerned with relations among objective probabilities in the real world. That is the sense in which height, not genotype, determines reproductive success. Sober is concerned with the relation between coefficients and variable values in a mathematical model. Mathematical determination in a model does not translate so simply to nature.

7. The distinction among external, ecological, and selective environments is introduced in Antonovics et al. 1988. For further discussion see that work or Brandon (forthcoming).

8. It is not completely clear what sorts of things should count as group properties. Obvious examples include the sorts of things that could not be properties of individual organisms—for instance, the relative frequency of certain alleles within the group, or the phenotypic distribution within the group. Other properties that might be selectively relevant are less obviously group properties. For instance, we may or may not want to count the ability to avoid predation as a group property. Whether or not that is a group property depends on whether the group's ability to avoid predation is something "over and above" the ability of each individual to avoid predation—that is, on whether there is some group effect on the individuals' abilities to avoid predation.

9. This need not be the case, but it is assumed in most models. For a review of these models see Wade 1978, Uyenoyama and Feldman 1980, Wilson 1983a, or the introduction to part III of Brandon and Burian 1984. Indeed, in one experimental treatment Wade (1977) selected for groups with the lowest numbers of organisms.

10. It goes beyond the scope of this chapter to apply this approach to one of the major conceptual problems concerning group selection, viz., whether group selection requires the nonrandom formation of groups. For arguments that nonrandom group formation is required, see Hamilton 1975, Maynard Smith 1982, and Nunney 1985. For opposing arguments see Wilson 1983a and Wade 1984. For an application of the approach of the present chapter to the problem, see Brandon (forthcoming).

11. If there is a hierarchy of interactors, then there is a corresponding hierarchy of selective environments. It is virtually inconceivable that all the organisms in a clade would share a common organismic selective environment. But the question that is relevant here is whether species in a clade share a common species-level selective environment. Damuth's point is that there is no reason to except that they do in general. This point holds even if it is not wildly implausible that in some instances species in a clade do share a common (species-level) selective environment.

12. I say apparently for the following reason: If you assume that every copy of a particular genotype has the same phenotype, then in standard cases of organismic selection there will be some genetic unit such that the variance in fitness at that level will be context-independent. But that assumption is not likely to be true for any real population. When the assumption fails, copies of a given genotype could be partitioned by phenotype in a way that would be relevant to fitness. Thus, the variance in fitness at the genotype level would not be context-independent. If all this is correct, I have no argument with Wimsatt's analysis; my argument would be against his application of that analysis.

13. For further discussion of the distinction between interdemic and intrademic group selection see Wade 1978 or the introduction to part III of Brandon and Burian 1984.

14. The "interactor" column is a hierarchy of inclusion if we ignore the first entry (i.e., the case of selection among RNAs within a primordial group). However, since that process is not concurrent with the others, there is a reason to ignore it when our concern is with a hierarchy of concurrent or possibly concurrent selection processes.

15. One might compare this dual hierarchy with those presented in Eldredge and Salthe 1985, Eldredge 1985, and Salthe 1985. There is one major difference: The hierarchy I have presented is relative to a specific process (namely selection). Theirs is not. Thus, Eldredge and Salthe take a broader view of interactors than I. According to Hull's definition, which I have adopted, interactors imply selection. But there are many forms of interaction (mass-energy interchange) with the environment that do not necessarily lead to selection. Perhaps, then, my dual hierarchy is a special case of theirs.

16. Vrba (1984) tests the alternative hypotheses of chance, organismic selection, and species selection among some monophylectic taxa of extinct and extant African mammals. Her data support the organismic-selection hypothesis, i.e. the hypothesis that the pattern of differential speciation is an *effect* (sensu Williams 1966) of organismic selection.

References

Antonovics, J., N. C. Ellstrand, and R. N. Brandon. 1988. "Genetic Variation and Environmental Variation: Expectations and Experiments." In *Plant Evolutionary Biology*, ed. S. K. Jain and L. D. Gotlieb. London: Chapman and Hall.

Arnold, A. J., and K. Fristrup. 1982. "The Theory of Evolution by Natural Selection: A Hierarchical Expansion." *Paleobiology* 8: 113–129.

Brandon, R. N. 1978. "Adaptation and Evolutionary Theory." *Studies in History and Philosophy of Science* 9: 181–206.

Brandon, R. N. 1981a. "Biological Teleology: Questions and Explanations." *Studies in History and Philosophy of Science* 12: 91–105.

Brandon, R. N. 1981b. "A Structural Description of Evolutionary Theory." In *PSA 1980*, volume 2, ed. P. Asquith and R. Giere. East Lansing, Mich.: Philosophy of Science Association.

Brandon, R. N. 1982. "The Levels of Selection." In *PSA 1982*, volume 1, ed. P. Asquith and T. Nickles. East Lansing, Mich.: Philosophy of Science Association.

Brandon, R. N. 1985. "Adaptation Explanations: Are Adaptations for the Good of Replicators or Interactors?" In *Evolution at a Crossroads: The New Biology and the New Philosophy of Science*, ed. B. Weber and D. Depew. Cambridge, Mass.: MIT Press. A Bradford Book.

Brandon, R. N. Forthcoming. *Adaptation and Environment*.

Brandon, R. N., and R. M. Burian, eds. 1984. *Genes, Organisms, Populations: Controversies over the Units of Selection*. Cambridge, Mass.: MIT Press. A Bradford Book.

Crow, J. F. 1979. "Genes that Violate Mendel's Rules." *Scientific American* 240, no. 2: 134–146.

Damuth, J. 1985. "Selection among 'Species': A Formulation in Terms of Natural Functional Units." *Evolution* 39: 1132–1146.

Dawkins, R. 1976. *The Selfish Gene*. Oxford University Press.

Dawkins, R. 1978. "Replicator Selection and the Extended Phenotype." *Zeitschrift für Tierpsychologie* 47: 61–76.

Dawkins, R. 1982a. "Replicators and Vehicles." In *Current Problems in Sociobiology*, ed. King's College Sociobiology Group. Cambridge University Press.

Dawkins, R. 1982b. *The Extended Phenotype*. Oxford: Freeman.

Doolittle, W. F., and C. Sapienza. 1980. "Selfish Genes, the Phenotype Paradigm and Genome Evolution." *Nature* 284: 601–603.

Eigen, M., W. Gardiner, P. Schuster, and R. Winkler-Oswatitsch. 1981. "The Origin of Genetic Information." *Scientific American* 244, no. 4: 78–94.

Eldredge, N. 1985. *The Unfinished Synthesis*. Oxford University Press.

Eldredge, N., and J. Cracraft. 1980. *Phylogenetic Patterns and Evolutionary Process*. New York: Columbia University Press.

Eldredge, N., and S. Salthe. 1985. "Hierarchy and Evolution." In *Oxford Surveys of Evolutionary Biology*, ed. R. Dawkins and M. Ridley. Oxford Univeristy Press.

Endler, J. A. 1986. *Natural Selection in the wild*. Princeton University Press.

Gould, S. J., and N. Eldredge. 1977. "Punctuated Equilibria: The Tempo and Mode of Evolution Reconsidered." *Paleobiology* 3: 115–151.

Hamilton, W. D. 1975. "Innate Social Aptitudes of Man: An Approach from Evolutionary Genetics." In *Biosocial Anthropology*, ed. R. Fox. New York: Wiley.

Hull, D. 1980. "Individuality and Selection." *Annual Review of Ecology and Systematics* 11: 311–332.

Hull, D. 1981. "Units of Evolution: A Metaphysical Essay." In *The Philosophy of Evolution*, ed. U. L. Jensen and R. Harre. Brighton: Harvester.

Jablonski, D. 1986. "Background and Mass Extinctions: The Alternation of Macroevolutionary Regimes." *Science* 231: 129–133.

Lewontin, R. C. 1970. "The Units of Selection." *Annual Review of Ecology and Systematics* 1: 1–18.

Lewontin, R. C. 1974. *The Genetic Basis of Evolutionary Change*. New York: Columbia University Press.

Lewontin, R. C. 1978. "Adaptation." *Scientific American* 239, no. 3: 156–169.

Lewontin, R. C. 1983. "Gene, Organism and Environment." In *Evolution from Molecules to Man*, ed. D. S. Bendall. Cambridge University Press.

Maynard Smith, J. 1982. "The Evolution of Social Behavior—A Classification of Models." In *Current Problems in Sociobiology*, ed. Cambridge Sociobiology Group. Cambridge University Press.

Mayr, E. 1963. *Animal Species and Evolution*. Cambridge, Mass.: Harvard University Press.

Mayr, E. 1978? "Evolution." *Scientific American* 239, no. 3: 46–55.

Nunney, L. 1985. "Group Selection, Altruism and Structured-Dome Models." *American Naturalist* 126: 262–293.

Orgel, L. E., and F. H. C. Crick. 1980. "Selfish DNA: The Ultimate Parasite." *Nature* 284: 604–607.

Salmon, W. C. 1971. *Statistical Explanation and Statistical Relevance*. University of Pittsburgh Press.

Salthe, S. N. 1985. *Evolving Hierarchical Systems*. New York: Columbia University Press.

Sober, E. 1984. *The Nature of Selection*. Cambridge, Mass.: MIT Press. A Bradford Book.

Stanley, S. M. 1975. "A Theory of Evolution above the Species Level." *Proceedings of the National Academy of Sciences* 72: 646–650.

Stanley, S. M. 1979. *Macroevolution: Pattern and Process*. San Francisco: Freeman.

Uyenoyama, M., and M. W. Feldman. 1980. "Theories of Kin and Group Selection: A Population Genetics Perspective." *Theoretical Population Biology* 19: 87–123.

Vrba, E. S. 1984. "Evolutionary Pattern and Process in the Sister-Group Alcelaphini-Aepycerotini (Mammalia: Bovidae)." In *Living Fossils*, ed. N. Eldredge and S. M. Stanley. New York: Springer-Verlag.

Vrba, E. S., and S. J. Gould. 1986. "The Hierarchical Expansion of Sorting and Selection: Sorting and Selection Cannot Be Equated." *Paleobiology* 12: 217–228.

Wade, M. J. 1977. "An Experimental Study of Group Selection." *Evolution* 31: 134–153.

Wade, M. J. 1978. "A Critical Review of the Models of Group Selection." *Quarterly Reivew of Biology* 53: 101–114.

Wade, M. J. 1984. "Soft Selection, Hard Selection, Kin Selection, and Group Selection." *American Naturalist* 125: 61–73.

Williams, G. C. 1966. *Adaptation and Natural Selection*. Princeton University Press.

Wilson, D. S. 1983a. "The Group Selection Controversy: History and Current Status." *Annual Review of Ecology and Systematics* 14: 159–187.

Wilson, D. S. 1983b. "The Effect of Population Structure on the Evolution of Mutualism: A Field Test Involving Burying Beetles and their Phoretic Mites." *American Naturalist* 121: 851–870.

Wimsatt, W. C. 1980. "Reductionist Research Strategies and their Biases in the Units of Selection Controversy." In *Scientific Discovery*, volume 2, ed. T. Nickles. Dordrecht: Reidel.

Wimsatt, W. C. 1981. "The Units of Selection and the Structure of the Multi-Level Genome." In *PSA 1980*, volume 2, ed. P. Asquith and R. Giere. East Lansing, Mich.: Philosophy of Science Association.

Wynne-Edwards, V. C. 1962. *Animal Dispersion in Relation to Social Behaviour*. Edinburgh: Oliver and Boyd.

Chapter 4

Niche-Constructing Phenotypes

F. J. Odling-Smee

Any theory of evolution has to account for at least two fundamental phenomena. It has to account for descent, and it has to account for the modification of descent during time. Descent depends on between-organisms and between-generations inheritance. The modification of descent depends on whatever forces are capable of changing that inheritance over time. Among the modifying forces, any force that has the power to direct descent by causing it to deviate significantly from what can be expected to happen by chance is of paramount importance and is bound to demand the special attention of the theory. In addition, any theory of evolution must deal in one fundamental "currency": fitness (simply a measure of the capacity of diverse organisms to contribute to evolutionary descent in the face of modifying forces).

The present orthodoxy, the modern synthetic theory of evolution, exemplifies these points. It describes evolution in terms of both descent and modification. It models only one kind of descent (that based on genetic inheritance), and it assumes that only one kind of modifying force (natural selection) is capable of directing the course of evolution along nonrandom paths. All else—genetic drift or gene mutation, for instance—is a matter of chance. Consequently, the modern synthesis defines fitness in terms of the capacities of different organisms to contribute to genetic inheritance in the presence of both natural selection and chance.

This definition of fitness is responsible for determining how the modern synthesis explains the role of phenotypes in evolution, and their behaviors. Since the synthetic theory recognizes only one kind of inheritance—genetic inheritance—it cannot do other than evaluate phenotypes in terms of their capacity to contribute genes to subsequent generations, either by their own reproductive efforts or via the reproductive efforts of their kin (Hamilton 1964; Williams 1966; Dawkins 1982). So the only way in which the theory allows an organism's behavior to affect its fitness is by affecting its capacity to transmit its genes to subsequent generations. This is true regardless of whether or not the behavior itself is genetically encoded. If a behavior is genetically encoded, then it has a dual aspect: In the parent generation, it contributes to the process of evolution by affecting the capacity of organisms to survive and reproduce; in the offspring generation, it appears as a product of that process (namely a phenotypic trait which has itself been inherited). If, alternatively, a behavior is not encoded by genes but, for example, is learned, it still contributes to the parent generation's fitness; however, it no longer appears as a heritable product among its offspring. If the latter kind of behavior should recur at all (for instance, because it has been learned afresh by offspring who find themselves in environmental circumstances similar to those of their parents), it will now have a different etiology. Either way, the role of behavior in evolution is measured by the synthetic theory in the same way. Like every other aspect of phenotypic expression, it is evaluated in the currency of genes (Krebs and Davies 1984).

In this chapter I shall argue that the modern synthesis does not provide an adequate basis for understanding either phenotypes or behavior in evolution. Genetic fitness does not occur in vacuo. It always occurs relative to particular natural selection forces in particular organisms' environments. Yet developing and behaving organisms routinely select and perturb their own relative environments. Thus, at least some of the selection forces that ultimately select genes are themselves selected and modified by the behaviors, and other activities, of phenotypes. The consequent relativity of genes to environments is so fundamental that it implies the existence of two routes to fitness instead of one. Active organisms may bequeath either "better (or worse) genes" for "anticipated environments" or they may bequeath "better (or worse) environments" for "anticipated genes." I shall argue that both of these routes to fitness exist, and that the second cannot be reduced to the first because it introduces a second kind of inheritance, which is distinct from genetics, and a second kind of directing force in evolution, which is distinct from natural selection. I shall then sketch one way in which evolutionary theory might be extended to incorporate these ideas.

The Modern Synthesis: The Story So Far

The modern synthesis originated with the reconciliation of the Darwinian and Mendelian legacies. Darwin held that the form of an organism is due to the external forces of natural selection. Mendel proposed that it is due to internal "factors" (now called genes). These two starting points appear contradictory, and they were so in practice until they were reconciled on the basis of three simplifying assumptions, approximately as follows. First, it was assumed that all heritable traits are determined by genes. Second, it was assumed that natural selection is the only modifying force capable of selecting among different randomly arising heritable traits nonrandomly.

Third, it was assumed that the environment, including both its biotic and nonbiotic components, is the sole source of natural selection. When these three assumptions were eventually combined, they constituted the modern synthetic theory (Simpson 1967; Lewontin 1983; Stebbins and Ayala 1985). They were also responsible for the theory's two most salient characteristics. The theory is preoccupied with genetics because it can measure evolutionary descent only in terms of genes. Paradoxically, it is also an extremely powerful "environmentalist" theory because it holds autonomous events in the environment (that is, autonomous natural-selection forces) to be exclusively responsible for directing the course of evolution down nonrandom paths.

Arguably, this environmentalism is the synthetic theory's most important side effect. It leads directly to the separation of organisms from their environments (Patten 1982). On the one hand, the theory is able to model changes in organisms in terms of their genetic inheritance; on the other hand, it cannot model environmental changes in terms of anything at all. Environments include nonbiotic as well as biotic components, and there is no genetic inheritance—in fact, no internal inheritance system of any kind—available in the nonbiotic environment. Consequently the synthetic theory lacks any medium of inheritance which could allow it to describe environmental changes as an integral part of the evolutionary process. Instead it is forced to assume that the environment is autonomous and that environmental change is a separate matter from changing organisms. The result is two disciplines: ecology, which handles environmental change, and evolutionary biology, which deals with changing organisms.

The attraction of the synthetic theory's approach is that it is simple. It allows the evolution of organisms to be plausibly described as a function of their changing environments. Its disadvantage is that it forces us to treat biotic evolution as an inputs-only process, directed solely by naturally selecting inputs to organisms from their environments. The outputs emitted by active organisms back to their environments, often via behaviour, can only be handled self-referentially; this means that they can only be accounted for indirectly in terms of the genetic inheritance system, and therefore in terms of the genetic fitness of the organisms themselves. They cannot be described in terms of their direct impact on the environment, because the theory provides no way of measuring that impact. Hence, the modern synthesis has to rule out the possibility that the outputs of active organisms are capable of modifying their own subsequent inputs in evolutionarily significant ways. This is the principal limitation of the theory, and the central issue we shall be examining.

As far as I know, the first person to draw attention to this particular limitation in a clear way was the physicist Schrödinger (1956). He was soon followed by the developmental biologist Waddington (1959, 1960, 1969).

Like Schrödinger, Waddington realized that organisms don't just sit on the receiving end of naturally selecting inputs from their environments. On the contrary, they select (to varying extents) their own habitats, select their own mates, select and consume resources, generate detritus, and even construct parts of their own environments (such as nests, burrows, paths, dams, or pheromone trails). In addition, many organisms select, protect, and provision various "nursery" environments for their offspring. Therefore, Waddington argued, evolution cannot just depend on naturally selecting inputs from environments to organisms; it must also depend on the outputs emitted by active organisms back to their environments. Waddington called this phenotype-dependent component of evolution the "exploitive system" (see figure 1 in chapter 1 above), and he noted that it had been left out of the modern synthesis.

Waddington drew most of his examples from developmental biology, but here it makes better sense to choose behavioral illustrations. The first comes from the salt-and-pepper moth (*Biston betularia*) studied by Kettlewell (1956). Kettlewell not only showed that the light and dark forms of this moth are differentially selected by predators, depending on how well each morph is camouflaged relative to light lichen-covered trees or dark sooty trees; he also showed that the darker moths tend to settle on the darker areas of trees more frequently than could be expected by chance. This observation indicates alternative routes to the adaptation. Either only those morphs that happen to match their background fortuitously are likely to survive and reproduce (classical natural selection) or only those morphs that are capable of finding the appropriate background relative to their own particular coloration are likely to survive and reproduce (natural selection modified by the behavioural outputs of the moths). Obviously these alternatives are not mutually exclusive, and they could occur in many other instances of cryptic coloration.

A second, more complicated example is from the Galapagos woodpecker finch. This bird is famous for using a tool—a twig or a cactus spine—which it holds in its beak to poke out grubs from the barks of trees. It thereby achieves its woodpecking in a most unusual fashion. Probably its novel behavior is based on learning rather than on gene mutations (Alcock 1972). One apparent result is that these birds have never evolved either the typical beak or the typical tongue of other woodpeckers. The immediate question is Why not? This expands to a more interesting question: What exactly is being transmitted via evolutionary descent among successive generations of woodpeckers? Part of the answer is clear enough. If Alcock is right, a capacity for learning the tool-using skill must be transmitted via genes in the usual way. But that alone is not enough to account for the whole phenomenon. It is also likely that the particular "woodpecking niche" opened up for these birds by their own behavior is transmitted from generation to generation, not genetically, but via those environments which successive generations of woodpeckers are themselves ensuring they encounter. In that case, a transmitted niche could then explain the modification of the selection forces in the finches' environment which, on the one hand, are apparently selecting for tool-using skills but which, on the other hand, are clearly not selecting for the elongated beaks and tongues of typical woodpeckers. The fact that the nongenetic "inheriting" of environmental resources is possible can then be demonstrated by referring to the transmission of breeding territories from parents to offspring or to helpers in the Florida scrub jay (Woolfenden and Fitzpatrick 1978) or by the inheritance of burrows and coterie territorial limits by juveniles from adults in prairie dogs (King 1955; Smith et al. 1973; Wilson 1975).

On the basis of this kind of evidence, a similar theoretical argument has been raised (Lewontin 1978, 1982, 1983; Levins and Lewontin 1985): that there is something seriously wrong with the concept of adaptation. At present the synthetic theory holds that organisms adapt to their environments in reaction to natural selection. But, says Lewontin, "organisms do not adapt to their environments; they construct them out of the bits and pieces of the external world" (1983, p. 280). He therefore proposes replacing the "metaphor of adaptation" by a new "metaphor of construction."

Lewontin is overstating the case slightly. The idea that active organisms construct their own environments does not replace the idea of adaptation. It merely proposes that the adaptive fit which organisms regularly express in their environments could be arrived at by a different route from the one described by the modern synthesis. Instead of natural selection's causing organisms to adapt to their environments, it proposes that the constructive activities of phenotypes could cause their environments to become adapted to themselves. More plausibly, it suggests that the adaptive fit between organisms and their environments could be caused by both of these processes acting together in a manner reminiscent of Kettlewell's moths. Elsewhere, Lewontin indicates that this is what he has in mind anyway when he presents two contrasting pairs of differential equations. The first pair encapsulates the modern synthesis. Evolutionary change over time is described first as a function of organisms O in their environments E (equation 1) and second as a function of autonomous changes occurring in the environment (equation 2):

$$\frac{dO}{dt} = f(O, E), \tag{1}$$

$$\frac{dE}{dt} = g(E). \tag{2}$$

The crucial point here is that these two equations are uncoupled from each other. Organisms are not supposed to cause any of the environmental changes which subsequently change themselves. In contrast, the second pair of equations are coupled. They describe a situation in which "organism and environment coevolve, each as a function of the other" (Lewontin 1983, p. 282):

$$\frac{dO}{dt} = f(O, E), \tag{3}$$

$$\frac{dE}{dt} = g(O, E). \tag{4}$$

The latter, Lewontin claims, is the better model of what is actually happening in nature.

The fact that organisms can modify selection forces in their own environments is now quite widely recognized (Southwood 1977; Hamilton and May 1977; Piaget 1979; Bock 1980; May 1981; Hailman 1982; Patten 1982; Wilson 1985). However, the inference that Schrödinger, Waddington, Lewontin, and Levins all draw from it—that the synthetic theory therefore stands in need of a radical revision—is not yet widely accepted in spite of the growing restlessness among many biologists about the current status of the theory (Gould 1980; Bonner 1982; Vrba and Eldredge 1984; Salthe 1985; Depew and Weber 1985). It is this inference that I want to explore, because of its potentially revolutionary implications for the study of behavior. All the preceding criticisms imply that we shall never do justice to the role of either phenotypes or behavior in evolution until we have replaced the present one-way version of evolutionary theory, whose central tenet is that biotic evolution is directed only by naturally selecting inputs from environments to organisms, with a new two-way version of evolutionary theory that formally acknowledges that both organisms and their environments can cause coevolutionary changes in each other via their mutual inputs and outputs. The significance of this step for behavior is, of course, that the outputs of animals are so frequently mediated by behavior. I shall call such a two-way version of evolutionary theory *organism-environment coevolution*.

Organism-Environment Coevolution

The first requirement of organism-environment coevolution is that it provide some way of measuring the impact of organisms on their environments, as well as measuring the impact of environments on their organisms. This is necessary so as to allow the contributions organisms make to evolutionary descent (either via the genes they bequeath or via the environmental modifications they bequeath) to be assessed. At present the impact of environments on organisms is measured in terms of the genetic system of inheritance, to which the organisms contribute if they survive and reproduce in the face of naturally selecting inputs from their environments. We now need an additional system of inheritance in order to be able to describe the complementary impact that organisms have on their environments via their outputs. But how can this be provided, in view of the fact that environments include abiotic components that do not incorporate any kind of inheritance system of their own? The answer, I suggest, is that, although it is not possible to describe a succession of changing environments absolutely in terms of any kind of internal inheritance system in the environment, it is possible to describe a succession of environments relativistically as an ecological inheritance relative to successive generations of organisms. This may be quite enough to get a general theory of organism-environment coevolution off the ground.

The principal difficulty with this proposal does not lie with the notion that it is possible for organisms to "inherit" environments. The phenomenon of environmental inheritance is self-evident; it is just not usual to call it an "inheritance" (except in the special case where humans inherit environmental "property" via cultural mechanisms). The real problem is how to combine an organism's genetic inheritance with its ecological inheritance within the scope of a single unified theory, and in such a way that the contributions of both kinds of inheritance to evolutionary descent can be modeled. There are several reasons why this is difficult:

(1) There is a major asymmetry between genetic and ecological inheritance. The genes an organism inherits are entirely determined by the actions and fates of ancestral organisms, because genetic inheritance is completely biological in character; but the same is not true of ecological inheritance. One component of an organism's ecological inheritance—the one driven by the outputs of organisms—does depend on ancestral organisms, but a second component does not. It would occur anyway, in the complete absence of all organisms, as a function of cosmology and physics. This asymmetry between the two inheritance systems makes the modeling of ecological inheritance inherently more awkward.

(2) Genes and environmental modifications are transmitted from generation to generation via different mechanisms. Genetic inheritance depends on the mechanisms of reproduction. This means that genes can be transmitted to new organisms only once during their lives: at the moment of their origin. It also means that genes can be transmitted to offspring only via parents; and it means that genes can be transmitted in only one direction, from parents to offspring, and not the other way round. However, the organism-dependent

component of ecological inheritance works according to different rules. Environmental modifications can be transmitted among organisms within as well as between generations, and at all stages of organisms' lifetimes. It is also possible for some feedback to occur between generations: offspring can modify their parents' environments, and vice versa. Finally, environmental perturbations need not be transmitted by genetic relatives only. They may also be transmitted by "neighbors" who share, or who have previously shared, some common aspect of a mutual environment. Such neighbors have to be ecologically related but need not be genetically related.

(3) The modifying force that directs genetic inheritance is natural selection, but the modifying force that directs ecological inheritance is something else. It comprises the outputs from active organisms to their environments. Henceforth, and following Lewontin's lead, I shall call this second directing force *niche construction* (with the proviso that it also implicitly refers to its negative aspect, niche destruction). Like natural selection, niche construction is capable of exerting a directing influence over evolution by modifying evolutionary descent in nonrandom ways. The difference is that it exerts its influence externally via the environment instead of internally via genes.

The scheme we end up with is illustrated in figure 1, which shows two complementary systems of descent working via two different kinds of transmission mechanisms under the direction of two reciprocal modifying forces. Thus a *genetic inheritance* is transmitted from ancestral organisms (O) at time t_0 to successor organisms at time t_i via the mechanisms of reproduction and under the direction of natural selection. Also, an *ecological inheritance* is transmitted to successor organisms at time t_i via the external environment (E). One component of this ecological inheritance is directed by the niche-constructing outputs of ancestral organisms at time t_0; however, a second component is independent of the niche-constructing outputs of all ancestral organisms and arises in the rest of the environment. The task ahead is to combine all these disparate elements within a unified theory of organism-environment coevolution.

The crucial step is to find a way of replacing the simple linear causation of the modern synthetic theory (symbolized by equations 1 and 2) with the more complicated cyclic causation of the general coevolutionary theory (symbolized by equations 3 and 4). This is the only step likely to link all these elements together in a single dynamic system. At present the synthetic theory models only a single "causal arrow," namely natural selection. However, the proposed general coevolutionary theory will have to model two "causal arrows": natural selection (with its arrow pointing from environments to organisms) and niche construction (with its arrow

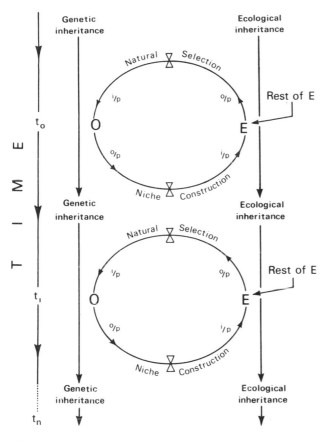

Figure 1
Organism-environment coevolution combines two kinds of descent, genetic and ecological, with two directing forces, natural selection and niche construction.

pointing in the opposite direction). It will also have to model the successive cycles of causation that are set up by the interactions of both these "causal arrows" with each other.

The Reference-Device Problem

This introduces the most fundamental reform of them all. Although the proposed coevolutionary theory is bound to be based on the foundations laid for it by the modern synthesis, it will not be possible to replace the synthetic theory's linear causation with the concept of cyclic causation without first abandoning the environmentalism of the synthetic theory.

The synthetic theory currently assigns a dual role to the environment. One role is explicit, pragmatic, and obvious. It is assumed that the environment is the sole source of natural selection. Its second role is implicit, philosophical, and far less obvious. Natural selection is assumed to be the only force capable of altering gene frequencies nonrandomly, and therefore to be capable of directing evolutionary descent down nonrandom paths. This second assumption is arbitrary in the sense that it does not necessarily follow from the first; but as soon as it is made, it converts the environment from being merely the source of *a* directing cause in evolution to being the source of *the only* directing cause. It thereby assigns a second metatheoretical role to the environment: that of acting as the ultimate "reference device" from which the synthetic theory derives its meaning.

The environment fulfills this second role simply by acting as the final source of the theory's explanations. In the guise of natural selection, environmental events are thought sufficient by themselves to explain the only phenomena in evolution that really require explanation: the non-randomness of evolutionary descent and its consequence, the existence of such improbable entities as living organisms. Everything else is explicable by chance. In its metatheoretical role, however, the environment is far from neutral. It duly supplies the synthetic theory, with its considerable explanatory power, but at the same time it limits the kinds of explanation that are possible by insisting that all the theory's causal explanations must now be cast in terms of natural-selection forces changing gene frequencies. The principal effect of this limitation is one that behavioral scientists have frequently discovered to their cost: It constrains evolutionary theory *a priori* in ways that prevent it from assigning any directing role in evolution to either the development or the behaviors of phenotypes. It follows that as long as the environment is maintained as the reference device for evolutionary theory, it will be bound to prevent such concepts as niche construction and ecological inheritance from ever being incoporated by the theory, no matter how strong the empirical evidence in favor of their incoporation. It is this deeply entrenched, covert prejudice that we shall have to abandon.

The issue is complicated enough to merit a digression. The environment as the ultimate source of the synthetic theory's explanations is only playing the same role as all the other reference devices that have ever been used in science (most clearly in physics) to serve as the origin of any theory's capacity to describe and explain natural phenomena. The main points to note are the following:

(1) To describe data it is always necessary to do so relative to some reference body, some point of origin, some system of coordinates, or some other kind of reference device. This is because it is impossible to describe anything relative to nothing, and equally impossible to describe anything exclusively relative to itself (Einstein 1956, 1960; Feynman 1965).

(2) In biology the description of data traditionally starts with the classification of organisms. Throughout prescientific history a great variety of reference devices were used as a basis for setting up diverse schemes of classification, some more florid than others. For example, the *scala naturae*, with its roots in Aristotle, graded organisms according to a scale of perfection, with formless creatures such as sponges at the bottom and man at the top (Lovejoy 1936; Ross 1949; Hodos and Campbell 1969). Primitive and medieval taxonomists, on the other hand, generally preferred to classify organisms more pragmatically, according to their usefulness to human beings (e.g., weeds versus flowers or vegetables). There were also some celebrated medieval attempts to classify animals according to their habitats (e.g. land, water, air; see Lovejoy 1936). The implicit reference device in this last case was the scheme of elements of antiquity (Russell 1946). Scientific classification of organisms began in the eighteenth century with the recognition by Linnaeus and others of natural affinities among organisms, and is now based on either phylogentic trees or cladograms.

(3) Explanation of data goes beyond description and requires less arbitrary devices to support it. To explain, it is necessary to tell a coherent causal story about the data, which means establishing a theory. To do that, it is necessary to continue to describe not only the data but also the cause or causes that account for them. Hence, an explanatory theory needs a reference device relative to which it is possible to describe both the data and their cause.

(4) If the data can be satisfactorily explained by a theory that appeals to simple linear causation only, then this extra requirement for achieving explanation raises no great difficulties. In such cases it

seems both natural and obvious to describe the cause and its effects (the data) relative to whatever reference device the theory proposes as the ultimate origin of the cause. In biology this point can again be illustrated by both prescientific and scientific examples. Prescientific explanations of life typically invoked, and still invoke, one or more creative deities. The logical function of such a deity is to serve as a reference device relative to which it then becomes possible to describe both the effect (phenomenal life) and the cause (mystical creation) with facility. Similarly, the contemporary scientific explanation proposed by the synthetic theory is based on simple linear causation. The observed data (phylogenetically related organisms) are explained by a single directing cause (the natural selection of genes), which in turn is described relative to the environment from which it originates. In this case, the environment acts as the reference device relative to which both the cause and its effects, organic evolution, are described.

(5) If, however, the observed data cannot be explained satisfactorily by a theory that depends exclusively on linear causation, but instead demand explanation by some other theory incorporating more than one cause and therefore more than one source of causation, then this simple kind of reference device no longer works (see Campbell 1985). This is because the joint effect of plural causes originating from diverse sources is not describable relative to any reference device that fails to support all of them. It is therefore not possible to use the source of just one cause as a reference device for a multicausal theory. Rather, it is necessary to find some alternative reference device relative to which all the putative causes and their effects can be described.

The proposed general theory of coevolution is the case in point. This theory sets out to explain contemporary biological data more satisfactorily than can the synthetic theory by appealing to cycles of causation driven by two directing forces. One "cause," natural selection, is readily described relative to the environment, because the environment is its origin and therefore its obvious reference device. However, the second "cause," niche construction, cannot be described relative to the environment, because organisms and not environments are the source of niche-constructing activities. Thus, any attempt to explain organism-environment coevolution exclusively relative to the environment must end up by explaining away the niche-constructing activities of organisms in terms of prior natural selection. But when that is done, phenotypes cease, *a priori*, to be the source of any kind of causal force in evolution that is even partly independent of their environments. Hence, one of the two causes of organism-environment coevolution is "written off" as a consequence of the other. The cost of this tactic is the destruction of coevolutionary theory's potentially superior powers of explanation by ensuring the cyclic causation on which it depends must regress to the linear causation of the synthetic theory. That reintroduces the anti-phenotypic bias that is the hallmark of the synthetic theory.

This is why the synthetic theory cannot accommodate the concept of niche-constructing phenotypes, and why it is not possible to develop a general theory of organism-environment coevolution without abandoning the concept of an autonomous environment as the reference device relative to which biotic evolution is described and explained.

The Inadequacies of Contemporary Models of Coevolution

How, then, do biologists regularly describe restricted coevolving systems relative to autonomous environments without apparently violating any of the assumptions of the synthetic theory (see, e.g., Maynard Smith 1974; May 1981; Roughgarden 1983)? Surely the above conclusion is wrong? No, because these restricted models only illustrate rather than refute the preceding argument.

Let us take a simple example. Two population models of predator-prey coevolution are typically described by translating the prior niche-constructing outputs of the predator species into subsequent naturally selecting inputs for the prey species and vice versa (Hassell 1981; May 1981; Bakker 1983). That allows the coevolution of both species to be treated as a matter of "reciprocal genetic changes" under the direction of reciprocal selection forces (Futuyma and Slatkin 1983, p. 3). This treatment redescribes the cyclic causation of a particular coevolutionary relationship by reducing its two directing causes to one. Each population responds to the naturally selecting inputs it receives from the other. Each population also emits niche-constructing outputs to the other. However, the contemporary coevolutionary models "write off" the latter by assuming that they are determined by the former, because that is the only way they can remain faithful to the tenets of the synthetic theory. But this step is tantamount to a claim that the relevant outputs of active organisms are always determined by previously selected genes. The claim is unsustainable for two reasons. First, although genes may determine proteins, they do not determine phenotypes (Mayr 1974; Suzuki, Griffiths, and Lewontin 1981; Bonner 1982; Lewontin 1982, 1983). Phenotypes are "underdetermined" (Dennett 1975) by their genes. Second, even though phenotypes are underdetermined by their genes, the genes in question may not have been naturally selected anyway. They could be carried by organisms for some other reason—genetic drift for instance, or perhaps molecular drive (Dover 1982).

This trick of equating outputs and inputs can, in any case, be used only to model the biotic components of organisms' environments. It cannot be used for any of the coevolutionary relationships between organisms and the abiotic components of their environments. Natural selection acts on genes via phenotypes. It can therefore be a directing force in evolution only relative to living systems that incorporate genetic inheritance. Thus, although it may be possible to redescribe the coevolution of a predator species A with its prey species B in terms of what A does to B's genes and vice versa, it is not possible to describe the coevolution of species A with some abiotic entity X in the same way, because X does not incorporate genes or any other kind of internal inheritance. In these circumstances it would be ludicrous to redescribe A's niche-constructing outputs as naturally selecting inputs for X. A's outputs can be understood only as outputs from A.

There is also another snag. The contemporary models of coevolution cannot be sufficiently generalized to act as a basis for a general coevolutionary theory, again for two reasons. First, they tend to become mathematically intractable as soon as they are extended (May 1981; Roughgarden 1983). Second, they progressively violate the environmentalism of the synthetic theory as they are extended, so they progressively undermine their own foundations.

Both points are illustrated by the Lotka-Volterra equations, which provide the historical starting point for most of these models. Equations 5 and 6, taken from May 1981 (p. 87), represent a simple model for the coevolution of any two competing species:

$$\frac{dN_1}{dt} = r_1 N_1 [1 - (N_1 + \alpha_{12}, N_2)/K_1], \tag{5}$$

$$\frac{dN_2}{dt} = r_2 N_2 [1 - (N_2 + \alpha_{21}, N_1)/K_2]. \tag{6}$$

N_1 and N_2 are two competing species. K_1 and K_2 are the carrying capacities of the environment from the point of view of species 1 and 2, respectively. r_1 and r_2 are the intrinsic rates of growth for the two species. α_{12} is the competition coefficient that measures the extent to which species 2 inhibits species 1; α_{21} is the corresponding coefficient that measures the extent to which species 1 inhibits species 2. The equations attempt to answer the question of how species 1 affects species 2, and vice versa, by focusing on the between-species interactions represented by the competition coefficients. Generalizing involves adding further species and further interactions to these equations (Pianka 1981), which rapidly makes them intractable.

The second restriction is more obscure. In equations 5 and 6 the special coevolutionary relation between species 1 and 2 is modeled cyclically by the two competition coefficients, but nothing else is. All else is left outside the coevolutionary analysis as either the rest of each species' environment (K_1 and K_2) or as some previously evolved product of natural selection by the environment (r_1 and r_2). "All else" is therefore the reservoir that contains the many other selection forces that are also acting on both species. These are still assumed to arise from an autonomously changing environment. The significance of this point is that it maintains the environmentalism of the synthetic theory nearly intact. If, however, the model were generalized, the number of environmental components treated "cyclically" would have to be increased, and the number treated "linearly" would decrease, thereby chipping away at the concept of an autonomously changing environment. Taken far enough, that would eventually mean that too little of the environment would be left to serve in its metatheoretical role of implicit reference device for the model. In practice it would mean that any attempt to explain organism-environment coevolution relative to the environment would become incomprehensible.

The present coevolutionary models are therefore incompatible with a general coevolutionary theory. The fundamental obstacle is the reference-device problem; until it is solved, it must hold up everything else. The solution is to start looking for an alternative reference device to replace the traditional concept of an autonomous environment. What is needed is a new device relative to which it is possible to describe both of coevolution's "causal arrows" without introducing any *a priori* biases in favor of natural selection and genetics or in favor of niche construction and phenotypes. The rest of this chapter is preoccupied with an attempt to supply this device. The device itself will be derived from one of the few general theories of organism-environment coevolution offered so far, that proposed by Patten (1982).

Terminology

Patten (1982) and Patten and Auble (1981) cast their theory in terms of general systems. This forces them to adopt a lexicon of six new words: holon, taxon, creaon, genon, environ, and enviroplasm. Briefly, a *holon* is any input-state-output system, either living or nonliving. A *taxon* is a special case of a *holon*, namely any living system. The *creaon* is any system's input environment. The *genon* is any system's output environment. The *environ* is any elementary ecological unit that contains an entire system of relationships between holons and taxons (n.b.: not taxa). "The environ is a construct which reunites organisms and their environments such that they coevolve." (Patten 1982, p. 214). Finally, the *environ* centre or "nucleus" is any uniquely defined holon or taxon with an environ relative to which

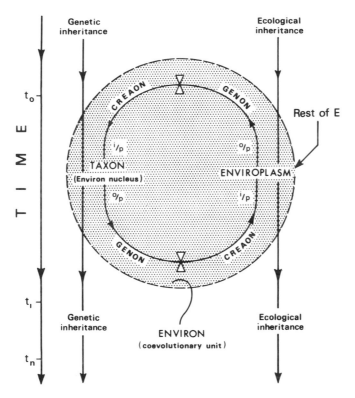

Figure 2
Patten's (1982) terminology illustrated in the context of organism-environment coevolution.

the remainder of the environ becomes its enviroplasm. The relationship between this terminology and that used in figure 1 is illustrated by figure 2.

The trouble with these terms is that they are so unusual. They make it hard to follow a sustained abstract argument. For this reason I shall translate four of them into familiar biological examples, and I shall initially present my argument with respect to these examples only. The key is to choose an appropriate living system to represent Patten's taxon. Because of the universality of Patten's theory, this choice is arbitrary. It is therefore possible to choose whichever living system is the most convenient to work with. In practice there are only two viable candidates: either a population or an individual organism. A population has the advantage of being the traditional subject matter of evolutionary theory, but it necessitates treating the niche-constructing activities of organisms stochastically on a population basis rather than an individual basis. An individual organism, on the other hand, has the advantage of being both a discrete actor, and therefore a discrete source of niche-constructing activities, and the discrete unit upon which natural selection acts; thus, it stands at the focus of both "causal arrows" of coevolution. For this reason an individual organism will be used here as the paradigm taxon in preference to a population. This choice determines the remaining translations. The paradigm enviroplasm becomes the individual organism's operational or "relative" environment. The creaon becomes its input environment, equivalent to the naturally selecting inputs or stimuli that constantly scan and irritate the organism throughout its life and which either permit it to survive and reproduce or eliminate it. The genon becomes the same organism's output environment, referring to every kind of niche-constructing activity emitted by the organism, including its behaviors. Of the remaining terms, *Holon* will be avoided and *environ*, which is Patten's crucial new concept and is untransalatable, will be used sparingly.

This choice of a paradigm taxon also determines that the first process to be considered will be ontogenesis rather than population evolution or phylogenesis. In the context of the synthetic theory that would be a drastic step to take, because the synthetic theory sees ontogenesis as fundamentally dissimilar from phylogenesis (Dawkins 1982). However, in the context of Patten's theory it is not a drastic step. The universality of his scheme makes it unimportant which process is looked at first. The coevolutionary logic should always be the same.

In addition to these translations, the analogy of a "game" will be borrowed from game theory as a further aid to communication. Game theory is not crucial to the present analysis, so it will not be used analytically. Instead it will be used loosely, as a means of providing a familiar scaffold on which to build an unfamiliar argument. The particular "game" chosen for this purpose is the existential game of "Gambler's Ruin" described by Slobodkin and Rapoport (1974). This is an especially apt but rather unusual game. In its original version the "game" is played between an evolving population and the rest of nature. Here the two "players" will initially be an individual organism and its relative environment. First, these two "players" and the "board" or reference device relative to which they play their "game" will be introduced. Then the "aims" of the two players and their respective "moves" will be described, followed by the "rules" and the players' "knowledge of the game."

The Organism-Environment Relationship

The "Players"
The first player is any individual organism, notated as O_i. This could be a single-cell or a multicell organism. It might be a plant, an animal, or a

Table 1
The relative environment (E_i) of any
organism O_i.

Physical space and time	Tolerance space
Present	*Present*
Here and now	Immediate
Past	*Past*
Here and earlier or Elsewhere and earlier	Post-interactive
Future	*Future*
Here and later or Elsewhere and later	Potential

microorganism. Anything that belongs to the class organism will do. Only two restrictions are necessary: The organism must express a phenotype, and it must possess some minimal assets at whatever arbitrary moment the game begins. Its assets will be twofold: The organism must possess an initial location in its environment in both space and time, and it must be adapted to its initial location. The latter means that O_i must be able to tolerate or use the initial inputs it receives from its environment, and it must possess sufficient free energy to fuel its initial outputs. It is assumed that the organism owes these assets to its prior interactions with its environment, and originally to its genetic and ecological inheritance.

The second player is the individual organism's operating or relative environment, notated as E_i. It is assumed to be heterogeneous in both space and time, and to contain other organisms besides O_i. Its heterogeneity ensures that O_i's adaptations cannot be constant but must fluctuate morphologically, metabolically, physiologically, and behaviorally across both space and time. E_i requires a double description. First, E_i's physical extension in both space and time needs describing relative to the organism's current location at any arbitrary moment. Second, the alternative locations in E_i, which O_i can potentially tolerate given its present adaptations and its potential adaptability, also need describing. One difficulty here is what to call this set of alternative possible locations for O_i. For a species the appropriate word is *niche*. However, only MacMahon et al. (1981) have used *niche* in connection with individual organisms. Hence, I shall use "tolerance space" for O_i. "Niche space" ($=$ tolerance space) will still be reserved for populations.

These two different descriptions of E_i are given in table 1. The environment's physical space and time is described in the left column in simple terms taken from Southwood 1977. They describe environmental space and time exclusively relative to the organism's current location. Thus, the organism's present location is called "here and now." Its past locations are either "here and earlier" or "elsewhere and earlier"; its future locations will be either "here and later" or "elsewhere and later."

The right column of table 1 depicts the same environment as a tolerance space, and likewise provides three descriptions. One relates to the organism's present state of adaptedness, one to its past states of adaptation, and one to its adaptability relative to its future. At any given moment the organism's immediate tolerance space comprises the source of its immediate inputs and the sink for its immediate outputs. The boundaries of this immediate space are set by the organism's "observational horizon" on the input side (which determines how much of the physical environment the organism can currently monitor "here and now") and by its "action horizon" on the output side (which determines how much of its environment the organism can currently perturb by its activities "here and now") (von Uexkull 1926; Patten and Auble 1981). Relative to where it is now, the organism's postinteractive tolerance space then becomes all those environmental locations which it has already visited, while its potential tolerance space refers to all those other environmental locations which the organism could tolerate and might yet visit in its future.

The "Board"

We now reach the heart of the matter. We need a new way of describing organism-environment coevolution that does not automatically break the coevolutionary cycle between organisms and their environments in any way. For that we need a new reference device, one roughly analogous to the board relative to which the game between O_i and E_i is played.

Figure 3a, which is compatible with figures 1 and 2, is based on figure 3b of Patten and Auble 1981. It represents any two coevolving systems, in this case O_i and E_i, and it illustrates two points. First, these two systems are linked by a cycle of causation based on the interactions of their mutual inputs and outputs. Second, each system is underdetermined by the other; its outputs are partly determined by the inputs it has previously received from the other, but they are also partly independent. This underdetermination is indicated by the diagonal lines separating inputs from outputs in each box.

In several respects, figure 3a is unrealistic. For instance, it only models a single cycle between the organism and its environment. A more realistic picture is that in figure 3b, which shows organism-environment coevolution as a function of multiple cycles of causation based on multiple input × outputs interactions between diverse subsystems in the organism and diverse components in its environment. It also shows that the local

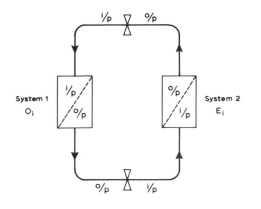

a.

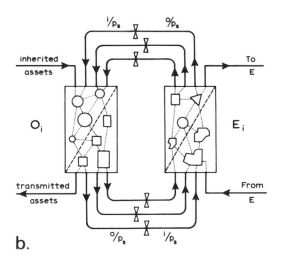

b.

Figure 3
Two coevolving systems: any organism O_i and its relative environment E_i. (a) Simple closed coevolution. (b) A more complicated example that is not completely closed.

coevolving system is never completely closed. Rather, there are limited connections between O_i and its population via the inheritance and transmission of genetic and ecological assets. There is also an additional connection between the organism's environment E_i, its population's environment (not shown), and the universal environment E (which contains E_i). The significance of this latter link is that it acknowledges that biotic and abiotic changes may occur in E which are initially autonomous relative to both O_i and E_i but which could subsequently affect E_i and thereby initiate a new coevolutionary cycle between O_i and E_i. Therefore, figure 3b illustrates the kind of scenario for which a new reference device is needed.

Most candidates for this job can be ruled out rapidly. The organism's environment has already been ruled out, because its use ultimately biases coevolutionary theory in favor of natural selection and genetics and against niche construction by phenotypes. The organism itself can also be ruled out, because its use would simply bias coevolutionary theory in the opposite direction: in favor of niche construction and phenotypes and against natural selection and genetics. That might promote an intriguingly subjective theory of evolution, like Lamarck's, but it would otherwise be useless. A third possibility is to use the universal environment E as a common matrix for both O_i and E_i. But that too is impractical, because it is not possible to establish a sufficiently clear boundary between E and E_i (Patten 1982).

The one remaining candidate is the mutual relationship between any organism O_i and its relative environment E_i. This relationship is expressed at the meeting point between these two systems. Simon (1982) describes such a meeting point as the *interface* between the inner organization of the organism and the outer organization of its environment. From here on this relationship will be referred to as the *organism-environment relationship*, notated (OE) in the general case and (O_iE_i) in the local case being considered here. At first sight this candidate may not appear promising, because of its intangability, but it offers real advantages over all its rivals. I will therefore use it and try to demonstrate some of its principal advantages. Thus, instead of trying to understand organism-environment coevolution relative to either the organism or its environment, I propose trying to understand it relative to their mutual (O_iE_i) relationship. In the context of Patten's theory this is equivalent to explaining the coevolution of organisms and their environments relative to the one unit that combines them both: their mutual environ. The present proposal goes beyond Patten only in stressing that the (O_iE_i) relationship is the functional center of whatever environ includes O_i as its nucleus, and that as such it makes a suitable reference device for explaining organism-environment coevolution.

The essence of this proposal can be illustrated by replacing Lewontin's pair of coevolutionary equations (equations 3 and 4 above) with a triplet of equations:

$$\frac{dO}{dt} = f(OE), \tag{7}$$

$$\frac{dE}{dt} = g(OE), \tag{8}$$

$$\frac{d(OE)}{dt} = h(O, E). \tag{9}$$

In the limited case where O_i represents any individual organism, the corresponding equations are the following:

$$\frac{dO_i}{dt} = f(O_i E_i), \tag{10}$$

$$\frac{dE_i}{dt} = g(O_i E_i), \tag{11}$$

$$\frac{d(O_i E_i)}{dt} = h(O_i, E). \tag{12}$$

Here $(O_i E_i)$ represents the mutual relationship between the organism O_i and its relative environment E_i in their environ, and $E = (E_i + \text{rest of } E)$ represents the universal environment.

We can now consider some of the advantages offered by the $(O_i E_i)$ as a reference device for a general coevolutionary theory.

(1) The $(O_i E_i)$ relationship between any organism and its environment is indifferent as to whether any particular component of their relationship is changed either by naturally selecting inputs from the environment or by niche-constructing outputs from the organism. The $(O_i E_i)$ relationship models both of these "causal arrows" even-handedly, thereby immediately eliminating the anti-niche-construction bias of the synthetic theory.

(2) The $(O_i E_i)$ reduces both organism changes and environmental changes to a single common currency: changes in the $(O_i E_i)$ relationship. This is because any coevolutionarily significant change in either O_i or E_i must drive a corresponding change in their mutual relationship. One unwelcome consequence of the cyclic causation of coevolution can therefore be avoided: Usually it is not possible to describe changing organisms and changing environments relative to each other simultaneously. Either the environment is "stopped" while organism changes are described (for example, evolutionarily stable strategies assume an at least temporarily stabilized environment

[Maynard Smith 1982] or else the organism is "stopped," or more likely ignored altogether, while changes in its environment are described independently. Yet either tactic leads to a break in the continuous cycle of causation which we need to model. The (O_iE_i) relationship, however, because it can reflect both organism changes and environment changes simultaneously, has no need to break the cycle at any point.

(3) The (O_iE_i) relationship is potentially capable of modeling an unlimited number of interactions between any organism and its environment, including both biotic and abiotic components. It is therefore capable of acting as the basis of a reference device for a general coevolutionary theory. In this respect it is not possible for the (O_iE_i) relationship to model all these interactions simultaneously, but it is possible for it to model them successively and in the sequence in which they actually occur.

The key here is the arbitrary definition of any organism O_i as the "nucleus" of its environ (Patten 1982). This step immediately converts the multiple components of an *environ* into just two coevolving systems: the organism, O_i, and its relative environment, E_i. The inputs and outputs of these two systems can then be redescribed relative to each other in terms of their mutual (O_iE_i). At any given moment only a small subset of the total interactions among the components of the environ are likely to be relevant to the (O_iE_i) relationship, and these can be modeled in terms of the changes of state which they cause to the (O_iE_i) relationship at that moment. Subsequently, at each successive moment, different interactions may occur, promoting further changes to the (O_iE_i) relationship. However, if it proves possible to model all these successive changes in terms of a dynamic model of the (O_iE_i), then such a model should continuously reflect all the interactions occurring anywhere and at any time within the environ that are relevant to the coevolution of O_i and E_i. The (O_iE_i) reference device should therefore convert the complex web of interactions that occur among multiple components in an environ back to the more familiar and tractable problem of understanding the ontogenesis or life history of any organism O_i relative to its heterogeneous environment E_i. There is, however, one major novelty: We are now seeking to understand O_i's life history relative to the (O_iE_i) relationship (equation 10) rather than relative to a supposedly autonomous environment. We can therefore understand it as a function of both naturally selecting inputs from E_i to O_i and niche-constructing outputs from O_i to E_i.

Further generality is provided by the arbitrariness of the choice of the organism O_i as the nucleus of its environ. Any other organism O_j can easily be substituted for O_i. Doing so simply generates a different (O_jE_j)

relationship in a different, but possibly overlapping, environ. Hence, the (O_iE_i) relationship is an extremely flexible device that provides a way of switching from one organism to another "ad lib."

A Dynamic Model of the (O_iE_i) Relationship

The next task is to try to build a dynamic model of the (O_iE_i) relationship. We can start by recalling that organisms relate to their environments in two different ways (see table 1). First, any organism is always at a specific location in environmental space and time. Second, wherever an organism is located in space and time, it must be adapted to that place and moment. These two relationships constitute the two different aspects of the (O_iE_i): a *space-time relationship* and an *adaptational relationship*. The adaptational relationship consists of the succession of input × output interactions between any organism and its relative environment at each successive point of contact. The space-time relationship determines where and when those interactions occur. As neither relationship is independent of the other, they must be represented simultaneously. That means modeling the adaptational relationship in the context of a constantly shifting space-time frame, which is equivalent to inserting the organism's tolerance space into physical space and time.

Figure 4a illustrates one way in which this might be done. It shows a three-dimensional organism growing larger and changing its location in space during time. The trouble with this diagram is that it is overrestricted. In particular, it doesn't represent the four dimensions of space and time clearly enough. The standard solution to that problem is to use a space-time diagram, as in figure 4b. Here all three spatial dimensions have been collapsed along a single axis (the y axis), leaving the x axis free to represent time. The same three-dimensional organism appears again, but it is now symbolized by the single thick black line O_i drawn in for the same two moments as before (t_0 and t_i). It is also possible to represent the organism's environment at these same two moments by the longer, thinner line E_i, thereby providing a preliminary model of the mutual (O_iE_i) relationship between O_i and E_i at moment t_0 and again at the later moment t_i.

The main advantage that figure 4b has over figure 4a is that it makes it far easier to illustrate the accumulating history of the (O_iE_i) relationship throughout any interval of time. For instance, during the interval t_0–t_i the organism O_i interacts with its environment inside the volume of space bounded by the coordinates p_0–p_k. The history of the (O_iE_i) relationship, however, is confined to the four-dimensional space-time volume (shaded) actually swept by the organism during the interval t_0–t_i. This history is bounded by the coordinates $[t_0, (p_0$–$p_i)$–$t_i, (p_j$–$p_k)]$. The difference between this four-dimensional environ history and the three-dimensional volume of environmental space which the organism interacts with during time is due to the organism's visiting different locations in space at different moments in time.

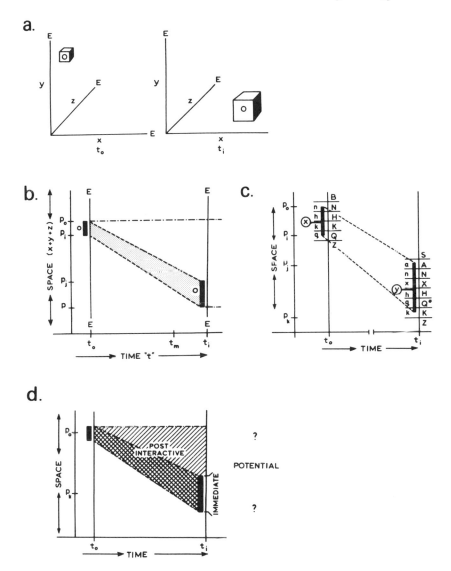

Figure 4
Changes in the $(O_i E_i)$ relationship in space and time. (a) A conventional representation of an organism O_i growing larger and changing location in space during time. (b) The same depicted in a space-time diagram. (c) The same with feature × factor changes superimposed. (d) The organism's tolerance space in physical space and time.

The adaptational relationship between the organism and its environment can be superimposed on this space-time diagram in the manner shown in figure 4c. The scheme illustrated is based on the work of Bock (1980). It assumes that any organism can be decomposed into subsystems called *features*, and that its environment can be similarly decomposed into subsystems called *factors*. Whether a feature is an adaptation depends on whether it is matched adaptively with a selection force arising from a specific environmental factor at a specific space-time location. Bock calls this matching condition *synerg*. If a feature is matched to a factor, then it qualifies as an adaptation. If there is a mismatch, it will have some other nonadaptive status and will constitute some kind of phenotypic redundancy (Bock 1980; Gould and Vrba 1982). The adaptational relationship between any organism and its environment can therefore be symbolized by the degree of correspondence between any two sets of symbols. Here the organism's features are represented by lower-case letters behind the line O_i, while the environment's factors are represented by upper-case letters behind the line E_i. A feature-factor match is symbolized by the correspondence of lower- and upper-case letters, a mismatch by a lack of correspondence. In this particular example, the organism O_i carries two kinds of redundancy. Its feature q is sufficiently general in purpose that it is able to match a range of alternative environmental factors, including both Q and Q^*. Its feature x, however, is simply a spare capacity, or an "exaptation" (Gould and Vrba 1982), at moment t_0, although by moment t_i it has become an adaptation; y is newly required redundancy at moment t_i. Thus, figure 4c shows the same organism as figures 4a and 4b, but it now demonstrates that this organism is differentiating and possibly behaving, and that it is growing as well as changing its location in space during time relative to its coevolving environment.

It is also possible to use the same space-time diagram to illustrate how this organism's tolerance space looks when it is inserted into physical space and time. Figure 4d combines the two columns of table 1 to show that this organism is currently encountering an immediate tolerance space "here" (p_k) and "now" (t_i). Its postinteractive tolerance space (shaded) trails behind it and is bounded by the coordinates p_k–p_0 "here or elsewhere" and t_i–t_0 "earlier"; its potential tolerance space is unspecified somewhere in its future, either "here and later" or "elsewhere and later." Finally, the history of the ($O_i E_i$) relationship itself comprises the four-dimensional space-time volume indicated by the darker shading.

The Aims of O_i and E_i
Next the aims of these two players need introducing. The aims of both the organism and its environment are initially assumed to be the same as those assigned by Slobodkin and Rapoport (1974) to a "population"

and to "nature" in their original version of "Gambler's Ruin." There the population's aim was to avoid extinction for as long as possible. Nature, however, was credited with no aim; it was considered indifferent to the population's fate. Here it will be assumed that O_i's aim is to survive as an individual organism for as long as it can. It will be assumed that E_i has no aim and is indifferent to O_i's continuing existence. The game itself is still the same as Gambler's Ruin, but the way it is played can be further specified. It consists of a feature-factor matching game played by O_i and E_i relative to their mutual $(O_i E_i)$ relationship wherever and whenever O_i contacts E_i in space and time. The organism stays in the game by surviving as long as there is a sufficient adaptive match between its features and the environment's factors. It loses the game by dying as soon as there is a sufficiently serious mismatch. The environment, on the other hand, never loses the game. Relative to O_i, "nature . . . has unlimited capital," so nature's ruin is "inconceivable" (Slobodkin and Rapoport 1974, p. 189).

Both of these assignments require some further comment. The organism's aim stems from the fact that it is a purposive system. Every organism is an improbable unstable system relative to its environment, and it can stay that way only by purposefully importing resources and exporting detritus (Conrad 1983). To do that, however, any organism must continuously utilize and tolerate its environment. Hence, its feature-factor matching game must serve these basic ends. To start with, it will be assumed that these are the organism's only ends, and that O_i's sole aim is survival. Later this assumption will be modified to take account of the organism's reproductive activities.

By contrast, the environment is not a purposive system relative to the organism. However, the environment is likely to contain many other organisms all of which will have the same basic aim as O_i. Some of these other organisms may not be indifferent to O_i's fate, because their own fates may be linked to that of O_i or to O_i's population. These will include O_i's parasites, predators, prey, competitors, symbionts, mates, and relatives. The environment will therefore contain some purposive components relative to O_i, in spite of its general indifference.

In this case, how should purposive components in an otherwise in-different environment be modeled relative to O_i? There are two possible solutions. The policy adopted here is to ignore the purposes of all other organisms except O_i by assuming that they are merely additional factors, and perhaps also additional selection forces, that are either especially capricious and malign or especially reliable and benign in O_i's environment. Under this assumption there is no need to give any of these other organisms a special status merely because they happen to have aims of their own. This is a crude but tractable solution. The alternative would be to generalize the coevolutionary game from a two-player game to an

n-player game in which the nth player always represents an aimless rest of nature and the remaining $n - 1$ players are each assigned some specific purpose relative to O_i and are modeled accordingly. This solution is compatible with the present approach so long as n remains a small number, but it is intractable otherwise.

The Moves of O_i and E_i

The organism and its environment must also be equipped with a capacity for action relative to each other. This means providing each of these players with a repertoire of moves. Given the initial states of O_i and E_i, a move is any subsequent change in either the organism or its environment that causes or cancels a change of state in their mutual $(O_i E_i)$ relationship.

Potentially, both the organism and its environment make many different kinds of moves. However, no matter what moves they make they can alter the $(O_i E_i)$ relationship in only a few ways. The derivation of this limited set of $(O_i E_i)$ state-changes from the very large set of all possible moves depends on four points: (i) Both the organism and its environment may initiate new moves relative to each other. (ii) Both the organism and its environment can affect both aspects of the $(O_i E_i)$ relationship. (iii) Both the organism and its environment can alter the adaptational relationship between them in two ways: either by changing themselves or by changing the other. (iv) Both the organism and its environment can change the space-time relationship in two ways also: either by changing O_i's location in space during time or by influencing O_i's endurance in time without necessarily affecting its location in space. (The last distinction is necessary in spite of the fact that every move will take some time to occur and will always affect O_i's endurance in time. It is needed partly because plural moves can happen simultaneously at approximately the same place in space and partly because O_i may or may not stay in the same place during time.) These four points give rise to eight different kinds of change to the $(O_i E_i)$ relationship, as indicated in figure 5. (O_i's moves are shown on the left and E_i's on the right to be consistent with figure 4). This scheme is exhaustive: any move made by either O_i or E_i must fall into one or another of these eight categories.

The detailed mapping of the subprocesses of ontogenesis into these $(O_i E_i)$ changes of state is beyond the scope of this chapter, but it is possible to provide a preliminary sketch. The right column of figure 5 shows the four different kinds of $(O_i E_i)$ changes initiated by the environment. Each cell represents a major category among the total set of naturally selecting inputs that scan the organism during its life. Cell 1 refers to all those components of environmental evolution that occur independently of the organism's activities. The notation indicates that this is one point at which the coevolution between O_i and E_i is not completely closed. It is possible

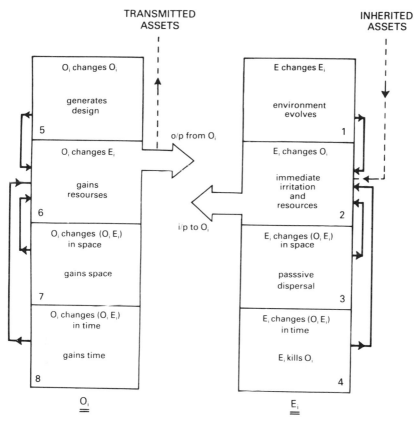

TRANSMITTED
ASSETS

INHERITED
ASSETS

O_i changes O_i	E changes E_i
generates design	environment evolves
5	1

o/p from O_i

O_i changes E_i	E_i changes O_i
gains resources	immediate irritation and resources
6	2

i/p to O_i

O_i changes $(O_i E_i)$ in space	E_i changes $(O_i E_i)$ in space
gains space	passsive dispersal
7	3

O_i changes $(O_i E_i)$ in time	E_i changes $(O_i E_i)$ in time
gains time	E_i kills O_i
8	4

$\underline{\underline{O_i}}$

$\underline{\underline{E_i}}$

Figure 5
The moves of the coevolutionary game classified in terms of the set of possible changes in the $(O_i E_i)$ relationship.

for an event to originate outside the organism's relative environment in the universal environment E, and for it to initiate a new coevolutionary cycle between O_i and E_i by causing a change in E_i that subsequently affects O_i. Cell 2 refers to the immediate irritants and resources within the scope of the organism's environment "here and now." Cell 3 refers to any environmental agent that is capable of displacing the organism across space. Cell 4 refers to the environment's capacity to terminate the organism's lifetime by killing it.

The left column of figure 5 shows the four different $(O_i E_i)$ changes initiated by the organism. Here each cell represents a different category among the organism's niche-constructing activities. Because the organism is a purposive system, each of these four cells represents a major subgoal or subaim for O_i. Cell 5 concerns the organism's capacity to generate and maintain its own internal organisation or "design." It refers primarily to the developmental processes of differentiation, pattern formation, and morphogenesis, as well as to processes of internal repair. Initially the moves in this cell are possible only because of the organism's inherited assets. They subsequently remain possible only as long as the organism can carrry out its other moves too. Cell 6 represents the organism's immediate niche-constructing outputs and refers primarily to its capacity to gain resources of all kinds and to emit waste products. Cell 7 refers to the organism's capacity to alter its own location in space during time, either by growth or by locomotion. Cell 8 refers to the organism's capacity to stay alive throughout an interval of time.

The most complicated cell is cell 8. To remain alive during time, any organism not only needs to emit a variety of niche-constructing acts; it also needs to integrate all its acts in such a way that the succession of its acts constitutes a viable life-history strategy relative to the heterogeneity of its environment (Stearns 1982; Horn and Rubenstein 1984). Furthermore, its overall life-history strategy must satisfy its total aims of survival and reproduction, and not just the limited aim of survival. It is therefore at this point that the organism's aims have to be extended to incorporate the production of offspring as well as the survival of itself.

In the present context there is ultimately only one reason why organisms ever reproduce. It stems from the fact that any organism is bound to lose its coevolutionary game in the end. Technically, organism O_i is equivalent to a finite-state machine, which means that at best it can express a limited number of alternative possible changes to itself. Its environment, however, is an infinite-state system, if only because it is open to inputs from the universal environment E (Waddington 1969). Therefore, E_i has the potential to generate an unlimited number of alternative states relative to O_i. We thus have a situation in which a limited organism is required to play a game of feature × factor matching against an unlimited environment.

Such a game is manifestly "unfair." Sooner or later there is bound to be a fatal mismatch between the organism and its environment. Hence the name of the game, "Gambler's Ruin." This assured mortality of organisms, however, raises a simple question: How do organisms exist at all? The answer is that in the long run the only kinds of organisms that can exist are those that happen to be instructed by their genes to reproduce within a time span for which they are likely to survive. Such genes are "selfish" (Dawkins 1976) because they commit organisms to the transmission of genes via reproduction rather than to the survival of phenotypes. But this does not mean that the only role of phenotypes in evolution is to transmit genes. That is a different idea, one stemming from the environmentalism of the synthetic theory and not from the existence of "selfish genes."

Reproduction works because the effect of producing offspring sufficiently early in a lifetime is to initiate a new instance of the coevolutionary game based on new, rejuvenated, and probably changed "nuclear" organisms in new environs. Since each of these new games will have a fate separate from O_i's, it is likely that at least some of them will persist after O_i's own game is over. It is therefore likely that among any set of reproducing organisms there will usually be some that are currently still alive and still in the game for a much longer time than O_i's own lifetime. This introduces a second point at which the coevolution of O_i and E_i is not completely closed: The organism O_i not only inherits its initial assets from its ancestors, both genetic and ecological; it is also likely to transmit some of its own assets, both genetic and ecological, to its offspring during its game.

One final point is also illustrated in figure 5. Regardless of kind, the environment's moves can only act as naturally selecting inputs to the organism via the organism's immediate environment "here and now" (cell 2). Similarly, the organism's moves can only act as niche-constructing outputs "here and now" (cell 6).

The Rules
These moves grant the organism and its environment their capacity to act on each other. However, their freedom of action is limited by numerous constraints which collectively demarcate between allowed and disallowed moves within each class of moves. These constraints are analogous to the rules of the game. There are two sets of rules: the "physical rules" (the relevant laws of physics, which apply equally to both the organism and its environment, particularly to that component of ecological inheritance which is independent of biotic evolution) and the "biological rules" (all additional constraints that refer only to living systems).

The Physical Rules   The physical rules constrain both aspects of the $(O_i E_i)$ relationship. Some constrain the freedom of both players to change the

Table 2
The physical "rules."

	Changes in space	Changes in time
Allowed changes of	Two directions in three dimensions	One direction in one dimension
location in E_i for O_i	Variable rate (can stop)	Fixed rate (cannot stop)
	Unlimited distance	Unlimited duration
Disallowed changes	Quantum jumps Physical competitive exclusion	

organism's location in space and time; others constrain the adaptational relationship instead. The most notable among the latter are the laws of thermodynamics (Conrad 1983), but gravity, geometry, and mechanics all play their parts too (Thompson 1917; McMahon and Bonner 1983). The physical rules that affect the adaptational relationship will be taken for granted here, but the rules that affect the space-time relationship will be summarized briefly even though they are so much a matter of common sense that they are usually taken for granted too. A brief restatement will help reorientate them around the $(O_i E_i)$ relationship.

Table 2 indicates that organisms are far freer in space than in time. Organisms can move or be moved across physical space in two directions in any of three spatial dimensions. Their rates of motion may vary from zero to some upper limit set by the laws of mechanics and the availability of energy. The distance they can potentially travel through space is unlimited. By contrast, in time an organism can only travel in one direction—from past to future—and at a fixed rate, which is determined by its environment's clock rather than by any clock of its own. For practical purposes an organism's endurance in time is, nevertheless, limited not by physical constraints but only by biological constraints. There are also two further rules, shown at the bottom of table 2: When an organism's space-time location changes, its translation in both space and time must be continuous—quantum jumps are not allowed. And there is a primitive form of competitive exclusive. No physical system can occupy exactly the same location as any other. Any organism may therefore have to compete for its space-time locations, even under the laws of physics.

The Biological Rules   The biological rules are far less obvious. They arise because organisms are not just physical systems but also living systems which have to earn their lives at their environment's expense. These rules are summarized in table 3. The top right cell refers to the fundamental thermodynamic requirement imposed on every organism to gain sufficient

Table 3
The biological "rules."

Design in space during time	Resources in time from space
Requirements	
Adaptation to immediate environment	Net inflow of energy from E_i to O_i ...
Adaptability to potential environment	at a sufficient rate ...
	on a lifelong basis
Constraints	
	Benefits of adaptation > Costs
	Biological competitive exclusion

resources from its environment to sustain life during time. The first rule requires the entropy relations between O_i and E_i to be such that a net inflow of energy from the environment to the organism is possible (Conrad 1983). The second states that although the rate at which any organism gains, stores, or uses energy may vary, the overall rate at which the organism gains energy must be sufficient to allow it to remain alive continuously and to make its next moves at each successive moment. The third rule simply requires the organism to meet these energy requirements on a lifelong basis.

The top left cell indicates the overall design requirements which any organism must meet relative to its environment in order to satisfy its resource needs. First, at any arbitrary moment t_0 the organism must be adapted, which means its design must be such that it can both tolerate and exploit its immediate environment. Second, throughout any arbitrary interval of time $t_0 - t_i$ the organism must remain adapted to its immediate environment at each successive moment. However, its environment is likely to change from moment to moment, so it follows that at each successive moment the organism must not only be adapted "here and now" but must also carry sufficient general-purpose adaptability to allow it to remain adapted "elsewhere and later" relative to the variety of alternative environments in its potential tolerance space which it may encounter at later moments (Levins 1968; Conrad 1983).

These energy and design requirements are also jointly responsible for the first constraint shown at the bottom of table 3. The achievement of adaptive design is bound to cost the organism energy and resources. Hence, the organism's design costs must be more than offset by the resources which the design itself permits it to gain. This must include the extra cost of the organism's redundancy and adaptability relative to its potential tolerance space, as well as the cost of its adaptation relative to its immediate environment (Thoday 1953; Levins 1968; Plotkin and Odling-Smee 1979; Conrad 1983). The second constraint is competition.

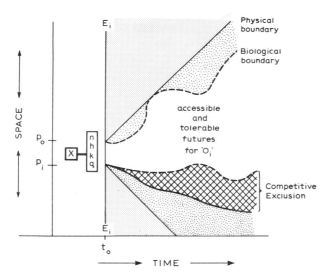

Figure 6
The physical and biological boundaries of O_i's potential tolerance space in physical space and time.

No organism can benefit from exactly the same environmental resources as another, so any organism is likely to have to compete with other organisms for its resources.

The main effect of both the physical and the biological rules is to establish boundaries within the organism's potential tolerance space beyond which the organism cannot go without immediately losing the game. These boundaries are indicated in figure 6. Those physical rules that constrain the space-time relationship do so by demarcating between zones of accessible and inaccessible futures for the organism in space and time relative to the organism's immediate location. They therefore impose an outer "physical boundary" on the organism's potential tolerance space beyond which the organism cannot go. The zones themselves are determined by the maximum rate at which any organism can either move or be moved across space during time. Their effect is to limit the alternative places to which the organism could get in space at later moments in time from the starting point of its present location.

The biological rules, as well as the remaining physical rules, which constrain the adaptational relationship, then determine a second "biological boundary" inside the primary physical boundary. This second boundary does not refer directly to any particular zone is space and time; it merely describes the set of alternative environments which the organism could tolerate and use if it happened to encounter them later on. For a species, the usual way of differentiating between tolerable and intolerable futures is by using Hutchinson's (1957) concept of the niche as a multidimensional hypervolume of tolerances relative to a potentially unlimited set of different environmental variables (Vandermeer 1972). This concept can also be used to describe any individual organism's tolerance space (MacMahon et al. 1981). Thus, each dimension in an individual organism's hypervolume of tolerances refers to a single feature × factor matching relationship between the organism and its environment at the $(O_i E_i)$ interface. The total hypervolume then refers to the totality of the organism's feature × factor relationship with its environment, including those potential relationships that depend on the organism's adaptability and redundant features.

Within limits, this makes it possible to insert the organism's potential tolerance space into physical space and time by anchoring its hypervolume of tolerances to its immediate space-time location. Thus in figure 6 a zone of tolerable futures is shown for O_i extending from its "here and now" location to enclose the alternative environments that O_i should be able to tolerate and use "elsewhere and later." This zone incorporates all the environmental regions that are both accessible to the organism given its current location, $(p_i - p_0)$, (l_0), and tolerable to the organism given its current set of features $[n, h, x, k, q]$. As long as the organism remains inside this zone, it will stay in the game. If it departs from it, it will lose the game. One weakness of this scheme is that the biological boundary can be sketched only on a probabilistic basis, because neither the organism's future moves nor those of its environment can be predicted with sufficient accuracy to do better; which leads to the organism's final requirement.

Knowledge of the Game
Because O_i is such a highly improbable system relative to its environment, it may lose its game at any moment. Hence, O_i cannot afford to play its moves haphazardly. If it did, it would be unlikely to survive for more than a very brief span of time. The organism must therefore demarcate between allowed and disallowed moves as defined by the rules of the game *a priori*. To do that, however, any organism must enjoy at least a minimal capacity to "predict" the future of the $(O_i E_i)$ relationship. Three different kinds of "prediction" are necessary: O_i must be able to "predict" at least some of E_i's future moves correctly, it must be able to "predict" its own future resource needs correctly, and it must be able to "predict" at least some of the outcomes of its own actions in its environment. Given these capacities, the organism may have some chance of "predicting" the future of the $(O_i E_i)$ relationship correctly, and of constraining its moves according to its "predictions" for a significant if still brief span of time. No equivalent obligation is imposed on the environment, because it cannot lose this game. Hence, the environment needs no predictive powers. Other orga-

nisms in O_i's environment do need predictive capacity for the same reason that O_i does. From the point of view of O_i, however, the "predictive" capacities of other organisms will merely increase or decrease the capriciousness of its own environment, depending on whether these other organisms are antagonistic or mutualistic relative to O_i (Law 1985).

In this context, the word *predict* does not imply cognitive knowledge on the part of organisms. Minimally, it need only imply apparent prediction and preparative design. Thus, any organism must be at least partly prepared in advance of its encounters with its environment for survival and reproduction. Yet whatever preparative design the organism expresses, structural or functional, it will be logically equivalent to predictive "information" or "knowledge" about its forthcoming game with its environment— albeit knowledge from which cognition is either partly or completely absent.

The primary source of any organism's knowledge is its genotype. To the extent to which an organism's genes have been naturally selected by ancestral environments, the knowledge they encode for must relate to previously successful ancestral designs relative to previously encountered ancestral environments. In fact, O_i's individual genotype will simply contain a sample of whatever knowledge is stored in its population's gene pool. The essence of this knowledge is therefore that of a "remembered history"—in this case, the history of a particular population-environment relationship, or (O_{pop}/E_{pop}) relationship (see "Generalizing the Game," below). The reuse of this genetic knowledge, and its contemporary reexpression by the individual organism O_i relative to its own relative environment E_i, therefore amounts to the gamble that O_i's future is going be the same as was its ancestors' past. This crucial inductive step constitutes the gamble at the heart of "Gambler's Ruin" (Slobodkin and Rapoport 1974). Very likely the gamble will fail, in which case all that any organism can do is to fall back on knowledgeless chance in the form of its genetic mutations and genetic recombinations. It will then have at least a remote chance of survival even in an environment that it has failed to "predict" (Campbell 1979; Odling-Smee 1983). It may also be able to amplify that chance slightly by its own subsequent niche-constructing activities, if it can survive for long enough to do so.

In addition to their inherited knowledge, some organisms may benefit from extra knowledge which they may gain for themselves by "remembering" their own individual history of interactions with their own relative environments, and by using what they remember to constrain their future niche-constructing acts. In this case the history that they must remember is the history of their own (O_iE_i) relationship (the dark shading in figure 4d) and not the (O_{pop}/E_{pop}) history on which their inherited genetic knowledge is based. However, an organism will be able to gain this extra knowledge only if it is equipped by its genes with subsystems, such as a central nervous system, which are themselves specialized for autonomous within-phenotype knowledge-gaining processes, such as learning. In a few cases, organisms may also gain still further knowledge as a function of their membership of some culture (Boyd and Richerson 1985). If so, then the relevant history here will be the history of some culture × environment interactions, and not that of either the $(O_i E_i)$ relationship or the (O_{pop}/E_{pop}) relationship (Plotkin and Odling-Smee 1981; Odling-Smee and Plotkin 1984).

The Game Itself
The preceding subsections can now be summarized by allowing both the organism and its environment to play off a few moves in their game relative to each other. Figure 7 concerns the same organism and the same environment as figure 4, but it provides more information about the dynamics of their coevolution. The primary product of their game is neither the organism's evolution (ontogenesis) nor its environment's, but rather the evolution of their mutual relationship, and hence of the environ

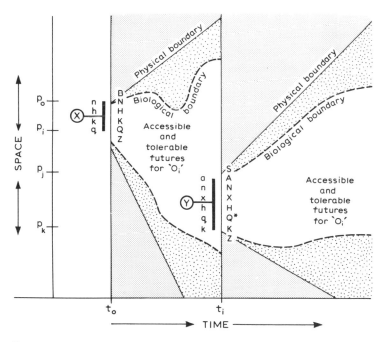

Figure 7
An extract from the game showing the primary evolution of the environ as a function of successive $(O_i E_i)$ changes of state and the evolution of the organism O_i and its environment E_i.

which they jointly constitute. This environ evolution is driven by both "causal arrows" of coevolution: natural selection and niche construction. Every move made by either O_i or E_i during their game will alter their (O_iE_i) relationship in some way and will therefore contribute to the evolution of their environ. Thus, in figure 7 the primary consequence of the interactions between the organism O_i and its relative environment E_i throughout the interval (t_0-t_i) is a progressively changing relationship between O_i and E_i on a move-by-move basis from the situation shown at moment t_0 to the situation shown at moment t_i, the overall result being the fragment of environ evolution shown here. (Figure 7 is closely comparable to figure 8 of MacMahon et al. 1981.)

The secondary products of the game are the evolution (ontogenesis) of the organism and the evolution of its relative environment. Each is a component process in the evolution of their environ. They can be considered separately, but only in the context of their shared environ and only relative to their mutual (O_iE_i) relationship. Neither can be considered with exclusive reference to the other, since neither is autonomous.

The environment E_i's evolution consists of all those changes to environmental heterogeneity in space and time that are due to the successive coevolutionary interactions of O_i and E_i. These are caused by the niche-constructing outputs from the organism and by whatever environmental agents are responsible for E_i's moves. In addition, some changes may originate from agents lying outside the local environ in the universal environment E. The net contribution of E_i's evolution to the game is simply to provide a space-time matrix, and a heterogeneous resource-bearing environment within that matrix, for O_i.

The organism's evolution (ontogenesis) is different because of two major asymmetries between O_i and E_i. First, the organism is a purposive system relative to its environment, whereas its environment is purposeless relative to it. Hence, O_i always has to be adapted to E_i, but E_i need not be adapted to O_i unless it is forced to be by the organism's own niche-constructing acts. Second, the organism is always located in space and time, whereas its environment merely provides the space-time matrix in which the organism is located. Hence, while O_i's location constantly changes during the game, the changes themselves must occur relative to space-time coordinates which are provided by its environment E_i and ultimately by the universal environment E. When these asymmetries are combined, they cause O_i's evolution to be isologous to the particular adaptive space-time path along which the organism travels in its environment E_i throughout its life. This path is analogous to a "world line" for a physical system in physics. It differs only in that the world line of any organism is a "biological world line" that necessarily incorporates the adaptation of the organism to its environment at each place and moment along its path.

The path itself is a function of the same coevolutionary interactions between O_i and E_i and the same succession of $(O_i E_i)$ states that are responsible for the evolution of E_i. In this case, whenever either the organism or its environment makes a move it changes the mutual $(O_i E_i)$ relationship. But every time that happens, the change of state to the $(O_i E_i)$ redefines all three aspects of the organism's environment E_i. Thus, any move from either player updates the organism's immediate tolerance space by altering the "here and now" state of the $(O_i E_i)$ relationship. It also alters the organism's potential tolerance space by revising the physical and biological boundaries that stem from the current state of the $(O_i E_i)$ relationship, and it updates the organism's postinteractive tolerance space by adding the previous $(O_i E_i)$ state to history. The net result is that the organism takes its next step along its particular world line.

The central problem for the organism is how to extend its own world line as far as possible, and at least far enough to allow it to reproduce. It can do that only as long as it obeys the rules. Hence, understanding O_i's evolution (ontogenesis) in the context of its environ is largely a matter of understanding the particular sequence of moves which the organism emits throughout its life. That reduces to understanding the sequence of move-selecting "decisions" taken by O_i relative to the succession of $(O_i E_i)$ states it encounters "here and now" and relative to the succession of $(O_i E_i)$ states it "predicts" it will encounter "elsewhere and later" in the light of its aims and in light of whatever knowledge of the game it manages to carry forward from a remembered "elsewhere and earlier." That, of course, is equivalent to the task of explaining the life-history tactics of any organism O_i, with this task now reorientated around the new coevolutionary reference device provided by the $(O_i F_i)$ in lieu of the synthetic theory's allegedly autonomous environment.

Generalizing the Game: Evolution's Hierarchies
The last step is to return to Patten's (1982) universal scheme. Thus far, any organism O_i has been treated as the paradigm living system or taxon, and ontogenesis has been treated as the paradigm coevolutionary process. As these examples were originally chosen to illustrate a particular instance of a general argument, it should now be possible to substitute any other taxon for O_i, that taxon's enviroplasm for E_i, the taxon-enviroplasm relationship for the $(O_i E_i)$ relationship, and any other coevolutionary process for ontogenesis without materially altering any part of the previous argument.

The simplest way to test this claim is to substitute the organism's population O_{pop} for the organism O_i, the population's environment E_{pop} for the organism's environment E_i, the mutual (O_{pop}/E_{pop}) relationship for the

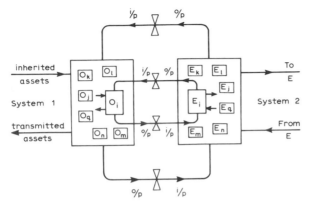

Figure 8
The hierarchy of embedment: the relationship between any organism O_i and its population (system 1), and that between O_i's environment E_i and its population's environment (system 2). Note: Organisms O_j–O_k are components of both E_i and O_i's population. This figure illustrates the latter point only.

$(O_i E_i)$, and the process of population evolution for ontogenesis. According-ly, figure 8 shows the same situation as figure 1 except that the two coevolv-ing systems illustrated now represent an evolving population (system 1) and its relative environment (system 2). The primary product of this new coevolutionary game is the evolution of the (O_{pop}/E_{pop}) relationship and its associated environ. This environ's evolution continues to be driven by exactly the same two "causal arrows" as before: naturally selecting inputs from E_{pop} to O_{pop} and niche-constructing outputs from O_{pop} to E_{pop}. Also as before, the outputs of each of these two systems are underdetermined by the inputs from the other. The relevant triplet of summarizing equations are therefore the following, where once again $E = (E_{pop} + \text{rest of } E)$:

$$\frac{d(O_{pop})}{dt} = f(O_{pop}/E_{pop}), \tag{13}$$

$$\frac{d(E_{pop})}{dt} = g(O_{pop}/E_{pop}), \tag{14}$$

$$\frac{d(O_{pop}/E_{pop})}{dt} = h(O_{pop}, E). \tag{15}$$

These equations indicate that the evolution of the (O_{pop}/E_{pop}) relationship is codetermined by both O_{pop} and E_{pop}, and that the evolution of both O_{pop} and E_{pop} is a function of their coevolutionary relationship. They also show that the overall coevolutionary system illustrated in figure 8, like that illustrated in figure 3, is not completely closed but is open to some inputs from the universal environment E.

The main difference between figures 8 and 3 is that the subsystems shown inside the boxes in figure 8 consist of diverse individual organisms $O_i, \ldots, O_q$ and their diverse relative environments $E_i, \ldots, E_q$ instead of diverse within-organisms subsystems, and diverse components in some individual organism's environment. Thus, in this inclusive (O_{pop}/E_{pop}) coevolutionary system, each separate (O_iE_i); $(O_jE_j) \ldots$ pair is itself a coevolving subsystem (one shown only). The redescription of the coevolutionary game at a different level therefore introduces a hierarchy of embedment or "Chinese boxes" (Nelson 1973; Simon 1982), which when fully extended becomes the complete ecological hierarchy of life (Eldredge and Salthe 1985; Salthe 1985). In theory it should be possible to play the present coevolutionary game between any living system (taxon) and its relative environment (enviroplasm) at any level in this hierarchy, provided that both of these coevolving systems are correctly identified and that their respective inputs and outputs are correctly described.

Figure 9 illustrates a second consequence of these same substitutions. It shows that the eight major classes of moves are recursive in nature in spite of the substitution of O_{pop} for O_i, of E_{pop} for E_i, and of the process of phylogenesis for ontogenesis. This recursion occurs because these eight classes are all universals. They refer only to the limited number of different ways in which the relationship between any two coevolving systems can change. The rules of the game that govern these moves are likewise universals, as are the currencies in which they deal. Thus, cells 1, 2, 5, and 6 are all concerned with changes to the (OE) relationship between the internal organization of organisms (or sets of organisms) and the external organization of their environments. The underlying universal currency here is entropy (Conrad 1983). Cells 3 and 7 both deal in the universal currency of space; time is the universal currency for cells 4 and 8.

Figure 9 also illustrates the inheritance links between any organism and its population. O_i receives its inherited assets from its ancestors O_{pop} before making its initial moves. Later it is likely to transmit some of its own assets on to its offspring and back to its population as a function of its own reproductive activities. These inherited and transmitted assets include both genetic and ecological assets. Thus, O_i inherits preparative knowledge (in the form of naturally selected genes) from its genetic ancestors and whatever organism-induced modifications are present in its initial environment E_i from its ecological ancestors. Likewise, when the same organism O_i reproduces, it transmits genes to its offspring and whatever additional modifications it has inflicted on the environment as a consequence of its own habitat-selecting and -perturbing activities.

The principal routes via which these assets are received and transmitted are sketched in figure 9. They give rise to a second hierarchy, sometimes called a hierarchy of connection (Nelson 1973; Simon 1982). In this particular example, the organism O_i receives both its genetic and its ecological

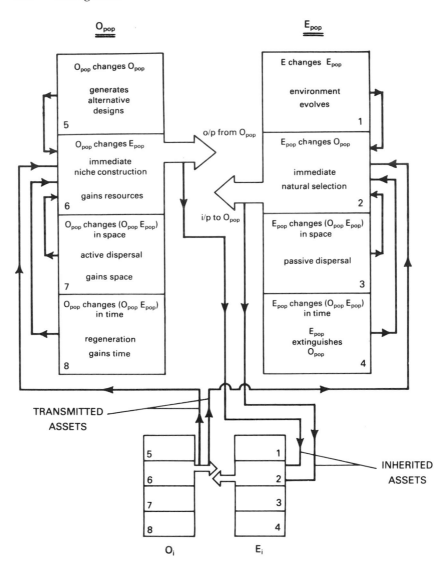

Figure 9
The hierarchy of connection: the relationship between any organism O_i and its population O_{pop}, and that between O_i's environment E_i and its population's environment E_{pop}.

assets from its population, O_{pop}, and from its population's environment, E_{pop}, via its own relative environment E_i. The routing via E_i is due to the fact that all the other organisms in O_i's population, including its own parents, are components of O_i's environment. Conversely, O_i bequeaths its own offspring to its population, O_{pop}, directly because it is simultaneously a member of that population. O_i also makes a direct contribution to its population's environment, E_{pop}, and therefore to its offspring's environment, by contributing additional perturbations to that environment. The extension of this hierarchy of connection beyond the two levels illustrated is less clear than the extension of the hierarchy of embedment (figure 8), but tentative steps toward exploring different fragments and different aspects of its extension have been made by Vrba and Eldredge (1984), Odling-Smee and Plotkin (1984), Eldredge and Salthe (1985), and Salthe (1985). (See also O'Neill et al. 1986.) It should also be noted that figure 9 is an oversimplification. It assumes that O_i's ecological ancestors are identical to its genetic ancestors, and that its ecological successors are identical to its genetic successors. In reality that is likely to be only partly true.

Finally, the generality of the present theory potentially extends beyond terrestrial populations and terrestrial ecosystems, because nothing in the foregoing analysis requires the nuclear living system (taxon) or its relative environment (enviroplasm) to be terrestrial. The coevolutionary game is truly a universal game, and it should be capable of describing and explaining a universal biology.

Implications of a Relativistic Biology

The preceding theory may appear complex, if only because of its novelty, but the central innovation is quite simple. It is the proposition that evolutionary theory be reorientated around the the (OE) instead of being described relative to the traditional concept of an autonomous environment, or (E). I have been arguing that this reform is necessary for two reasons: First, the evidence suggests that evolution cannot be just an inputs-only process. Rather, it appears to be an inputs-plus-outputs process based on both the natural selection of heritable genes by environments and the niche construction (or niche destruction) of heritable environments by phenotypes. Second, it isn't possible to model either this extra system of ecological inheritance or this extra directing force of niche construction without abandoning the environmentalism of the synthetic theory. That, however, will require nothing less that the replacement of the environment in its covert metatheoretical role of reference device for evolutionary theory by the (OE).

Deriving the (OE), however, is only the first step toward developing a full general theory of organism-environment coevolution. Subsequent steps must include (i) demonstrating in detail how the subprocesses of ontogenesis and phylogenesis translate into the scheme of moves illustrated in figures 5 and 9; (ii) elucidating the genetic and ecological links between levels in the kinds of hierarchies depicted in figures 8 and 9, with emphasis placed on ecological inheritance to balance the emphasis now placed on genetic inheritance; (iii) deriving coevolutionary life-history tactics; and (iv) building formal models, based on a general coevolutionary theory, which are capable of competing with the current models in explaining data and generating predictions. There is, in other words, a long way to go. Nevertheless, it is already possible to discuss some of the major implications of the present approach. Three issues will be discussed here: fitness, the role of behavior in evolution, and the capacity of evolutionary theory to provide the necessary biological infrastructure for the remaining behavioral, social, and political sciences.

Fitness
If fitness means contributing to evolutionary descent in the face of modifying forces, then for the modern synthesis fitness becomes a quantity that is maximized by the single "causal arrow" of natural selection. Qualitatively, it comprises whatever "preparative knowledge" about "design" is encoded in the genes that are transmitted from generation to generation relative to supposedly autonomous environments. Only one currency is necessary for the measurement of fitness: transmitted genes.

In contrast, the present general coevolutionary theory proposes that fitness comprises whatever quantity is maximized by both natural selection and niche construction. Qualitatively, this becomes both the "preparative knowledge" encoded in genes, plus whatever environments have been selected, spoiled, ameliorated, or built for the organisms which are carrying those genes, and which their "preparative knowledge" must address. Hence, the present theory assumes that ancestral organisms don't just bequeath genetically equipped successors to evolutionary descent via genetic inheritance. Rather, it proposes that they bequeath successor organism-environment (*OE*) relationships via both genetic and ecological inheritance. In that case, it is misleading to measure fitness exclusively in genes. Instead we need a more comprehensive currency, one capable of combining both an organism's genetic and ecological contributions to descent. Ideally this currency should measure the adaptive correspondence, or synerg (Bock 1980), between both the transmitted genes and the transmitted environments relative to each other.

At present the only fitness score that comes near satisfying this requirement is "lifetime reproductive success," which counts the total number of viable offspring produced by any parent organism throughout its life (see, e.g., Clutton-Brock et al. 1982). Viability means the survival of the offspring to some criterion age. This concept of viable offspring has two points in common with the proposed concept of viable new (*OE*)s. It tacitly acknowledges that organisms can transmit modified environments as well as selected genes to their offspring, and it tacitly acknowledges that there are two routes to fitness rather than one: Parents can increase the viability of their offspring either by giving them "better genes" relative to their environments or by supplying them with "better environments" relative to their genes.

There are numerous examples of investment in this second route to fitness. In many species, parents don't just transmit genes to their offspring; they also select their offspring's initial habitat in space or time or both, doing so with greatly varying degrees of energy, skill, and discrimination. In addition, many organisms prepare, protect, and provision juvenile environments for their offspring by means of a huge variety of parental caring activities. Beyond that, some organisms continue to help their adult offspring, for instance by transmitting breeding territories to them (e.g., the Florida scrub jay again). Others help remoter relatives as well via the mechanisms of kin selection (Hamilton 1964); still others help genetically unrelated conspecifics (Axelrod and Hamilton 1981; Emlen 1984; Axelrod 1984) or symbionts (Law 1985) via diverse reciprocal altruistic acts. All these niche-constructing activities contribute something to the lifetime reproductive success of the organisms that emit them by ultimately affecting the total number of viable offspring they themselves produce.

However, in spite of these merits, the lifetime reproduction score still falls short of the requirements of the present theory. First, it measures the investments organisms make in their niche-constructing acts only in terms of the time or energy they allocate to specific acts relative to their total time or energy budgets (Southwood 1981; Clutton-Brock et al. 1982; Wootton 1984). This is tantamount to evaluating the niche-constructing outputs of organisms exclusively self-referentially, in terms of the costs and benefits that accrue to the organisms themselves. Such costs and benefits can then be reduced to genes and thus to the genetic inheritance system only. No attempt is made to measure the perturbations in the environment that are caused by those same niche constructing outputs. There is therefore nothing to indicate the extent to which the outputs of organisms are actually driving the coevolution of their environments and contributing to an ecological inheritance for their succesors. Second, although it acknowledges that the fitness of organisms is affected by both the transmission of genes and the transmission of environmental modifications, lifetime reproductive success continues to overlook the fundamental point that genetic inheritance and ecological inheritance are achieved by different mechanism. Genetic inheritance depends on the mechanisms of reproduction, whereas ecological inheritance depends on the mechanisms of niche construction. These two kinds of mechanisms do not work in the same way. They are not constrained by the same rules (see above). They don't even necessarily work together. To take the extreme example, it is at least logically possible for an organism to transmit no genes at all, thereby achieving a conventional fitness score of zero, yet to transmit significant environmental modifications to its successors via ecological inheritance. A childless human inventor could do just that via culture (see below); so could an inventive potato-washing macaque (Kawamura 1963) that has no offspring.

For these reasons, fitness must be measured not just by genes but also by the environmental modifications induced by the outputs of organisms. Only then will it be possible to assess the total contribution organisms make to evolutionary descent. This is a tall order because as yet there is no unit in sight, comparable to the gene, that might be used for measuring either the selection or the perturbation of environments by phenotypes. All that now exist are the many diverse biogeochemical measures used by ecologists. Some universal and probably symbolic unit of exchange, a kind of "ecological dollar," is required to calculate the equivalent environmental value of every kind of niche-constructing act (Conrad 1983). In the meantime, the absence of an appropriate currency for measuring ecological inheritance should not be allowed to obscure the significance of niche construction as a directing force in evolution any more than the prevailing absence of the "gene" allowed biologists to forget about the significance of natural selection in Darwin's day.

If we could find a way of doing it, one extra advantage of measuring fitness in terms of both genes and environments is that it would finally close the gap between evolutionary biology and ecology. Evolutionary biology focuses on genetic inheritance and ignores the inheritance of organism induced modifications in environments. Ecology, on the other hand, is predominantly concerned with the measurement and transmission of all kinds of perturbations in the environment. As long as fitness is scored in genes alone, the gap between these two disciplines is likely to remain intact. If fitness could be measured in terms of both the transmission of genes and the transmission of environments, then the gap should disappear.

The Role of Behavior in Evolution
Behavior affects the evolution of organisms primarily by contributing to their life-history strategies. This much is agreed upon by both the modern synthesis and the present general theory of organism-environment coevolution. Beyond this initial consensus, however, the two theories diverge quite sharply. The modern synthesis seeks to understand the life histories of organisms exclusively in terms of naturally selecting inputs to

organisms from environments, and it assumes that the diverse life histories of species are caused by different sets of selection forces arising from their different environments. Organisms react to these selection forces across successive generations, and "track" whatever changes occur in their environments during time, albeit in "clever" ways. Their status is therefore that of "problem solvers" only. Given the right combination of luck and naturally selected genes, they may be able to "solve" the problems "set for them" by their environments, but that is all.

In contrast, the kind of general coevolutionary theory proposed here understands the life histories of organisms in terms of both their naturally selecting inputs and their niche-constructing outputs. It therefore allows organisms to act as well as react on either side of the (OE) interface without their actions necessarily being determined by naturally selected genes. So organisms can "track" changes in their environments by changing themselves on the (O) side of the (OE); or they can avoid changing themselves by "counteracting" the changes that occur in their environments, or by "seeking" new environments, on the (E) side of the (OE). But these additional options change the status of organisms. They now become not just "problem solvers" capable of solving the adaptational problems set for them by their environments; but also "problem setters" who can set themselves and their successors at least some of their own problems by modifying their environments and by redefining their problems.

One way to illustrate the difference between these two theories is in terms of the familiar, though still controversial, r versus K life-history strategies (Pianka 1970; Stearns 1976, 1977; Boyce 1984; Horn and Rubenstein 1984; Begon et al. 1986). A population of r strategists is generally thought of as living in a habitat that is either unpredictable or ephemeral and that tends, in consequence, to select for organisms that demonstrate early breeding, high fecundity, semelparity, rapid development, small size, and little or no parental care. Conversely, a population of K strategists is thought of as living in a habitat that is either constant or predictably seasonal and that tends to select for organisms that demonstrate late breeding, low fecundity, iteroparity, slow development, large size, and extensive parental care. For the modern synthesis, the only reason different species express these alternatives is that they live in different environments that incorporate either "r selection" or "K selection" forces. No other explanation is possible, because the theory allows organisms only a genetic route to fitness, and that route is directed exclusively by natural selection.

A general coevolutionary theory, however, supposes two routes to fitness rather than one—the genetic and the ecological—and acknowledges that any organism can contribute to both. It is therefore worth noting the near correspondence between the r and K strategies and these two alternative routes to fitness. Suitably reinterpreted, r strategists become organisms that invest primarily in the genetic route to fitness, by maximizing their efforts to transmit genes and by minimizing everything else; K strategists are organisms that invest much more heavily in ecological inheritance, by investing in parental care, for instance, and by reducing their fecundity. However, the main point of the contrast is that for the synthetic theory the "choice" between these and all other possible strategies is "decided" by natural selection alone; for the proposed general coevolutionary theory it is only partly "decided" by natural selection, and is otherwise "decided" by the many ways in which organisms modify their own naturally selecting inputs by their niche-constructing outputs.

The latter include at least three kinds of niche-constructing acts, all of them involving behavior: phenotypic selection, phenotypic perturbation, and "prediction" by organisms of their own relative environments. Phenotypic selection refers to all those organismic activities whose main effect is to change the particular environment which the organism itself confronts. It could refer either to the selection of an alternative environment as a whole (as occurs in habitat selection, dispersal, and migration) or only to the selection of specific components in an environment (for example, the selection of a mate, the selection of a breeding territory or refuge, or—on the micro scale—the selection of a song perch by a bird or the bark of a tree by a moth [Kettlewell 1956]). Some of these activities— dispersal, for instance—are already known to complicate attempts to understand the life histories of organisms exclusively in terms of r and K selection, just as one would expect on the present theory (Horn and Rubenstein 1984).

Phenotypic perturbation is similar to phenotypic selection but refers to the qualitative changes which organisms inflict on their environments rather than to the selection of different environments. These changes include the depletion of resources, hoarding, the dumping of detritus, and more exotic acts such as building nests, dams, and burrows, making paths and trails, and signaling with scent marks.

The third activity, "prediction," is not so straightforward. When organisms invest in additional "knowledge-gaining" processes (learning, for example), their activities do not by themselves change their environments, but they may redefine an organism's problems. For example, learning can change an objectively complex and superficially capricious environment into one that is subjectively ordered and stable simply because the organism may now "anticipate" what is coming next (Piaget 1971). The importance of this kind of action derives primarily from the fact that environmental capriciousness is known to be a powerful determining influence on life-history strategies (see the comments on "r selection" above), whereas environmental capriciousness is relative to "knowledge" about the environment.

One further point applies to all these niche-constructing acts. A critic of the proposed theory might complain that any organism's capacity to change the environment is negligible, and that its contribution to an ecological inheritance system may therefore be safely ignored, just as it now is by the synthetic theory. Other sources of perturbation or stability in the environment will always override anything the organism can do for itself or for its successors. Several answers can be given to this objection. The first is to stress again that the present coevolutionary theory does not ask any organism, O_i, to modify the general environment, E; it only asks O_i to modify its own relative environment, E_i. So even if O_i's capacity to modify E is puny, that doesn't matter, because O_i's capacity to modify E_i is typically quite considerable, and O_i's fitness depends on its $(O_i E_i)$ relationship and not on its relationship to E. Second, the same objection might just as well be leveled at O_i's contribution to genetic inheritance. Any organism's capacity to change its population, and thence life on Earth, by transmitting its genes to the next generation may also be puny. However, the genetic transmissions of individual organisms gear up via the sheer multiplicity of organisms to become highly significant on a very large scale. The same is true of the contributions of individual organisms to ecological inheritance. They may start as extremely modest interactions between individual organisms and their relative environments, but they gear up via the multiplicity of organisms, and via the hierarchical links shown in figures 8 and 9, until they too can become significant on the largest scale. An example is the apparent involvement of organisms in the replacement of the Earth's early oxygen-free atmosphere by its present atmosphere, which contains about 21 percent oxygen. Third, the evolution of learning and culture, which are rare in nature, may amplify the power of individual organisms to perturb their own and their neighbors' environments very considerably. The contemporary human environment is the obvious example.

If we accept that organisms not only "solve" the problems set for them by natural selection but also "set themselves" some of their own problems via these various niche-constructing acts, there is still one difficulty: It will no longer be any good to try to understand the life histories of different species exclusively in terms of different sets of natural selection pressures (r versus K selection, for instance). Instead it will be necessary to understand them in terms of both natural selection and niche construction. In that case, they will have to be explained relative to the only reference device that is capable of combining natural selection and niche construction, the (OE). That must mean giving up our contemporary efforts to understand the life histories of organisms relative to alternative environmental (E) states, and trying to model them relative to alternative (OE) states instead.

This need not be as formidable as it sounds, because the options open to organisms will still be severely constrained. Figure 5 shows that it is possible for any organism O_i to alter its own (O_iE_i) relationship in only a strictly limited number of ways. Thus, the classificatory scheme of "moves" given in figures 5 and 9 should provide a nonarbitrary basis for exploring all the possible tradeoffs in any sequence of outputs (niche-constructing acts) emitted by any organism, versus any corresponding sequence of inputs (natural selection forces) it receives from its environment.

A provisional and extremely tentative indication of the logic governing these tradeoffs is shown in figure 10, which is derived by combining the physical and biological rules of tables 2 and 3, the cells of figure 5, and O_i's "knowledge" of the coevolutionary game. This figure illustrates an organism's needs and costs and the benefits that should accrue to it from a successful integration of its various moves or niche-constructing acts relative to its own needs and its environment's moves.

Any organism's chain of needs runs as follows: Life means staying alive during time (cell 8); but O_i is an improbable system relative to its environment E_i, which means that to gain lifetime it must first gain resources from E_i (cell 6); yet O_i can gain resources from E_i only if it first makes physical contact with E_i across space during time (cell 7). Contact with environmental space, however, demands continuously adaptive "design" (cell 5). That, in turn, is impossible without some *a priori* knowledge about both self and relative environment—the (O_iE_i) relationship. This knowledge (plus some initial resources) is originally provided by O_i's inherited assets, but it doesn't come free. It has to be paid for by diverting some of the resources already gained away from the business of extending the organism's own lifetime and toward additional knowledge-gaining activities; these activities ultimately include the production of offspring by the organism and the transmission of both genetic and ecological assets to the next generation. Reproduction is therefore a cost forced on O_i by the same "selfish genes" it originally inherited from its ancestors as a part of its own initial birthright. At this point we arrive at the kernel of the life-history-strategy story: the tradeoff between survival and reproduction (see, e.g., Southwood 1981). If O_i gets its tradeoffs right, then benefits start to flow in the opposite direction. Relevant knowledge confers adaptive design. Adaptive design permits contact with an environment across space during time. That permits resource gaining from space during time. The resources gained may then grant O_i a further extension of lifetime, which may be sufficient to allow it to reproduce and to generate new viable (OE)s during time, each with a separate fate.

The last point refers to the influence of niche-constructing acts on genetic inheritance. The vast majority of the genes which an organism inherits have already been selected by ancestral environments. In fact, the total collection of those ancestral environments contains the interactive

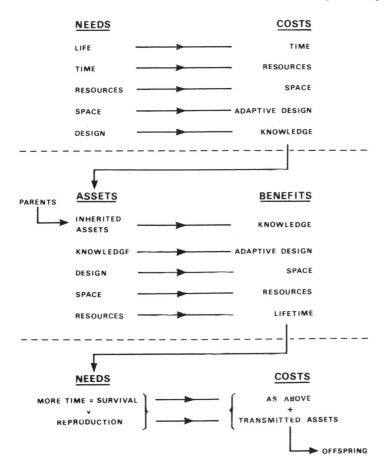

Figure 10
The logic governing the life-history strategies of organisms.

history of an organism's population. However, this population history has not been determined solely by prior natural selection. Rather, it is a function of both prior natural selection and prior niche construction. This is because each ancestral organism has already played exactly the same co-evolutionary game that the contemporary organism, O_i, is now playing. Hence, the "knowledge" encoded in O_i's genes will reflect not only the environmental selection forces that once acted on its ancestors but also the niche-constructing activities emitted by those same ancestors, including behavior. By the same token, if O_i is able to gain extra knowledge during its lifetime by remembering its own past encounters with its relative environment, E_i, then what it remembers will be a function of its individual interactive history, which is identical to the history of its $(O_i E_i)$ relationship (see the dark shading in figure 4d). This history will likewise be the product of both prior naturally selecting inputs to the organism and its own prior niche-constructing outputs. Should an organism belong to a culture and receive culturally transmitted knowledge as well, the same logic will apply once again, this time to the interactive history of its culture.

The result is that according to the present general coevolutionary theory, but not according to the modern synthesis, active phenotypes are causal agents in biotic evolution. They are not driven into their futures simply by their reactions to autonomously changing environments. Instead they are driven by changing $(O_i E_i)$ relationships, which are partly changed by the organisms thesmselves. In this manner, niche-constructing organisms become partly responsible for their own evolutionary futures, along with their naturally selecting environments. This is exactly what Waddington's "exploitive system" originally proposed. The role of behavior in evolution is therefore that of a contributory cause. Behavior is not just another phenotypic product of evolution. It is not just an effect. It is causal, and it is more interesting that we used to think.

Biological Infrastructure for the Social Sciences

Some of the ideas discussed in this chapter are directly relevant to those other behavioral sciences, social, economic, and political, that lie beyond the immediate scope of behavioral biology and which usually apply either chiefly or exclusively to human beings. Space is limited, so the point will be illustrated will respect to psychology and the human end of the sociobiology debate only.

Psychology

The history of psychology reveals that, like the modern synthesis, it is unable to handle the dynamics of the two-way relationships between active organisms and their relative environments. The simplest way to

demonstrate this is to consider the three principal traditions that constitute contemporary psychology: behaviorism, psychoanalytic theory, and
cognitive psychology.

In behaviorism the relationship between any organism and its environment can be characterized by a single "causal arrow" pointing from the
environment to the organism. Here we have stimulus inputs (S) from
an environment held responsible for determining an organism's response
outputs (R) in much the same way that naturally selecting inputs are
supposed by the modern synthesis to determine phenotypic expression
among populations. In its most extreme form, this kind of "S-R" psychology makes no attempt to understand the active processes that occur
within organisms. Indeed it shuns such attempts on the grounds that
internal mental events can never be observed and are therefore illegitimate
phenomena for psychologists to study (Skinner 1953). The result is that
organisms are treated by behaviorists as if they are nothing but reac-
tive systems whose behaviors are driven by impinging events in their
environments.

The approach of the psychoanalysts can also be characterized by a single
"causal arrow," but this time the arrow is pointing the other way: from the
organism to its environment. This tradition typically takes internal mental
events (particularly affective events) seriously, and it avoids the aridity of
behaviorism by explaining the behavioral outputs of human beings largely
in terms of those inner events. Consequently it ends up explaining how
human behavior is "caused" by internal psychodynamic events. True, many
of these internal mental events are assumed by psychoanalysts to have
been caused (or at least triggered) by prior environmental events—the
childhood traumas of an individual human being, for example. However,
such assumptions are usually left "loose." Psychoanalysts are therefore
vulnerable to the criticism, which they receive from behaviorists, that they
fail to demonstrate any lawful dependence of inner mental events on prior
external events. In this respect psychoanalysts are inclined to generate
plausible "just so stories," much as certain biologists are inclined to invent
untestable hypotheses about natural selection forces in order to "explain"
phenotypes (Gould 1978; Gould and Lewontin 1979; Gould and Vrba
1982).

Cognitive psychology was born out of a profound dissatisfaction among
many psychologists with the failure of behaviorism to handle data indicat-
ing vigorous psychological activity inside organisms (for instance, with
respect to memory and attention [Neisser 1967], perception [Lindsey
and Norman 1972], reasoning, [Bruner et al. 1956; Wason and Johnson-
Laird 1972], and human language [Chomsky 1957], and was provided with
the opportunity to make a fresh start by the advent of computers (Mayer
1981). In spite of several successes, cognitive psychology has not yet

managed to model the two-way relationships between active organisms and their environments in a manner clearly superior to those of the other two traditions. At present there is an incipient danger that cognitive psychology will end up by describing organism-environment relationships exclusively in terms of "programs' inside the heads of animals and therefore, like psychoanalysis before it, with a single "causal arrow" pointing from organisms to environments. Cognitive psychologists defend themselves from this charge of "subjectivity" by demonstrating how their hypothetical mental programs can be translated into working algorithms. However, this defense, impressive though it sometimes is, glosses over substantive points—among them the point that natural systems are ultimately self-designing systems relative to the selection forces in their environments whereas computers and robots are not (Dennett 1975; Searle 1980). Cognitive psychology may yet succeed, but if the arguments in this chapter are correct it will not be until it models the two-way relationship between any organism and its environment relativistically, which means relative to the (OE).

The tension among these three traditions in psychology recalls an earlier tension between empiricism and nativism in philosophy. Empiricist explanations make use of a single "objective causal arrow" pointing from environments to organisms. Nativist explanations use a single "subjective causal arrow" pointing from organisms to environments (Russell 1946). From the present point of view, the ensuing conflicts between the empiricists and nativists are simply one more symptom of our widespread historical failure to appreciate the relativistic nature of the two way (inputs plus outputs)-relationships that actually link active and behaving organisms to their coevolving worlds.

Sociobiology
Sociobiology is the latest in a long line of attempts to build a bridge between genetic evolution and sociocultural evolution (especially human cultural evolution). Like many of its predecessors it is firmly rooted in the modern synthetic theory. It is therefore forced *a priori* to explain the evolution of both societies and cultures exclusively in terms of the natural selection of heritable genes (Wilson 1975; Alexander 1979). Two consequences flow from this approach. First, it strongly inclines sociobiologists to the view that cultural traits are ultimately determined by naturally selected genes (Lumsden and Wilson 1981). Second, it commits sociobiologists to the notion that fitness means contributing to descent via the genetic system of inheritance only. The idea that fitness might also include the transmission of modified environments via ecological inheritance is not incorporated.

Sociobiology's critics have attacked both of these commitments. They point out that human phenotypes express many traits that are not genetically determined (Sahlins 1976; Rose et al. 1984), and they emphasize that cultural evolution does not necessarily maximize genetic inclusive fitness as a "genetics only" sociobiology requires. (It can do precisely the opposite; see Vining, 1986.) They also argue that the human environment is in many respects artificial, because it is itself largely a product of cultural evolution, and that it has become so unlike the natural environments that originally selected for human genes that the whole sociobiology debate is irrelevant to human affairs. Even some sociobiologists agree with this last point (see, e.g., Dawkins 1982), although in so doing they are retreating and are perpetuating the schism between evolutionary biology and the human social sciences.

There have been several attempts to settle the issue of genetic determinism. The most common has been to advocate either a dual-process (Durham 1982; Boyd and Richerson 1985) or a multiple-process (Plotkin and Odling-Smee 1981) model of evolution, and to spell out how culture can escape from genetic determination without escaping from the overall evolutionary process. All these models propose a second phenotypic channel of communication between organisms via which "culturally based knowledge" is both transmitted and received by organisms within and between generations, in addition to the genetic instructions which are transmitted intergenerationally during reproduction.

However, no previous attempt to satisfy the above-mentioned criticisms has focused primarily on the construction of artificial and novel environments through cultural activities. In this respect the present theory offers a contribution. Not only is this theory compatible with the dual-process or multiple-process models of evolution; because it introduces the concepts of niche construction and ecological inheritance, it provides a mechanism whereby novel environments could be constructed and transmitted by cultural activities. For general coevolutionary theory, culturally induced environments are only a special case of organism-environment coevolution. If they are of extra interest it is only because culture amplifies the power of niche-constructing acts, and hence the magnitude of the perturbations that may be caused by cultural organisms in their own environments.

To take this last point further, the proposed theory provides a second possible basis for social cooperation—one based on ecological inheritance—in addition to that already provided by inclusive fitness and genetic inheritance. Organisms that share overlapping environmental resources are usually expected to compete with one another unless they are genetically related. However, an alternative is possible: Organisms that are not genetic relatives may, nevertheless, cooperate via reciprocal altruistic acts to ameliorate, protect, and exploit their mutual environment for the ecological benefit of each individual. In fact, in any circumstances where the benefits of cooperation exceed the benefits of successful competition among populations of organisms, this kind of mutualism ought to appear. This point obviously bears on the evolution of mutualistic relationships (Law 1985), and it heralds the prospect of a viable group-selection hypothesis (Wilson 1983; Wynne-Edwards 1986) based on group niche construction.

When all these threads are brought together by combining heritable genetic instructions and cultural knowledge with the proposed ecological inheritance, and when fitness is redefined to refer to both the transmission of "knowledge" about environments and the transmission of the environments themselves (the two relative to each other), then we should end up with a new infrastructure for sociobiology. A general coevolutionary theory may be able to provide the framework, which has eluded us so far, for a genuine "new synthesis" between evolutionary biology and the social sciences. Here at last we may have the beginnings of a theory rich enough to cope with the actual complexities of human socio-cultural life. The framework will never be provided by the modern synthesis, because that theory's internal assumptions are too limiting. As most biologists are aware, evolutionary theory has a vast untapped capacity to inform the behavioral and social sciences, including all the human sciences. However, as long as evolutionary theory remains equated with the modern synthesis, most social scientists, and probably most human beings, will continue to believe that it has not.

Acknowledgments

Many people have helped me with the preparation of this chapter and I am grateful to all of them. However, I should particularly like to thank David Hull (Northwestern), Richard Lewontin (Harvard), Larry Slobodkin (Stony Brook), and Henry Plotkin (University College London) for their constructive criticism and comments.

References

Alcock, J. 1972. "The Evolution of the Use of Tools by Feeding Animals." *Evolution* 26: 464–473.

Alexander, R. D. 1979. *Darwinism and Human Affairs*. Seattle: University of Washington Press.

Axelrod, R. 1984. *The Evolution of Cooperation*. New York: Basic Books.

Axelrod, R., and W. D. Hamilton. 1981. "The Evolution of Cooperation." *Science* 211: 1390–1396.

Bakker, R. T. 1983. "The Red Deer Flees, the Wolf Pursues: Incongruencies in Predator-Prey Coevolution." In *Coevolution*, ed. D. J. Futuyma and M. Slatkin. Sunderland, Mass.: Sinauer.

Begon, M., J. L. Harper, and C. R. Townsend. 1986. *Ecology: Individuals, Populations and Communities*. Oxford: Blackwell.

Bock, W. J. 1980. "The Definition and Recognition of Biological Adaptation." *American Zoologist* 20: 217–227.

Bonner, J. T., ed. 1982. *Evolution and Development*. New York: Springer-Verlag.

Boyce, M. S. 1984. "Restitution of r- and K-selection as a Model of Density-Dependent Natural Selection." *Annual Review of Ecological Systems* 15: 427–447.

Boyd, R., and P. J. Richerson. 1985. *Culture and the Evolutionary Process*. University of Chicago Press.

Bruner, J. S., J. J. Goodnow, and G. A. Austen. 1956. *A Study of Thinking*. New York: Wiley.

Campbell, D. T. 1979. Descriptive Epistemology: Psychological, Sociological, and Evolutionary. Unpublished.

Campbell, J. H. 1985. "An Organizational Interpretation of Evolution." In *Evolution at a Crossroads*, ed. D. J. Depew and B. H. Weber. Cambridge, Mass.: MIT Press.

Chomsky, N. 1957. *Syntactic Structures*. The Hague: Mouton.

Clutton-Brock, T. H., F. E. Guiness, and S. D. Albon. 1982. *Red Deer: Behavior and Ecology of Two Sexes*. Edinburgh University Press.

Conrad, M. 1983. *Adaptability*. New York: Plenum.

Dawkins, R. 1976. *The Selfish Gene*. Oxford University Press.

Dawkins, R. 1982. *The Extended Phenotype*. Oxford: Freeman.

Dennett, D. C. 1975. "Why the Law of Effect Will Not Go Away." *Journal For the Theory of Social Behavior* 5: 169–187.

Depew, D. J., and B. H. Weber, eds. 1985. *Evolution at a Crossroads*. Cambridge, Mass.: MIT Press.

Dover, G. 1982. "Molecular Drive: A Cohesive Model of Species Evolution." *Nature* 299: 111–117.

Durham, W. H. 1982. "Interactions of Genetic and Cultural Evolution." *Human Ecology* 10: 289–323.

Einstein, A. 1956. *The Meaning of Relativity*. Sixth edition. London: Methuen.

Einstein, A. 1960. *Relativity*. London: Methuen.

Eldredge, N., and S. N. Salthe. 1985. "Hierarchy and Evolution." *Oxford Surveys in Evolutionary Biology* 1: 184–208.

Emlen, S. T. 1984. "Cooperative Breeding in Birds and Mammals." In *Behavioral Ecology: An Evolutionary Approach*, ed. J. R. Krebs and N. Davies. Second edition. Oxford: Blackwell.

Feynman, R. 1965. *The Character of Physical Law*. London: Cox and Wyman.

Futuyma, D. J., and M. Slatkin, eds. 1983. *Coevolution*. Sunderland, Mass.: Sinauer.

Gould, S. J. 1978. "Sociobiology: The Art of Story Telling." *New Scientist* 8: 530–533.

Gould, S. J. 1980. "Is a New and General Theory of Evolution Emerging?" *Paleobiology* 6: 119–130.

Gould, S. J., and R. C. Lewontin. 1979. "The Spandrels of San Marco and the Panglossian Paradigm: A Critique of the Adaptationist Programme." In *The Evolution of Adaptation by Natural Selection*, ed. J. Maynard Smith and R. Holliday. London: Royal Society.

Gould, S. J., and E. S. Vrba. 1982. "Exaptation—A Missing Term in the Science of Form." *Paleobiology* 8: 4–15.

Hailman, J. P. 1982. "Evolution and Behavior: An Iconoclastic View." In *Learning, Development and Culture*, ed. H. C. Plotkin. Chichester: Wiley.

Hamilton, W. D. 1964. "The Genetical Evolution of Social Behavior." *Journal of Theoretical Biology* 7: 1–32.

Hamilton, W. D., and R. M. May. 1977. "Dispersal in Stable Habitats." *Nature* 269: 578–581.

Hassell, M. P. 1981. "Arthropod Predator-Prey Systems." In *Theoretical Ecology*, ed. R. M. May. Second edition. Oxford: Blackwell.

Hodos, W., and C. B. G. Campbell. 1969. "Scala Naturae: Why There Is No Theory in Comparative Psychology." *Psychological Review* 76: 337–350.

Horn, H. S., and D. I. Rubenstein. 1984. "Behavioral Adaptations and Life History." In *Behavioral Ecology: An Evolutionary Approach*, ed. J. R. Krebs and N. B. Davies. Oxford: Blackwell.

Hutchinson, G. E. 1957. "Concluding Remarks." *Cold Spring Harbor Symposia on Quantitative Biology* 22: 415–427.

Kawamura, S. 1963. "The Process of Sub-culture Propagation among Japanese Macaques." In *Primate Social Behavior*, ed. C. H. Southwick. New York: Van Nostrand.

Kettlewell, H. B. D. 1956. "A Resume of Investigations on the Evolution of Melanism in the Lepidoptera." *Proceedings of the Royal Society B* 145: 297–303.

King, J. A. 1955. "Social Behavior, Social Organization, and Population Dynamics in a Black-Tailed Prairiedog Town in the Black Hills of South Dakota." *Contributions from the Laboratory of Vertebrate Biology* (University of Michigan, Ann Arbor), no. 67: 123.

Krebs, J. R., and N. B. Davies, eds. 1984. *Behavioral Ecology: An Evolutionary Approach*. Second edition. Oxford: Blackwell.

Law, R. 1985. "Evolution in a Mutualistic Environment." In *The Biology of Mutualism*, ed. D. H. Boucher. Beckenham: Croom Helm.

Levins, R. 1968. *Evolution in Changing Environments*. Princeton University Press.

Levins, R., and Lewontin, R. C. 1985. *The Dialectical Biologist*. Cambridge, Mass.: Harvard University Press.

Lewontin, R. C. 1978. "Adaptation." *Scientific American* 239, no. 3: 156–169.

Lewontin, R. C. 1982. "Organism and Environment." In *Learning, Development and Culture*, ed. H. C. Plotkin. Chichester: Wiley.

Lewontin, R. C. 1983. "Gene, Organism and Environment." In *Evolution from Molecules to Men*, ed. D. S. Bendall. Cambridge University Press.

Lindsey, P. H., and D. A. Norman 1972. *Human Information Processing*. New York: Academic.

Lovejoy, A. O. 1936. *The Great Chain of Being*. New York: Harper.

Lumsden, C. C., and E. O. Wilson. 1981. *Genes, Mind, and Culture: The Coevolutionary Process*. Cambridge, Mass.: Harvard University Press.

MacMahon, J. A., D. J. Schimpf, D. C. Anderson, K. G. Smith, and R. L. Bayn. 1981. "An Organism-centred Approach to Some Community and Ecosystem Concepts." *Journal of Theoretical Biology* 88: 287–307.

McMahon, T. A., and J. T. Bonner. 1983. *On Size and Life*. New York: Freeman.

May, R. M., ed. 1981. *Theoretical Ecology*. Second edition Oxford: Blackwell.

Mayer, R. E. 1981. *The Promise of Cognitive Psychology*. San Francisco: Freeman.

Mayr, E. 1974. "Behavior Programs and Evolutionary Strategies." *American Scientist* 62: 650–659.

Maynard Smith, J. 1974. *Models in Ecology*. Cambridge University Press.

Maynard Smith, J. 1982. *Evolution and the Theory of Games*. Cambridge University Press.

Neisser, U. 1967. *Cognitive Psychology*. New York: Appleton-Century-Crofts.

Nelson, K. 1973. "Does the Holistic Study of Behavior Have a Future?" In *Perspectives in Ethology*, ed. P. P. G. Bateson and P. H. Klopfer. New York: Plenum.

Odling-Smee, F. J. 1983. "Multiple Levels in Evolution." In *Animal Models of Human Behavior*, ed. G. C. L. Davey. New York: Wiley.

Odling-Smee, F. J., and H. C. Plotkin. 1984. "Evolution: Its Levels and Its Units." *Behavioral and Brain Sciences* 7: 318–320.

O'Neill, R. V., D. L. DeAngelis, J. B. Waide, and T. F. H. Allen. 1986. *A Hierarchical Concept of Ecosytems*. Princeton University Press.

Patten, B. C. 1982. "Environs: Relativistic Elementary Particles for Ecology." *American Naturalist* 119: 179–219.

Patten, B. C., and G. T. Auble. 1981. "System Theory of the Ecological Niche." *American Naturalist* 117: 893–922.

Piaget, J. 1971. *Biology and Knowledge*. Edinburgh University Press.

Piaget, J. 1979. *Behavior and Evolution*. London: Routledge and Kegan Paul.

Pianka, E. R. 1970. "On r- and K-Selection." *American Naturalist* 104: 592–597.

Pianka, E. R. 1981. "Competition and Niche Theory." In *Theoretical Ecology*, ed. R. M. May. Second edition. Oxford: Blackwell.

Plotkin, H. C., and F. J. Odling-Smee. 1979. "Learning, Change and Evolution." *Advances in the Study of Behavior* 10: 1–41.

Plotkin, H. C., and F. J. Odling-Smee. 1981. "A Multiple-Level Model of Evolution and Its Implications for Sociobiology." *Behavioral and Brain Sciences* 4: 225–268.

Rose, S., L. J. Kamin, and R. C. Lewontin. 1984. *Not in Our Genes*. London: Penguin.

Ross, W. D. 1949. *Aristotle*. London: Methuen.

Roughgarden, J. 1983. "The Theory of Coevolution." In *Coevolution*, ed. D. J. Futuyma and M. Slatkin. Sunderland, Mass.: Sinauer.

Russell, B. 1946. *History of Western Philosophy*. London: Allen and Unwin.

Sahlins, M. 1976. *The Use and Abuse of Biology*. Ann Arbor: University of Michigan Press.

Salthe, S. N. 1985. *Evolving Hierarchical Systems*. New York: Columbia University Press.

Schrödinger, E. 1956 "Mind and Matter." In E. Schrödinger, *What Is Life?* Cambridge University Press, 1967.

Searle, J. R. 1980. "Minds, Brains and Programs." *Behavioral and Brain Sciences* 3: 417–424.

Simon, H. A. 1982. *The Sciences of the Artificial*. Second edition. Cambridge, Mass.: MIT Press.

Simpson, G. G. 1967. *The Meaning of Evolution*. New Haven, Conn.: Yale University Press.

Skinner, B. F. 1953. *Science and Human Behavior*. New York: Free Press.

Slobodkin, L. B., and A. Rapoport. 1974. "An Optimal Strategy of Evolution." *Quarterly Review of Biology* 49: 181–200.

Smith, W. J., S. L. Smith, E. C. Oppenheimer, J. G. de Villa, and F. A. Ulmer. 1973. "Behavior of a Captive Population of Blacktailed Prairie Dogs: Annual Cycle of Social Behavior." *Behavior* 46: 189–220.

Southwood, T. R. E. 1977. "Habitat, the Templet for Ecological Strategies?" *Journal of Animal Ecology* 46: 337–365.

Southwood, T. R. E. 1981. "Bionomic Strategies and Population Parameters." In *Theoretical Ecology*, ed. R. M. May. Second edition. Oxford: Blackwell.

Stearns, S. C. 1976. "Life-History Tactics: A Review of the Ideas." *Quarterly Review of Biology* 51: 3–47.

Stearns, S. C. 1977. "The Evolution of Life History Traits: A Critique of the Theory and a Review of the Data." *Annual Review of Ecological Systems* 8: 145–171.

Stearns, S. C. 1982. "The Role of Development in the Evolution of Life-Histories." In *Evolution and Development*, ed. J. T. Bonner. New York: Springer-Verlag.

Stebbins, G. L., and F. J. Ayala. 1985. "The Evolution of Darwinism." *Scientific American* 253, no. 1: 54–64.

Suzuki, D. T., A. J. F. Griffiths, and R. C. Lewontin. 1981. *An Introduction to Genetic Analysis*. San Francisco: Freeman.

Thoday, J. M. 1953. "Components of fitness." *Symposia of the Society for Experimental Biology* 7: 96–113.

Thompson, D. A. W. 1917. *On Growth and Form*. Cambridge University Press.

Vandermeer, J. H. 1972. "Niche Theory." *Annual Review of Ecological Systems* 3: 107–132.

Vining, R. V. 1986. "Social versus Reproductive Success: The Central Theoretical Problem in Human Sociobiology." *Behavioral and Brain Sciences* 9: 167–216.

von Uexkull, J. 1926. *Theoretical Biology*. London: Kegan, Paul, Trench, Tubner.

Vrba, E. S., and N. Eldredge. 1984. "Individuals, Hierarchies and Processes: Towards a More Complete Evolutionary Theory." *Paleobiology* 10: 146–171.

Waddington, C. H. 1959. "Evolutionary Systems: Animal and Human." *Nature* 183: 1634–1638.

Waddington, C. H. 1960. "Evolutionary Adaptation." In *The Evolution of Life*, ed. S. Tax. University of Chicago Press.

Waddington, C. H. 1969. "Paradigm for an Evolutionary Process." In *Towards a Theoretical Biology, 2: Sketches*, ed. C. H. Waddington. Edinburgh University Press.

Wason, P. C., and P. N. Johnson-Laird. 1972. *Psychology of Reasoning*. London: Batsford.

Williams, G. C. 1966. *Adaptation and Natural Selection*. Princeton University Press.

Wilson, A. C. 1985. "The Molecular Basis of Evolution." *Scientific American* 253, no. 3: 148–157.

Wilson, D. S. 1983. "The Group Selection Controversy: History and Current Status." *Annual Review of Ecological Systems* 14: 159–187.

Wilson, E. O. 1975. *Sociobiology: The New Synthesis*. Cambridge, Mass.: Harvard University Press.

Woolfenden, G. E., and J. W. Fitzpatrick. 1978. "The Inheritance of Territory in Group-Breeding Birds." *Bioscience* 28: 104–108.

Wootton, R. J. 1984. *A Functional Biology of Sticklebacks*. London: Croom Helm.

Wynne-Edwards, V. C. 1986. *Evolution through Group Selection*. Oxford: Blackwell.

Chapter 5

Learning and Evolution

H. C. Plotkin

Learning is used in this chapter as a generic term refering to the acquisition by an individual animal of information or knowledge about some aspect of that animal's world or of its relationship to that world, the storage of that information, and its integration into already existing behavior patterns such that it may alter the future behavior of that animal. The cognitive processes of experimental psychology—including those commonly known as thinking and problem solving, which are considered essential to many forms of learning—are considered to fall within the limits of the term *learning* as it will be used here. Such a fuzzy and imprecise definition is excusable because the nature of the processes and mechanisms that result in learning is of little importance to this chapter. What *is* important are the consequences that such learning processes have for behavior, which may be of evolutionary significance.

Psychology has long been dominated by the study of learning in one guise (or approach) or another. Although classical ethology placed much less emphasis upon learning, contemporary behavioral biology is increasingly mindful of it. This is not because learning is a universal feature of animal behavior, which it probably is not. Indeed, its phylogenetic distribution is poorly documented. It is widely present in vertebrates, of course, and it occurs in numerous species of *Mollusca* and *Arthropoda* (though how commonly is unclear). It has been sporadically reported in representatives of some other phyla (see Corning et al. 1973a, 1973b, and 1975 for extensive reviews), but it is almost certainly not present in all animal species. Now, a lack of universality cannot be the reason for the deep interest that learning arouses. Anthropocentrism doubtless can account for a large part of it. But there is, it is suggested, another reason. This is the widely shared intuition of biologists, often poorly articulated if articulated at all, that when learning is present it is a powerful device by which individuals exploit, and adapt to, their environments; and that the power and efficacy of learning as such as device stems from its adding a potent dynamic to behavior. (I intend the word *dynamic* here to suggest, as in its ordinary sense, the opposite of *static*—i.e., that forces are not in equilibrium.)

This chapter will consider this learning-induced behavioral dynamism in the context of how such learned behavior may then play a causal role in the evolution of the population to which the individual learners belong. There have been a number of reviews and analyses (which will be cited in the appropriate sections) of specific ways in which learning affects behavior that may have evolutionary significance. However, I know of no previous attempt at an overview. The way that I have gone about providing one here is doubtless incomplete, and in part arbitrary; however, it is entirely guided by the general aim of the book, which is to examine the role of behavior in evolution.

The use of the term *learning* in so encompassing a manner may be offensive to those who spend their time teasing apart the detailed mechanisms of different forms of learning using phylogenetic, ontogenetic, neurobiological, and experimental-psychological methods. These details and differences are not doubted, and it is not the intention of this chapter to trivialize such studies. The distinctions that this chapter does attempt to draw are, however, rather different from those of these more usual approaches to learning. This is because the contribution of individual learning to the evolution of the population to which the learner belongs is an opportunistic process into which, frequently, any number of different forms of learning, with possible different mechanisms, can enter. Thus, the form of analysis adopted here forces a generic use that may seem to be at odds with an approach based upon mechanisms of learning. This should not, however, be taken to mean that viewing individual learning as a systemic property of an evolving system necessarily denies the importance of the mechanisms of that learning. It merely considers the latter irrelevant to the issue of the role that learning plays in evolution.

In addition to reviewing the ways in which learning and learned behavior may (theoretically) be causal factors in evolution, this chapter is also concerned with the those areas and issues that lend themselves to empirical study. This is obviously a crucial issue. If this review does not suggest alternative and more embracing explanations of known phenomena, and/or novel lines of empirical research, then it is simply a theoretical exercise that is going nowhere. Thus, in the sections and subsections that follow, empirical lines are drawn, but very broadly. This is because at this stage the intention is to indicate fruitful areas of empirical study. It obviously cannot be the business of a chapter of this kind to outline specific details of required experiments or observations.

The Evolution of Learning

It is now widely accepted that for much of this century laboratory-based studies of learning were carried out mostly with a view to explaining learning in terms of its proximate causes, and without regard to evolution-ary considerations. Evolution was often paid fleeting lip service, but the notion that learning is a phenotypic trait or set of traits that has evolved played no role whatever in the development of learning theory until the 1960s. (See Plotkin and Odling-Smee 1982 and Roper 1983 for more detailed reviews of how this occurred and what its implications for tradi-tional learning theory were.) The strongest evidence that learning is an evolved trait came, ironically, from laboratory studies, and it confirmed what Lorenz and Tinbergen had been insisting on for decades, viz. that learning is constrained and not an all-purpose generalist capacity. Studies on imprinting, birdsong, dietary choice, and foraging—so-called natural-istic learning situations and tasks—confirmed the message coming from the learning laboratories that, to a lesser or greater degree determined by the species of learner and the nature of the task, animals are primed to learn certain kinds of relationships and not others. No learner, and that includes humans, is a *tabula rasa*. It is this priming that makes learning an adaptive trait, because without it learning would be an unfocused, slow, inefficient process. (See Revusky 1985 for an alternative, generalist account of learn-ing. Details of the argument as to what is general and what species-specific about learning, and of what is right and what is wrong about the *tabula rasa* conception of learning, are of little consequence to this chapter and so are not presented here. What small importance the issue has for the role of learned behavior in evolution will be brought out in the next section.)

Subsequent developments in learning theory that are explicitly based on the view that learning has evolved have taken several different, albeit related, paths. One has been to forge closer links between traditional accounts of learning and behavioral ecology (see, e.g., Shettleworth 1984). Another has been to explore the ways in which learning can be analyzed in terms of the "ecological" theory of J. J. Gibson (see Johnston and Pietrewicz 1985 for a collection of essays). A third path has continued the development of evolutionary epistemology as a framework for understand-ing learning as a part of a hierarchy of knowledge-gaining and knowledge-storing processes (Plotkin 1988 is a recent review). The fourth has con-cerned the extension of the conception of evolutionarily stable strategies to developmental stable strategies (Harley 1981; Maynard-Smith 1982). This last is an especially interesting approach, since it uses a highly success-ful analytical device, the theory of games, as a method of modeling evolu-tion, on the explicit assumption that the dynamics of competing strategies are the same whether they are genetically and developmentally or cogni-tively based.

Whatever the details of the differences of these various theoretical lines, on one thing they are entirely agreed: that learning is a phenotypic trait that has evolved, the assumption of its evolution being crucial to a full understanding of learning. Nothing in this chapter is at variance with this central and essential point, and everything that follows is based upon it.

What the next four sections attempt to do, however, is to explore the ways in which the circle relating evolution and learning can be closed: learning has indeed evolved, but in what ways is learning also a cause in the total process of evolution?

Four Roles of Learning in Evolution

Learned Behavioral Adaptations
Learning is adaptive. This is the most commonplace view of the role of learning in evolution, and it is closely related to the generally accepted notion that learning is an evolved trait or set of traits. More specifically, the assumption that learning is adaptive is the assumption that learning operates to increase the adaptedness of behavior. This is so widely held an intuition among biologists that it has seldom been explicitly articulated, and even less often formalized. Despite the common-sense nature of this view, it has rarely been tested; and when it has been, serious problems of interpretation have arisen. Such problems apart, learning seen in this way is being ascribed a conservative, indirect role in evolution, no different in kind from the roles of other adaptive phenotypic traits that increase mean phenotypic fitness and hence contribute to the reproductive competence of phenotypes.

The phrase "learned behavioral adaptation" refers to a complex of adaptive behaviors formed out of the effects of learning on existing behavior. The precise nature of this complex remains unknown and is subject to much argument; it has always been a source of deep controversy in the social sciences, where it is referred to as the nature-nurture problem. It is not merely an ideological issue, though; it touches upon the question whether the fundamental biological nature of learning is that of a generalist, cross-species ability or that of a more constrained, species-typical trait. Early formulations of the problem rather blurred the matter. Lorenz stated that "we can observe behavioral chains which are not inherited as a unitary whole but always possess 'gaps' which are appropriately filled up by self-conditioning or insight behavior during the ontogeny of the individual.... For instance, the recognition of the 'appropriate' object for particular behavior is frequently *not* inherited as an integral part of instinctive systems adapted to respond to a given object. Instead, there is an instinctive tendency to try out various objects, the range of which is gradually restricted to appropriate objects." (Lorenz 1932 [1970, pp. 60–61]) But what are these gaps? Are they really gaps in the sense of empty spaces that can be filled by anything? If they are, then Lorenz would seem to be arguing that learning is a generalist capacity, divorced from the requirements of any specific behavioral chain, that is able to fill any gap.

Hull's (1943) position was also ambiguous. If he were writing today, Hull would be described as an adaptationist. He claimed that one of the main objectives of molar behavioral science is to understand why behavior "is so generally adaptive" (p. 19). Hull also recognized that "innate behavior tendencies vary about a central range" and are never fixed and invariant (p. 58). Such inherent variation, however, is not sufficient to ensure the adaptiveness of the behavior in question. Behavior, despite its inherently variable form, "will hardly be optimally effective for the survival of organisms living in a complex, highly variable, and consequently unpredictable environment. For the optimal probability of survival of such organisms, inherited behavior tendencies must be supplemented by learning." (p. 68) But here Hull too is unclear about whether that supplemental process of learning is some kind of free-floating, generalist ability or one that is very specifically fixed to the behavior that has to be so supplemented. However, from the general tenor of Hull's writings it is reasonable to assume that he considered learning to be a generalist trait. Skinner (1953) also seems to have been plumping for a generalist interpretation when he wrote that "where inherited behavior leaves off, the inherited modifiability of the process of conditioning takes over" (p. 55). But it is by no means clear that the opposite cannot be read into that statement—i.e., that since inherited behavior is not general (in the sense of a generalist trait), then neither is the process of conditioning that "takes over." This ambiguity suggests that the problem of the specialist versus the generalist nature of learning was not a focus of attention at the time.

Sommerhoff (1950, 1969) developed a more specific view of learning within a highly original approach to the concept of adaptation. It is also one of the few formalized accounts of learning as a form of adaptation. He did not tie the notion of adaptedness to Darwinian fitness in terms of reproductive competence; instead he attempted an account of the goal-directed nature of adaptation. Thus Sommerhoff provided an analysis of adaptations, in a mathematically formalized manner, as "directive correlations." A directive correlation describes a flexible relationship between some feature of a phenotype and an aspect of its environment, the conjunction of the two being the goal of the adaptation. Furthermore, Sommerhoff's position was unusual in recognizing that adaptations can be differentiated on the basis of the lag time that is required to establish the correlation. Long-term directive correlations, which he called phylogenetic adaptations, have a lag time of at least one generation and furnish, among other kinds of adaptations, unlearned behaviors. Short-term directive correlations refer to reflexive and spatially orienting devices, such as taxes, whereby behavioral adjustments to rapid fluctuations in the environment are achieved. Sommerhoff referred to medium-term directive correlations as "ontogenetic adaptations." These involve adaptive adjustments to conditions in the environment that have a degree of stability relative to the life span of the organism but are too short to be encompassed by phylogenetic adaptations. He singled out learning as an example of such medium-term directive correlations. Thus, for Sommerhoff learning *is* a specific, behaviorally integrated, medium-term set of adaptations. It is difficult to read into Sommerhoff's scheme the notion that learning is a generalist capacity that floats about, separate from the behaviors that is shapes.

Another approach that is important in this respect is that of Mayr (1974), who coined the phrase "open program," one effect of which is to present a position that makes the specificity of learning quite clear. If Mayr's "open program" concept is translated into a Lorenzian behavioral chain with gaps, the gaps become those parts of the chain that are relatively unspecified. Certain experiences allow those gaps to be differentiated into specific behavioral tendencies. Thus, for Mayr, too, learning is not a generalist capacity but one that is tied to specific aspects of behavioral ontogeny.

With certain differences that are not important for present purposes, Plotkin and Odling-Smee (1979) and Johnston and Turvey (1980) developed slightly further this kind of thinking, in which learning is envisaged as a means by which behavior is fine-tuned to the specific conditions of the learner's interaction with its environment. Briefly, the argument goes as follows: Behavioral adaptations are furnished by genetic and epigenetic means in a relatively crude form. This is because the precise nature of the learner-environment interaction cannot be predicted; it can only be specified, on the basis of *a posteriori* selection, as falling within certain limits. Subsequent experience of the individual fills in the precise values of certain parameters (spatial coordinates, visual characteristics, etc.) and so sharpens the fit between behavior and the learner's world.

Many biologists and psychologists consider the views expressed in the preceding paragraphs to be simply the explication of the obvious. Yet, however, unsurprising such arguments might be as to the role of learning in enhancing the adaptedness of behavior, they place learning within a genetic, epigenetic, and ecological framework that itself raises certain serious empirical problems. This is because when learning is viewed in this way, further complexity is bestowed upon the already complex system within which learning operates. It is this system's complexity that raises empirical problems not faced by approaches (and sciences at large) that deal with intrinsically simple systems. The physicist is confident that the behavior of subatomic particles in an accelerator reflects the behavior of subatomic particles outside that accelerator. This is because no matter how contrived and artificial the physics laboratory, it has validity as a test bed for events in the world at large. But as complexity increases, as it quickly does when learning is considered in the context of evolution, laboratory study is in danger of progressively degrading that complexity and hence reducing the validity of the studies. The more complex a phenomenon in its relationships with the natural world, the more degraded and invalid might be its laboratory study. On the other hand, field studies of learning (i.e., investigations set in the natural world) face formidable problems of disentangling the variables contributing to the behavior which learning is assumed to be influencing. And whether set in the laboratory or in the field, all research on learning has difficulty answering the seemingly self-evident question as to its adaptedness. Every attempt to understand learning in an evolutionary context suffers from these twin difficulties: the tendency simply to assume what is thought to be obvious, and the very real difficulty of demonstrating it.

The assumption that learning is adaptive comes from the gradual acceptance of the claims of the classical ethologists and is a theoretical assertion, not an empirical finding. There *does* seem to be empirical support from studies that show learning to have a goal directedness and an apparent efficiency that are widely held to be the hallmarks of adaptation. For example, in a widely cited study, Kamil (1978) showed that a species of nectar-feeding bird, the amakihi of Hawaii, appears to forage efficiently by remembering what flowers it has recently visited. The pattern of foraging seems not to be accounted for by the systematic movement patterns of individual birds or by some overt form of marking. Further, that birds have a memory capacity equal to the task of such foraging efficiency has been shown independently by the studies of Shettleworth and her colleagues (described in Shettleworth 1983), which show that several North American and European species of birds appear to be able to commit to memory the positions of thousands of food hoards over periods of months. Also, the ability of nectar-foraging birds to learn the strategies appropriate to such foraging has been confirmed by the laboratory work of Cole et al. (1982).

How, then, can it be claimed that "there is no body of acceptable evidence demonstrating that learning unequivocally improves the adaptiveness of behavior under natural conditions" (Hailman 1985, p. 38)? Hailman's case, presumably, is as follows: Traditionally, the claim that an attribute is adaptive is tied to the notion that such an attribute increases mean phenotypic fitness (Williams 1966). Mean phenotypic fitness is measured by reproductive competence. Yet no published study, as far as I am aware, has ever shown that learning in general, or some specific form of learning, increases reproductive competence. This is an extraordinary gap in our knowledge. It may not be too long before such studies can be performed. There is an increasing understanding about how to eliminate specific forms of learning, such as spatial memory or pattern recognition, at least in mammals, by appropriate neurological intervention. It may also eventually be possible to bring about such selective learning impairments by genetic manipulation. Both field and laboratory studies of the effects of such impairments on mean phenotypic fitness may then become feasible. This is an area that is ripe for investigation.

A perhaps less tractable problem posed by empirical studies under natural conditions concerns knowing when learning is responsible for changes in behavior. Shettleworth (1984) shows how several variables that enter into foraging behavior, (for example, switching from one prey item to another, changing the search area, or altering the pattern of movement in space) could be the result of the operation of either cognitive processes or unlearned rules of thumb. Kamil's study of the amakihi and Tinbergen's (1938) classic experiments on homing behavior in the digger wasp (*Philanthus triangulum*) are rare examples of field work that seem unequivocally to establish learning as one of the causes. Doubtless ingenious experimenters will supply other examples in the future, but the requirements for controlled manipulation of variables will make laboratory investigation indispensable, especially if such work incorporates a degree of natural complexity. This is just what certain recent studies, both empirical and theoretical, have attempted by modeling controlled laboratory studies on naturalistic settings within which learning is almost certainly operating. Examples are operant studies serving as analogies for foraging (Kamil and Sargeant 1981; Pietrewicz and Richards 1985), formalized modeling of foraging as partly a problem of learning (Kacelnik and Krebs 1985), investigations of hoarding (Shettleworth 1983), and learning by observing conspecifics (C. M. Heyes et al., unpublished data).

There is, finally, a cluster of social behaviors for which learning is essential. Here not only individual fitness but also inclusive fitness is increased as a result of learning abilities. Such behaviors involve biased responsiveness, including the giving of reciprocal aid, based on the recognition of individual animals and on memory of the history of previous interactions with individuals (see Hepper 1986 and Trivers 1985 for recent reviews). There is also the possibility, as Dunbar suggests in the next chapter of this book, that some of the cost-benefit analyses involved in social interactions are carried out by individual animals using complex cognitive processes. The same problems of measuring actual adaptiveness and of teasing apart unlearned rules of thumb from learned strategies apply here that apply to, say, foraging. This is an area of animal behavior, however, where the last decade has produced remarkable technical and theoretical advances. There is no reason to doubt that knowledge about the role of learning in social relationships will continue to expand rapidly.

The study of the adaptedness of learning may offer rich empirical pickings. I doubt that investigators will be put off by my insisting that adaptedness be measured in terms of increased fitness and reproductive competence. A mix of formal modeling, field work, and laboratory experimentation will supply the answers in time. The investigations that are needed may be technically difficult, but their aim is easy to formulate. This is not the case for the next possible role of learning in evolution.

The Exploitive System
Waddington uses the term "exploitive system" to describe the ability of some animals to select (choose) the environments in which they will live, these choices having an effect on the selection pressures to which the animals will be subjected. In chapter 1 of this book I considered the exploitive system within the more general context of the history of attempts to examine the role of behavior in evolution. Here the concern is to focus upon the exploitive system as a specific instance of how learning might affect the role of behavior in evolution.

As was noted in chapter 1, Waddington was not the only writer to envisage the operation of something like an exploitive system. Another was Mayr:

> Mayr showed that different kinds of behavior play different roles in evolution. Behavior that serves as communication, for instance courtship behavior, must be stereotyped in order not to be misunderstood. The genetic program controlling such behavior must be "closed," that is, it must be reasonably resistant to any chances during the individual life cycle. Other behaviors, for instance those that control the choice of food or habitat, must have a certain amount of flexibility in order to permit the incorporation of new experiences; such behaviors must be controlled by an "open" program. New selection pressures, *induced by changes in behavior*, may lead to morphological changes facilitating the occupation of new ecological niches or adaptive zones.... Many if not most acquisitions of new structures in the course of evolution can be ascribed to selection forces exerted by newly acquired behaviors. *Behavior thus plays an important role as the pacemaker of evolutionary change*. Most adaptive radiations were apparently caused by behavioral shifts. (Mayr 1982, p. 612; italics added)

This is a very strong statement. As was noted in chapter 1, it echoes others that Mayr has previously made and which have also been made in slightly different form by other evolutionists. Waddington's conception of an exploitive system is a virtually identical claim, but it is more explicit in that it is consistently presented as a subprocess of evolution, coequal in status with genetic, developmental, and natural-selective subsystems. In a number of places, Lorenz (1966, for example) also referred to behavior as an evolutionary pacemaker, though in certain respects his position was quite the opposite to that of Mayr. Mayr wrote:

> A shift into a new niche or adaptive zone is, almost without exception, initiated by a change in behavior. The other adaptations to the new niche, particularly the structural ones, are acquired secondarily. With habitat and food selection—behavioral phenomena—playing a major role in the shift into new adaptive zones, the importance of behavior in initiating new evolutionary events is self-evident. Sibling species, in spite of their morphological similarity, often show remarkable behavioral differences. (1963, p. 604)

Lorenz would certainly have agreed with the last sentence, since he often pointed out that certain behaviors showed remarkable variation between closely related species whereas other kinds of behavior, and morphology at large, were more conserved, and that one needed to make comparisons at the taxonomic rank of family before observing differences of similar magnitude. However, Lorenz most frequently singled out ritualized communication as the behavioral pacemaker for evolution, whereas Mayr (1974) specifically claimed for such behavior the characteristic of "closed" behavioral programs. As in the quote above, this is because of the need for such signaling systems not to be misunderstood by the receivers of the signals.

These differences in emphasis between Mayr and Lorenz are due, it is conjectured, to differences in the focus of their thinking. As ardent Darwinists, both wished to see their own work most closely associated with the core issues of evolution, especially speciation. For Lorenz, because of his seminal contributions to ethology in general and to the study of signaling systems specifically, interspecific differences in communicative behavior were the obvious places to look for the crucial role of behavior in evolution. The evidence, he claimed, was differences in the signaling systems of closely related species. Mayr, as the originator of the "founder principle," looked to other ways by which speciation occurs, and saw in courtship rituals devices to *prevent* cross-breeding—a view quite contrary to that of Lorenz. And unlike Lorenz, Mayr adduced no evidence to support his conception of which behaviors contributed most to the evolutionary process. Furthermore, they differed in that Lorenz considered the behaviors to which they referred in these pacemaker roles unlearned whereas Mayr considered them at least partly learned.

Thus, whatever the finer details of their positions, these two eminent biologists adopted fairly similar positions on behavior as an evolutionary pacemaker. A. C. Hardy (1965) and E. O. Wilson (1975) made similar claims, as did Piaget (1979). Piaget was greatly influenced by Waddington, but he went well beyond support for Waddington's notion of the exploitive system; he championed the "Baldwin effect" and other rather Lamarckian notions by which behavior might directly affect the genotype—and for which no known mechanisms exist. For this reason Piaget is excluded as a serious proponent of an exploitive-system "view." All the other writers mentioned are, however, so considered. And what links them even further is the oddity of the contrast between the magnitude of the claim that behavior (including learned behavior) is a major factor in evolution and the sheer paucity of analysis with regard to the claim. This point is amplified and documented in chapter 1 of the present volume.

Any of three considerations might account for this curious lack of fit between the importance of the claim and the small amount of analysis devoted to it. All three reflect the real complexity of the analytical task of understanding the role of behavior in evolution, whether that behavior is learned or unlearned. Because these considerations raise issues that are of central importance to this whole book, I want to dwell a little on each of them.

The first of these three considerations is the potential for confusion between the various possible roles that unlearned behavior and learned behavior might have in evolution; and further confusion over both the kinds of relationships that may exist between these behaviors that are not distinguished from one another and the relationships between these behaviors and other factors in evolution, such as the issue of sympatric and allopatric speciation. It is precisely to avoid such confusion that the distinction was first raised in chapter 1. For the same reason, the present chapter has been organized, to the greatest possible extent, in terms of clearly demarcated; potentially different roles for learning in evolution. Thus, the next subsection considers whether learned behavior may directly affect gamete exchange and hence gene frequencies in the gene pool and gene combinations in offspring—a quite different issue from whether learning acts to sharpen behavioral adaptations, the concern of the preceding subsection. Both are different, again, from the issue of whether learned behaviors might lead to altered selection pressures, which is the concern of the present subsection. A failure to distinguish among these various possible roles, and the likely accompanying sense of unease that the relationship between learning and evolution is a complex matter and cannot be simply dispensed with by vague references to the importance of phenotypic behavior at large, might have contributed to the avoidance of serious analysis of the problem.

The second possible reason for the scant attention to such purportedly important matters (a reason alluded to in the preceding subsection and in chapter 1) is the very real difficulty of disentangling the behavior of the phenotype from nonbehavioral phenotypic attributes and of distinguishing between learned and unlearned behaviors. This may seem a somewhat picayune concern to the biologist who is not directly interested behavioral studies. But it clearly was not so to either Mayr or Lorenz, and it cannot be so to this chapter. The research program being advanced in this book requires clear distinctions to be drawn between (1) a phenotypic theory of evolution, (2) the more specific issue of the role of behavior in evolution, and (3)—as a sign of conceptual and analytical rigor—the ability to break the category "behavior" into finer components, such as learning, social interactions, and so on. Ultimately, certain distinctions may prove cumbersome, if not otiose; however, beginnings must be built on minimal distinctions, and if these are not drawn then the effort is likely to be stultified at the outset and to result in loose, if rather grand, claims of little substance.

The third consideration is lack of empirical support. Empirical study and theory feed off one another, of course. The notion that behavior is an evolutionary pacemaker has been around for at least four decades. Yet only one set of empirical studies by A. C. Wilson and his colleagues has been published, and that very recently. Without further empirical support, the claim that behavior is an evolutionary pacemaker will not survive another 40 years.

Before considering A. C. Wilson's work, I must spell out the precise nature of the assertions made for learning in this subsection. They are as follows. If behavior be taken to refer to whole-animal or near whole-animal interactions with the environment (typified for most biologists by gross locomotion in space or by more limited interactions between specialized effectors and specific features of the environment, such as biting or grasping an object), then such interactions, as components of the exploitive system, may alter the selection pressures acting on the organism. An exploring insect flees a noxious object; a forager comes upon a new resource or encounters a novel parasite or predator. Learning, as has already been pointed out, adds to the dynamism of the system because, although learning may evolve as specific adaptive skills, such skills are not necessarily closed abilities but may have potentially wide, generalized usage. An animal that can remember spatial features of its environment can use such a spatial mapping ability to enlarge the spatial range of its movements. Similarly, learned skills of manipulation using appendages such as limbs or mouth parts can be extended from the specific environment-posed problems for which they evolved to other tasks that require manipulative skills. One effect such enhanced learner-environment interactions might have is that they might expose the learner to novel selection pressures, which may, in turn, alter the selective advantages of certain phenotypic traits and their accompanying genetic instructions that were previously not strongly selected for or perhaps not selected for at all.

A. C. Wilson (1985) frames the point in slightly different terms. He argues that "the basic equation of evolution states that the rate of evolution within a population equals the number of mutations arising per unit of time multiplied by the fraction of those mutations destined to be fixed" (p. 155). If

$$E = rI, \tag{1}$$

where r is the mutation rate and I is the fraction of mutations fixed in a population, and if

$$I = f(\Delta_{sel}), \tag{2}$$

where Δ_{sel} is the change in selection pressures whereby mutations become fixed in populations, then E (the rate of evolution within a population) will increase with an increase in either r or I. Hence, the argument is that the exploitive system, by changing selection pressures, increases the fixation rate (I) of those mutations and so may change the rate at which evolution occurs.

This scenario will lead nowhere evolutionarily if one envisages it as operating only in reproductively isolated or reproductively limited "clever" exploiters of their environment. Evolution, as most biologists understand the term, is something that happens in populations of organisms. If an exploitive system that learns is to be envisaged as having a causal role in evolution, then the exploitive system must involve either highly reproductively successful individuals or groups of learners of the same species being subjected in this opportunistic fashion to new environmental pressures, and there must be the possibility that such small groups of animals will become isolated breeding populations.

How can this be tested? If learning-exploitive systems lead to novel selection pressures, then the descendent populations of such "learning exploiters" should be adapted to a wide range of environmental features, which means that they should be morphologically and behaviorally more diverse. This is exactly what Wyles, Kunkel, and Wilson (1983) claim to have shown using morphological measures. They used the method of Cherry et al. (1982) to measure overall morphological differences between species. This method employs as an estimator of such differences the formula

$$H = 100 \sum_{i=1}^{N} (x_i - y_i), \tag{3}$$

where x_i is the mean value of the ith morphological feature in species X, and y_i is the corresponding value for the homologous trait in species, Y. In the study of Wyles et al., $N = 8$ specific traits. They examined such differences in birds because of the traditional assumptions by biologists that birds of different species are morphologically very similar owing to the constraints imposed upon their morphology by the requirements of flight. In the event, they found, using 239 species of birds belonging to 26 different orders, that the H values for birds were similar to those of

Table 1
Brain size in relation to rate of anatomical evolution. Source: Wyles et al. 1983. Used with permission.

Taxonomic group	Relative brain size	Anatomical rate
Home	114	> 10
Hominoids	26	2.5
Songbirds	23	1.6
Other mammals	12	0.7
Other birds	4.3	0.7
Lizards	1.2	0.25
Frogs	0.9	0.23
Salamanders	0.8	0.26

mammals, with similar correlations between H value and taxonomic ranking. That is, morphological differences increased with supposed phylogenetic distance. In itself this is an unsurprising finding. However, they further took into account the putative "ages" of the living genera of amphibia, reptiles, birds, and mammals that they examined, (the age estimates being based on both fossil and molecular difference data), and they concluded that "anatomical divergence among birds has been unusually fast in relation to both point-mutational divergence and to time. The only other groups of land vertebrates with comparable rates of anatomical evolution are the mammals." (p. 4396)

Wyles et al. account for their findings by the hypothesis of "behavioral drive," which is a hypothesis identical to that outlined above for an exploitive system that learns. They provide support for this hypothesis by pointing to the relationship between relative brain size (defined by $yx^{-0.67}$, where y is brain weight in grams and x is body weight in kilograms, from Jerison 1973) and anatomical rates of evolution (i.e., mean divergence in body shape per million years, based on the intrageneric morphological distance H given in equation 3 above). Their results are reproduced here in table 1.

Wilson and his colleagues have reported two other studies (Larson, Prager, and Wilson 1984; Sage, Loiselle, Basasibwaki, and Wilson 1984). These reports enlarge their data base to include rates of chromosomal rearrangement, rates of speciation, and population structures. These measurements have been extended beyond birds to include various groups of mammals, reptiles, amphibia, and a particular group of fish, viz. African cichlid fish. The latter are of especial interest because the "explosive evolution" shown by the cichlid fish of Lake Victoria rival the rates of evolution in birds and mammals. But though the rates of evolution are high in these fish, nothing is known of the details of their relative brain size. Also unknown, and of great importance to Wilson's case, is anything of their behavior, especially their communication and social behavior.

Wilson is very specific in giving social learning a central position among the cognitive skills that contribute to his idea of behavioral drive. Thus, on his account, the behavioral innovations that arise in the course of the interaction between the learner and a novel environment are transmitted, or at least are potentially transmissable, between conspecifics by a further act of learning. For this reason, we will have cause to return to this account of the work of Wilson and his colleagues in the subsection on social learning. But to conclude this review of their studies, it must be stressed that their position depends upon a number of connected assertions, all of them approached empirically in an indirect manner: (1) that morphological divergence results from divergent selection pressures, (2) that these wider selection pressures are caused by learned behavioral innovations, (3) that these innovations are transmitted by learning to conspecifics, and (4) that such cognitive abilities are related to brain size. The last assumption at least is questionable; Bennett and Harvey (1985) and Martin (1981) offer alternative explanations of differences in brain size among species, though Jerison (1985; 1986) should be consulted for a staunch defense of the view that increases in relative brain size are correlated with increases in intelligence (learning ability, in the generic terms of this chapter). The first three assertions also lack direct empirical support. Nonetheless, despite their indirect nature, the findings of Wilson et al. are intriguing, and obviously supply some support for the claims that have been made about the exploitive system and the role of learning in evolution. In order to refine the question in terms specific to learning, more work of this kind is needed in which knowledge of learning abilities from comparative laboratory and field studies guides the choice of species whose morphological divergence, rates of anatomical change, and brain size are then subjected to statistical tests of correlation.

In summary, it may yet be possible to define properly, and then to analyze more rigorously, the role of learning in revealing novel selection pressures, and it *is* possible to establish an empirical program to test the resultant claims using studies along the lines of those of Wilson et al. One or two studies do not make an empirical science out of an idea. But they are a start, and Wilson points with some precision to the sorts of the empirical studies that are needed. This surely is better than merely making unfounded assertions. I will return to the issue of social learning in the final section of this chapter.

Mate-Choice Learning
In sexually reproducing animals, the individuals that are reproductively successful contribute directly to the gene frequencies of the gene pool.

Thus, of all behaviors, mating behavior is the most direct determinant of the constitution of the gene pool, and hence mating behavior is the behavior of the phenotype that is most closely related to what many biologists consider to be the quintessence of evolution: gene-frequency changes in the gene pool of a breeding population. When mating behavior deviates from what would be expected on the basis of chance encounters alone, and when that deviation is due to processes occurring inside the animal, then mate choice is assumed to be operating (Halliday 1983). If that mate choice is influenced by some form or forms of learning—i.e., if the internal processes that are partially causing the mate choice are processes of learning—then mate choice constitutes the most direct potential causal role for learning in evolution.

Mate choice is assumed to have many possible functions. These include increasing access to resources, retaining adaptive attributes to local environmental conditions by maintaining particular genetic combinations of co-adapted gene complexes in descendent generations of offspring, enhancing inclusive fitness, and maintaining optimal inbreeding:outbreeding ratios. (These and others are reviewed by various authors in Bateson 1983.) Some of these functions are not exclusive, and mate choice within some species may represent the outcome of simultaneously acting selection pressures for such devices arising from more than one source. There are also likely to be different functions subserved by similar mate-choice devices in different species. In certain instances, mate choice might be the cutting edge of evolution by which lineages are split, though at present there is no direct evidence to support such an assertion.

If, as seems likely, mate choice does indeed subserve different functions in different species, it is just as likely that different mechanisms exist for establishing mate choice in widely different species. And when mate choice is a result of learning processes, there is no good reason to assume that only one form of learning is involved. Indeed, it is quite the opposite. The two best-known forms of learning that have been implicated in mate choice in certain species, notably birds, are sexual imprinting (Bateson 1978; Immelmann 1972) and acquired dialect (usually bird-song dialect) (Kroodsma et al. 1982). In the case of sexual imprinting, exposure to particular individuals directly affects subsequent choice of mate. In the case of bird-song dialect, when and if it does affect mate choice, the manner in which it does so may be as direct as in sexual imprinting (e.g., exposure to dialect at an early phase of life later results in those dialect characteristics acting as positive or negative attractors in choosing a mate) or may be indirect (e.g., dialect leads to exclusion of males from an area, which then acts as an indirect determinant of mate choice). Whatever the similarities or differences of function, the consensus for the present is that sexual imprinting and dialect learning in birds are neurologically different forms of learning

(Kroodsma 1984). The latter is important because it raises the strong possibility that they differ in terms of mechanism.

Furthermore, similar or identical kinds of learning may subserve quite different functions. Some forms of song-dialect learning may be functionally similar to sexual imprinting; however, a wide range of other possible functions have been put forward for dialect learning, often with little agreement as to what these might be (see Baker and Cunningham 1985 and the responses of commentators to that paper). It is also quite conceivable that other forms of learning, which result in particular biases toward food or habitat choices and which affect (albeit indirectly) patterns of mating behavior, may have similar functions.

There is thus a welter of possible mechanisms and functions in this general area of early learning and mate choice, which at present is engendering a great deal of empirical work. However, as far as I know, none of it is directed at the question raised by this chapter, namely whether mate-choice learning devices alter gene frequencies in breeding populations and are thus directly involved in evolution. With the increasing understanding of the neurological basis of some of these forms of learning (Bateson 1984; Konishi 1984) and hence the technical potential for eliminating these forms of learning in particular animals, and with the growth in techniques for monitoring changes in gene pools, such studies are becoming eminently feasible.

Mate choice, and the kinds of mate choice determined by learning, are by no means confined to birds. There seems little doubt, though, that they are especially prominent in birds, and this raises certain other issues about mate-choice learning mechanisms and evolution. Immelmann (1984) makes two interesting points in this regard. The first is that avian ontogeny is exceptionally rapid, with most birds reaching adult form within 1 percent of their total life expectancy. The second is that extensive parental care is a feature of most modern birds, and that the assured presence of parents as models for learning may have relaxed the selection pressures for unlearned recognition devices and hence made intraspecies communication more available to "open programs."

Immelmann's second point may be the clue to the difference between the views of Mayr and Lorenz as regards the distribution of open programs in behavioral repertoires and as to how such open programs may operate as evolutionary pacemakers. It is possible that it is the reliability of parental care in birds that has resulted in their being an exception, if indeed they are an exception, to Mayr's claim that intraspecific communication in general and mating behavior specifically should be protected from the vicissitudes of unreliable learning mechanisms by being controlled by relatively closed developmental programs. This consideration, together with Immelmann's first point, suggests that the relationships between mate choice, learning,

and evolution are bound up in the broader problem of life-history strategies, and that behavior as an evolutionary pacemaker may be quite
closely bound to the issue of mate choice. Empirical study of this problem is
likely to reveal that it is extremely complex, but the pursuit of relatively simple empirical ends may reveal some kind of structure to that complexity.

Is there any way to bring conceptual order to this topic? One possibility
is to consider the role of mate-choice learning in evolution as an instance
of *downward causation*. This term was introduced by Campbell (1974), who,
along with many other biologists, recognized the hierarchical structure of
life. This recognition is more than just an ontological statement. The reason
why the idea of the hierarchical nature of living systems has been attractive
to so many is that it promises a conceptual unification of seemingly refrac-
tory or unconnected problems. That is why Campbell's term is used here.
The notion of downward causation offers the possibility of a conceptually
unified view of all kinds of mate-choice learning devices and evolution,
even though the empirical issues might seem diverse and confusing.

Implicit in the most common understanding of hierarchical organization
is the view that the direction of influence or cause in a hierarchy goes from
lower (more fundamental) to higher (less fundamental) levels. There is a
great deal of confusion as to what *is* "lower" and what is "higher," but the
strongly held intuition is that in a hierarchy the direction of causal influence
is predominantly one-way. What Campbell's term *downward causation* does
is make explicit a fairly obvious feature of hierarchies that has been largely
hidden by this strong assumption of the unidirectional nature of hierarchical influence. The principle of downward causation states that "all processes at the lower levels of a hierarchy are restrained by and act in
conformity to the laws of the higher levels." This is the reverse of the more
common-sense view that lower, more fundamental levels of a hierarchy
"command" the higher, less fundamental levels—i.e., upward causation.
(Vrba and Eldredge [1984] use the concepts of upward and downward
causation in hierarchies in a single discussion.)

The importance of hierarchy theory to any discussion of the role of
learned behavior in evolution is that the relationship of learning processes
in general to events that occur at the genetical level is a hierarchical one.
Thus, the nature of this hierarchy and some general issues of hierarchy
theory must be expanded upon before the relevance to mate choice of
Campbell's notion of downward causation can be understood.

Living systems can be depicted in a variety of hierarchical schemes
(Eldredge and Salthe 1985; Simon 1973). The most commonly conceived
hierarchy is a structural one that has macromolecules at its most fundamental level, organs and organisms at intermediate levels, and populations,
societies, and ecosystems at the "highest" levels. The principal feature of
such a hierarchy is what Simon (1973) referred to as the "Chinese box"

characteristic, also sometimes called *containment* or *embeddedness*. Populations are made up of organisms; organisms are made up of organs, organs of cells, and cells of macromolecules. Thus, if one "opens up" any single entity at any one level (provided that it is not the most fundamental level) one finds it contains other entities, and if one "opens up" any of these one finds other entities. The fundamental level is reached when the entities at a level contain no further entities. Such structural hierarchies are not, however, the only kind.

Another form of hierarchy is one that has been called a *control hierarchy* (Pattee, 1973) or a *hierarchy of connection* (Dawkins 1976a). This kind of hierarchy is close to what was originally meant by the term, and refers to a partial ordering of entities on the basis of asymmetrical authority relations. Military hierarchies are a classical embodiment of such an ordering. Generals have authority over all ranks, and lower-ranking officers have authority over non-officers; but generals are not in any sense made up of their officers, and the latter do not contain private soldiers. The "Chinese box" characteristic is lacking in a control hierarchy.

Control hierarchies are prominent in biology as well as in the social sciences. Both sensory-analysis mechanisms and motor-control mechanisms in vertebrate nervous systems comprise control hierarchies. Ontogenesis occurs through a complex of control hierarchies. The relationship between learning and genetics is also that of a control hierarchy. In every individual learner, the knowledge that is coded into genetic structure is historically prior to, and has authority over (in the sense that it directs), individual development. Development proceeds by way of a series of control hierarchies to result in (among other things) the ability of certain animals to learn. The relationship

genes → developmental trajectories → cognitive mechanisms

is not one of containment. Genes are not contained or embedded in developmental pathways, and the latter are not made up of their end products (in this case, cognitive mechanisms). The relationship is one of asymmetrical authority. In populations, of course, genes are thought of as constituting gene pools. Thus, the relationship between the gene pool and individual learning mechanisms in phenotypes is a control hierarchy. A more detailed analysis of the relationship among genes, development, and learning can be found in Plotkin and Odling-Smee 1979, and a more recent statement in Plotkin 1988.

Let us return to the example of a military hierarchy. The asymmetry of authority relationships, an essential feature of the structure, represents upward causation—the general, as the highest authority, is the most fundamental level of the hierarchy. The private occupies the least fundamental level and has the least authority. (The "high" authority of the general occupying a "fundamental" level in a hierarchy strikes some people as contrary to commen sense and ordinary language. The problem that the hierarchy theorist faces, however, is the need to apply a consistent terminology to both structural and control hierarchies. "Most fundamental" refers to an entity that is not being "bossed by" and is not "made up of" other entities. Maintaining that consistency results in control hierarchies having an asymmetry that appears to go from down to up, just as molecules are thought of as "down" and populations as "up." Thus, we have the seeming contradiction of "high" authority being "down" in a control hierarchy. It is perfectly possible, of course, to turn both hierarchies upside down and reverse the directions, as long as one does it to both control and structural hierarchies. In any event, as long as one knows why one is ordering hierarchies in the way that one is, and does so consistently, there is no serious problem.) Generals give orders to lower-ranking officers, and officers to privates. But generals do not just shout their orders into the wind. The activities of the soldiers and the interaction between those soldiers and their environment are reported back to the general, who then modifies his orders in a way that is appropriate to the information received. This feedback, whether mediated by subordinate levels or direct observation, is downward causation—what is occurring at less fundamental levels of the hierarchy is causing "restraint" and "conformity of action" at more fundamental levels. Common sense dictates that downward causation is an essential feature of control hierarchies, for without it the structure becomes uncoordinated and unstable.

Now, apart from the obvious difference that conscious intention as such does not exist in hierarchies not made up of conscious and intending agents (though analogues of conscious intention might be construed as arising out of the dynamic constraints of a system—see Maynard Smith 1984), the reasoning of the previous paragraph applies to the control hierarchy of which individual learning is a part. The constitution of the gene pool at time t_1 results in (issues orders for) the construction of phenotypes p_1 having characteristics c_1, including certain forms of learning. If those forms of learning bias mate choice over a number of generations, then the action of those learning mechanisms will result in a constitution of the gene pool at time t_2, which will give rise to (issue orders for) phenotypes p_2, whose characteristics c_2 will be partially a result of the mate-choice learning of previous generations of phenotypes.

If the notion of downward causation is helpful in understanding the relationship between learning and gene-pool composition, it is important that the following two points be kept in mind.

(1) Campbell's original usage was intended to conceptualize the way in which *all* features of the phenotype might effect changes in the genotypes of later generation. In other words, it was meant to capture in hierarchical

terms the fact that selection operates upon phenotypes rather than upon genotypes. Insofar as all genotype-phenotype relationships constitute control hierarchies, Campbell's notion must be universally applicable. However, Campbell was considering only two levels, the genetic and the developmental, with selection operating upon the phenotype as the end point of development. If the phenotype is a learning phenotype, then there is a third level in the hierarchy which is itself a part determiner of behavior (see the Mars Rover analogy in chapter 1 of this book). If that is the case, then downward causation may act not only on the gene pool but also on development. Filial imprinting, where learning results in a protective parental buffer to later development and hence partly determines later development, is a good example of downward causation acting from a learning level to a developmental level in a control hierarchy that describes the learning phenotype. The parallel case in our three-level military hierarchy is where the activities of the soldiers effect changes in the behavior of the middle ranking officers as well as in that of the general. Thus, downward causation may act among all levels in a control hierarchy, and greatly complicates the causal nexus that operates in such a system.

(2) The second point, which is implicit in what has already been said, is that mate-choice learning has been labeled as an instance of downward causation not because downward causation is limited to mate-choice learning but because, as was stated above, mate-choice learning presents us with the most direct example of learning's being potentially able to alter the composition of the gene pool. However, learned behavioral adaptations contribute to mean phenotypic fitness and are thus also instances of downward causation. So, too, is the exploitive learning system, since changing selection pressures will eventually lead to an altered gene-pool composition. As will be seen below, social learning also enters into the downward causation relationship. The only difference among these various kinds of learning in this regard is in the directness of the relationship. It is difficult to conceive of a measure of this difference, but in the case of mate-choice learning the learning mechanism "sees more clearly and directly" to the genetic level; in other forms of learning the "vision" is obscured by a multitude of other phenotypic factors that are also contributing to individual fitness. The Weismann maxim, of course, is never violated by any form of learning. What learning may do is change the frequency of genes in a gene pool. It never alters the genes qualitatively.

So is there any real basis for the distinctions drawn in this chapter? As was noted, a first attempt at this problem is bound to be arbitrary and largely incorrect. But the need to draw distinctions is an essential part of any analysis, and it may yet be possible that, with regard to downward causation, the number of transition points involved in a learning mechanism *causing* a change in gene-pool composition may be a useful distinction to make between different learning forms.

The next form of learning to be considered, social learning, is also an instance of downward causation. However, it gives rise to a phenomenon so curious and unique in biology that a separate treatment of it is fully justified.

Social Learning

Among biologists who are interested in the phenomenon of culture, there is widespread agreement not only that human culture is a product of evolution (as, of course, it must be) but also that human culture is itself an evolutionary process (Boyd and Richerson 1985; Cavalli-Sforza and Feldman 1981; Dawkins 1976b; Durham 1982; Hull 1982; Plotkin and Odling-Smee 1981). In both biological and cultural evolution, variants are generated and selection operates to winnow out the unfit variants; the fit ones are then propagated by some kind of transmission process to descendent individuals. In the terminology of Dawkins, both types of evolution occur by the processes of replication and vehicular propagation of the replicanda. Because such an abstract description of evolution serves in both cases, it is indeed correct to refer to evolution in both cases. (An example of an explication of cultural evolution in terms of replicators and interactors—Hull's variation on Dawkins's conception—is given in chapter 2.)

Understanding cultural change as being due to evolutionary processes, however, requires the stipulation of the ways in which cultural evolution differs from "biological" evolution. Differences in mechanism are obvious, widely recognized, and of no conceptual significance. Nobody thinks that cultural evolution *is* biological evolution. The claim is that both cultural change and biological change can be understood in terms of the same set of processes that together define evolution. There are, however, "structural differences" between the two (Boyd and Richerson 1985), and it is these that result in the differences in how change occurs in cultures and biological systems. Among the most important differences suggested are those relating to "mating systems" (multiple parenting in cultural evolution, for example), the form of inheritance (for instance, blending is a distinct possibility in culture), and the relationship between the variants generated and the selection pressures (intentionality may be an important factor in cultural evolution). The analogies and disanalogies between biological and cultural evolution have been surveyed by Boyd and Richerson (1985), Heyes and Plotkin (1988), and Hull (1982).

The nature of the *relationship* between biological and cultural evolution has, in recent years, become a focus of considerable controversy—it is the nature-nurture argument in slightly different guise. Its controversial aspect apart, the problem raises important evolutionary issues which have empirical ramifications. One approach is to consider the relationship as one of synergism, with one form of evolution accelerating the other (Lumsden and Wilson 1981) or with the two forms acting in concert to accelerate overall organismic evolution in populations that have evolved culture (Wilson 1985). No biologist would concede the possibility of cultural evolution proceeding independently of biological considerations, but the very conception of culture as evolving admits of some degree of autonomy from biological evolution. Thus, another approach is to build on that conception of the partial autonomy of cultural evolution. Boyd and Richerson (1985) have done so by way of what they call a "dual inheritance" system, whereby behavior is determined by both a genetic-developmental line of information transmission and some form of social learning, and have presented the first attempt at formalizing in mathematical models the nature of the relationship between these two kinds of evolution as they jointly determine specific human behaviors, beliefs, and so on. A review of these issues and of the relative merits of the different approaches is beyond the scope of this chapter; suffice it to say that in the next decades these various models and approaches will be subjected to both empirical and theoretical scrutiny.

There is, though, one feature of cultural evolution on which there is general agreement. This is that some form or forms of social learning are essential to cultural evolution. The role (or, at any rate, the principal role) envisaged for social learning is as the transmission process by which the replicanda are propagated between individuals. Thus, the essence of cultural evolution—the nongenetic transmission between phenotypes of information about the world—occurs by way of social learning. Social learning is taken to be the analogue of the genetic processes of biological evolution. If, therefore, cultural evolution, with social learning as its transmission device, may act to influence significantly the course of biological evolution in a species, then social learning must have a causal role in that biological evolution.

Is this a credible description of the role of social learning in *biological* evolution, given that there is little doubt, in general, as to the place of social learning in cultural evolution? There is a consensus that cultural evolution may somehow change the fitness of the individuals making up that culture, and it is even more likely that culture is a strong force in some circumstances for assortative mating. Cultural injunctions powerfully determine mating patterns in human populations. Thus, even in this limited way, culture must have entered into the biological evolution of *Homo sapiens* in a causal manner. Social learning, therefore, because of its role in cultural evolution, must be a causal determinant of human evolution, at least. Furthermore, it is causal in two ways. This is because culture itself evolves;

that is its first role. Such cultural evolution is nested in and affects the course of biological evolution; that is its second role.

Now, social learning is not a uniquely human phenomenon. It must have precursors in other hominoids, and possibly in other primates. Social learning has certainly been documented in a wide range of other mammals, including rats (Galef 1976), bats (Gaudet and Fenton 1984), lions (Schenkel 1966), and red squirrels (Weigl and Hanson 1980). It has also been occasionally reported in other vertebrates, including birds (Sasvari 1979 [Song dialect not involved]) and coral-reef fish (Helfman and Schultz 1984). Thus, although culture may be unique to our species, precursor protocultures, in which social learning also plays a central role, are likely present in a limited number of species closely related to man; and protocultures may also have evolved independently in a number of other, unrelated species.

Thus, in very general terms, a case can be made for the importance of social learning in the evolution of at least a limited number of species. Few biologists would doubt that general case. But to get more precision into the argument, and to delineate specific lines of empirical research, is a less simple matter.

The difficulty with making any suggestions as to what might be fruitful empirical research lies in the complexity of the nexus of social learning, cultural evolution, biological evolution. One can try to break into the network of related processes at almost any point and via a wide range of disciplines. After all, culture is arguably the most complicated phenomenon in biology. It takes in large areas of neuroscience, cognitive science, and social science as well as genetics and ecology. This is not, therefore, a subject to be made light of in just a few paragraphs. The best strategy in a review such as this is to be highly selective. I shall do this by asking two questions, each of which bears on a single issue. Neither question relates directly to how social learning is a cause in biological evolution, and this is for the reason already outlined: The relationship is inherently indirect and always occurs by way of cultural evolution.

The first question is: Just what kind of phylogenetic distribution is there for culture? *Is* it a uniquely human phenomenon, or should we accept, for example, bird-song dialect learning and transmission as a form of culture— or, if one feels fussy about the word *culture*, protoculture? (Lumsden and Wilson [1981] skirted this terminological problem by suggesting the use of a graded series, based on the cumulative sequence [imitation] [imitation + teaching] [imitation + teaching + reification], as one moves from primitive protocultural to true cultural creatures. For *imitaton* read social learning, and for *reification* read abstraction and rule-making. Social learning occurs at every point in the series.) The second question is: What are the qualities of social learning that make it different from other forms of learning and which make it the basis of cultural evolution, whatever its phylogenetic distribution? These are closely related questions.

However one tries to avoid prematurely drawing overdetailed distinctions, the first of these questions comes dangerously close to fruitless arguments of definition. In an attempt to avoid these, let us look at the problem in a slightly different light. If we accept that social learning is to cultural evolution as genetics is to biological evolution, and if we also accept the presence of appropriate selection mechanisms, must we accept that cultural evolution is present when social learning is known to occur in a species? This raises, in turn, a definitional problem with regard to social learning. At the risk of offending some readers by refusing to be caught up in the finer details of differences between social facilitation, local enhancement, and imitation (Thorpe 1956), or between instinctive imitation, intelligent imitation, and inferential or reflective imitation (Lloyd-Morgan 1920), I will define social learning rather pragmatically as the acquisition of specific skills, information, or abstract rules by interaction with or observation of another animal or other animals, usually of one's own species. On this definition, bird-song dialect learning may be a manifestation of cultural evolution in those species of songbirds that show such learning. And, despite the doubt that Galef (1980) has cast on cultural transmission in wild rats of ways of gaining access to prey objects, there is enough evidence from laboratory studies of social learning in rats to suggest that at least this rodent species may also be a creature of culture or protoculture. But even if one accepts the existence of culture or protoculture in all species that display social learning, cultural evolution is nonetheless a characteristic of very few species, whereas learning of any kind is a much more common characteristic of species from several different phyla. In other words, social learning seems to be a much more restricted phenomenon than most other kinds of learning, and certainly is more restricted than all other kinds combined. Why is there this disjunction? What, if anything, do we know of social learning that makes it different from all other forms of learning?

Social learning has been studied in a rather desultory fashion for over a century. Darwin wrote about its existence in nonhumans as follows: "Animals ... sometimes imitate each other's actions: thus two species of wolves, which had been reared by dogs, learned to bark, as does sometimes the jackal, but whether this can be called voluntary imitation is another question.... Dureau de la Malle gives an account of a dog reared by a cat, who learned to imitate the well-known action of a cat licking her paws, and thus washing her ears and face...." Several other instances of cross-species imitation are cited by Darwin, who then writes: "The parents of many animals, trusting to the principle of imitation in their young, and more especially to their instinctive or inherited tendencies, may be said to educate them. We see this when a cat brings a live mouse to her kittens; and Dureau de la Malle has given a curious account of his observations on hawks which taught their young dexterity, as well as judgement of distances, by first dropping through the air dead mice and sparrows, which the young generally failed to catch, and then bringing them live birds and letting them loose." (Both quotations are from Darwin 1871 [pp. 451 and 452 of the Modern Library edition].) The second quotation instances behavior that Lumsden and Wilson would have accorded the status of a protoculture characterized by the presence of both imitation and teaching.

The early study of social learning was essentially the collecting and collating of anecdotes (Romanes 1885). The rise of comparative psychology, and later of ethology, led to more rigorous approaches. However, the aims and methods of social-learning studies have changed at least four times over the last 100 years, partly as a function of changes in the thinking of learning theorists and partly as the subject passed from the hands of evolutionary biologists to laboratory psychologists and back again. A reading of recent reviews (Davis 1973; Galef 1976; Heyes 1984) will show that we still know nothing of the ways in which social learning may differ from any other kind of learning—apart, of course, from the requirement that another animal be present during some part of the learning process. There is nothing known about the neurobiology, the ontogeny, or the phylogeny of social learning that one can point to and say "in this and that way social learning is different from other forms of learning." Nor is anything known about the mechanism of social learning that would allow us to distinguish it from other forms of learning—conditioning, trial-and-error learning, problem solving, or any other kind. In view of the intense interest aroused by cultural evolution, this is an astonishing lack. Our understanding of cultural evolution is equivalent to the pre-Mendelian understanding of biological evolution. We know that there is transmission of information between phenotypes, and we know that it occurs by way of some kind of learning. Beyond that, we know nothing. Empirical research on both social learning and cultural evolution must begin at this most basic level of charting something of the phylogeny and ontogeny of social learning and of establishing knowledge as to its neurological site and mechanism, as well as to its mechanism as a psychological process, relative to other forms of learning.

A plausible alternative view is that social learning is no different in essence from other forms of learning. What may be important is whether certain species are constrained to pay special attention to the behavior of conspecifics. Also, what may importantly determine the existence of cultural evolution is not just the ability to learn from conspecifics but, rather, the presence of selection processes that must lead to the differential propagation of learned behavior if cultural evolution is to occur. To settle all such questions will require more knowledge about social learning, particularly about how it differs from other forms of learning. Even if differences cannot be demonstrated, this is essential knowledge because we will then know whether a species must possess properties other than social learning if culture or protoculture is to evolve. And if there are differences, then we need to know whether they are constant across cultural and protocultural species; without this knowledge we will not really understand what is unique to human cultural evolution.

There is another important question that cannot be answered until we know whether and how social learning is different from other forms of learning. The sociobiological theory of cultural evolution reduces to an explanation of culture in terms of genetically transmitted developmental predispositions (Lumsden and Wilson 1981), which means that culture must always act, at least in the long term, to mold and maintain behavior that increases the reproductive fitness of individuals. However, if cultural evolution has a degree of autonomy from biological evolution, then cultural evolution may result in individual behavior that does *not* enhance individual or inclusive fitness. Boyd and Richerson (1985) develop and explore models of cultural evolution wherein such autonomy is the result of the "dual inheritance" by an individual member of a culture of information that determines that individual's subsequent behavior. As already noted, the one form of inheritance is genetic and the other is social learning. It is the latter that bestows some autonomy on culture. The significance of the work of Boyd and Richerson is that, in putting the models into mathematical form, they find that such a dual inheritance system may give rise to behaviors, beliefs, and traditions that do not enhance individual fitness and may even be injurious to it. Culture can, within their models, give rise to sustained "unbiological" behavior. Anyone who is familiar with the sociobiology controversy of recent years will understand the significance of Boyd and Richerson's results. But are they correct?

One assumption that is fundamental to all of Boyd and Richerson's modeling is "the idea that social learning and individual learning are *alternative* ways of acquiring a particular behavioral variant" p. 97; italics in the original). Any reasonable interpretation of their use of the word *alternative*, and of their italicizing it, must acknowledge the implications that cultural and protocultural animals have in their brains two *different* kinds of learning device, that either might be used to effect behavioral change, and that there must be a switching mechanism by which the animal can use either one or the other under different circumstances. Thus, a learner might acquire a dietary preference (for example) by observing other animals and using a social learning device, L_S, by which the appropriate information is encoded, stored, and subject to retrieval; or it might sample various dietary objects for itself, monitor the consequences of eating them, and encode and store the appropriate information using some individual learning device, L_I. L_S and L_I are different entities, have different operating costs, and yield different error rates during learning. This last characteristic is especially important to Boyd and Richerson. They establish a parameter a, which expresses the relative weighting or importance of L_S and L_I:

$$a = V_e/V_e + L,$$

where V_e is the variance of the errors made during learning and L is the propensity of a learner to rely on L_I. The parameter a "gives the fractional importance of cultural transmission in determining mature phenotype [sic]. Notice that the relative importance of individual learning depends on both an individual's propensity to rely on individual learning (measured by L) and the accuracy of the learning process (measured by V_e). When $L \gg V_e$, individual behavior is mostly determined by individual learning; when $L \ll V_e$, learning will have little effect on the initial phenotype." (p. 95). On the basis of these assumptions, Boyd and Richerson go on to develop their model. They explore what conditions of the environment (such as its spatial heterogeneity and fluctuations over time), and what characteristics of L_S and L_I in terms of relative costs and error rates, will give rise to behaviors of individuals that are predominantly culturally determined and hence potentially decoupled from considerations of reproductive fitness. Not only is their modeling explicit as to the discreteness of L_S and L_I; it also asserts explicitly that on occasion these might compete with one another.

Boyd and Richerson broach issues of great theoretical importance. They provide us with the most important, detailed, and formalized treatment of cultural evolution yet. Theirs is a severe challenge to sociobiological approaches to culture. But their models stand or fall on certain assumptions about learning which are not yet supported by empirical research. Such research, to be sure, is possible; and until we know more about social learning itself, theoretical exercises having to do with the evolution of culture and the relationship between cultural and biological evolution will remain uncertain and unverified.

Summary

I have tried to show in this chapter not only that there is a conceptual basis for the case that learning may have a causal role in the evolution of the populations of which the learners are a part but also that this case has either actual or potential empirical support. I am acutely aware of the fragile and arbitrary nature of the divisions drawn in this review. I am not confident that they will serve any purpose other than to provide a temporary categorization, around which a beginning analysis can be made. Nonetheless, I am convinced that, without the drawing of some distinctions, no analysis will be possible and we will be left only with grand statements of little substance. Since theory and empiricism go hand in hand, there will then be no compulsion to do the experiments and make the observations. And without the empiricism there will be no support for the notion that learning has a causal role to play in the process of evolution.

References

Baker, M. C., and M. A. Cunningham. 1985. "The Biology of Bird Song Dialects." *Behavioral and Brain Sciences* 8: 85–133.

Bateson, P. P. G. 1978. "Early Experiences and Sexual Preferences." In *Biological Determinants of Sexual Behavior*, ed. J. B. Hutchison. Chichester: Wiley.

Bateson, P. P. G., ed. 1983. *Mate Choice*. Cambridge University Press.

Bateson, P. P. G. 1984. "The Neural Basis of Imprinting." In *The Biology of Learning*, ed. P. Marler and H. S. Terrace. Berlin: Springer-Verlag.

Bennett, P. M., and P. H. Harvey. 1985. "Relative Brain Size and Ecology in Birds." *Journal of Zoology* 207: 151–169.

Boyd, R., and P. J. Richerson. 1985. *Culture and the Evolutionary Process*. University of Chicago Press.

Campbell, D. T. 1974. "'Downward Causation' in Hierarchically Organized Biological Systems." In *Studies in the Philosophy of Biology*. ed. F. Ayala and T. Dobzhansky. London: Macmillan.

Cavalli-Sforza, L. L., and M. W. Feldman. 1981. *Cultural Transmission and Evolution*. Princeton University Press.

Cherry, L. M., S. M. Case, J. G. Kunkel, J. S. Wyles, and A. C. Wilson. 1982. "Body Shape Metrics and Organismal Evolution." *Evolution* 36: 914–933.

Cole, S., F. R. Hainsworth, A. C. Kamil, T. Mercier, and L. L. Wolf. 1982. "Spatial Learning as an Adaptation in Hummingbirds." *Science* 217: 655–657.

Corning, W. C., J. A. Dyal, and A. O. D. Willows, eds. 1973a, 1973b, 1975. *Invertebrate Learning*, volumes 1–3. New York: Plenum.

Darwin, C. 1871. *The Descent of Man*. New York: Random House (Modern Library).

Davis, J. M. 1973. "Imitation: A Review and Critique." In *Perspectives in Ethology*, ed. P. P. G. Bateson and P. H. Klopfer. London: Plenum.

Dawkins, R. 1976a. "Hierarchical Organization: A Candidate Principle for Ethology." In *Growing Points in Ethology*, ed. P. P. G. Bateson and R. A. Hinde. Cambridge University Press.

Dawkins, R. 1976b. *The Selfish Gene*. Oxford University Press.

Durham, W. H. 1982. "Interactions of Genetic and Cultural Evolution." *Human Ecology* 10: 289–323.

Eldredge, N., and S. N. Salthe. 1985. "Hierarchy and Evolution." *Oxford Surveys in Evolutionary Biology* 1: 184–208.

Galef, B. G. J. 1976. "Social Transmission of Acquired Behavior: A Discussion of Tradition and Social Learning in Vertebrates." *Advances in the Study of Behavior* 6: 77–100.

Galef, B. G. J. 1980. "Diving for Food: Analysis of a Possible Case of Social Learning by Wild Rats." *Journal of Comparative and Physiological Psychology* 94: 416–425.

Gaudet, C. L., and M. B. Fenton. 1984. "Observational Learning in Three Species of Insectivorous Bats." *Animal Behavior* 32: 385–388.

Hailman, J. P. 1985. "Historical Notes on the Biology of Learning." In *Issues in the Ecology of*

Learning, ed. T. D. Johnston and A. T. Pietrewicz. Hillsdale, N.J.: Erlbaum.

Halliday, T. R. 1983. "The Study of Mate Choice." In *Mate Choice*, ed. P. P. G. Bateson. Cambridge University Press.

Hardy, A. C. 1965. *The Living Stream*. London: Collins.

Harley, C. B. 1981. "Learning the Evolutionary Stable Strategy." *Journal of Theoretical Biology* 89: 611–633.

Helfman, G. S., and E. T. Schultz. 1984. "Social Transmission of Behavioral Traditions in a Coral Reef Fish." *Animal Behavior* 32: 379–384.

Hepper, P. 1986. "Kin Recognition: Functions and Mechanisms." *Biological Reviews* 62: 63–93.

Heyes, C. M. 1984. Conspecific Learning in the Syrian Hamster. Doctoral thesis, University of London.

Heyes, C. M., and H. C. Plotkin. 1988. "Replicators and Interactors in Cultural Evolution." In *The Philosophy of David Hull*, ed. M. Ruse. Dordrecht: Reidel.

Hull, C. L. 1943. *Principles of Behavior*. New York: Appleton-Century-Crofts.

Hull, D. L. 1982. "The Naked Meme." In *Learning, Development and Culture: Essays in Evolutionary Epistemology*, ed. H. C. Plotkin. Chichester: Wiley.

Immelmann, K. 1972. "Sexual and Other Long-Term Aspects of Imprinting in Birds and Other Species." *Advances in the Study of Behavior* 4: 147–174.

Immelmann, K. 1984. "The Natural History of Bird Learning." In *The Biology of Learning*, ed. P. Marler and H. S. Terrace. Berlin: Springer-Verlag.

Jerison, H. J. 1973. *Evolution of the Brain and Intelligence*. London: Academic.

Jerison, H. J. 1985. "Animal Intelligence as Encephalization." *Philosophical Transactions of the Royal Society* B 308: 21–35.

Jerison, H. J. 1986. "Issues in Brain Evolution." *Oxford Surveys in Evolutionary Biology* 2: 102–134.

Johnston, T. D., and A. T. Pietrewicz, eds. 1985. *Issues in the Ecological Study of Learning*. Hillsdale, N.J.: Erlbaum.

Johnston, T. D., and M. T. Turvey. 1980. "A Sketch of an Ecological Metatheory for Theories of Learning." *Psychology of Learning and Motivation* 14: 147–205.

Kacelnik, A., and J. R. Krebs. 1985. "Learning to Exploit Patchily Distributed Food." In *Behavioral Ecology: Ecological Consequences of Adaptive Behavior*, ed. R. M. Sibley and R. H. Smith. Oxford: Blackwell.

Kamil, A. C. 1978. "Systematic Foraging for Nectar by Amikihi, *Loxops virens*." *Journal of Comparative and Physiological Psychology* 92: 388–396.

Kamil, A. C., and T. D. Sargent, eds. 1981. *Foraging Behavior: Ecological, Ethological, and Psychological Approaches*. New York: Garland.

Konishi, M. 1984. "A Logical Basis for Single-Neuron Study of Learning in Complex Neural Systems." In *The Biology of Learning*, ed. P. Marler and H. S. Terrace. Berlin: Springer-Verlag.

Kroodsma, D. E. 1984. "Biology of Learning in Nonmammalian Vertebrates." In *The Biology of Learning*, ed. P. Marler and H. S. Terrace. Berlin: Springer-Verlag.

Kroodsma, D. E., E. H. Miller, and H. Ouellet, eds. 1982. *Acoustic Communication in Birds*, volume 2. New York: Academic.

Larson, A., E. M. Prager, and A. C. Wilson. 1984. "Chromosomal Evolution, Speciation and Morphological Change in Vertebrates: The Role of Social Behavior." *Chromosomes Today* 8: 215–227.

Lloyd-Morgan, C. 1920. *Animal Behavior*. London: Arnold.

Lorenz, K. Z. 1932. "A Consideration of Methods of Identification of Species-Specific Instinctive Behavior Patterns in Birds." Reprinted in *Studies in Animal and Human Behavior*, volume 1 (London: Methuen, 1970).

Lorenz, K. Z. 1966. "The Evolution of Ritualization in the Biological and Cultural Spheres." *Philosophical Transactions of the Royal Society* B 251: 273–284.

Lumsden, C. J., and E. O. Wilson. 1981. *Genes, Mind, and Culture*. Cambridge, Mass.: Harvard University Press.

Martin, R. D. 1981. "Relative Brain Size and Basal Metabolic Rate in Terrestrial Vertebrates." *Nature* 293: 57–60.

Maynard Smith, J. 1982. *Evolution and the Theory of Games*. Cambridge University Press.

Maynard Smith, J. 1984. "The Evolution of Animal Intelligence." In *Minds, Machines and Evolution*, ed. C. Hookway. Cambridge University Press.

Mayr, E. 1963. *Animal Species and Evolution*. Cambridge, Mass.: Harvard University Press.

Mayr, E. 1974. "Behavior Programs and Evolutionary Strategies." *American Scientist* 62: 650–659.

Mayr, E. 1982. *The Growth of Biological Thought*. Cambridge, Mass.: Harvard University Press.

Pattee, H. H. 1973. "The Physical Basis and Origin of Hierarchical Control." In *Hierarchy Theory*, ed. H. H. Pattee. New York: Braziller.

Piaget, J. 1979. *Behavior and Evolution*. London: Routledge and Kegan Paul.

Pietrewicz, A. T., and J. B. Richards. 1985. "Learning to Forage: An Ecological Perspective." In *Issues in the Ecological Study of Learning*, ed. T. D. Johnston and A. T. Pietrewicz. Hillsdale, N.J.: Erlbaum.

Plotkin, H. C. 1988. "An Evolutionary Epistemological Approach to the Evolution of Intelligence." In *The Evolutionary Biology of Intelligence*, ed. H. J. Jerison. Heidelberg: Springer-Verlag.

Plotkin, H. C., and F. J. Odling-Smee. 1979. "Learning, Change and Evolution." *Advances in the Study of Behavior* 10: 1–41.

Plotkin, H. C., and F. J. Odling-Smee. 1981. "A Multiple-Level Model of Evolution and Its Implications for Sociobiology." *Behavioral and Brain Sciences* 4: 225–268.

Plotkin, H. C., and F. J. Odling-Smee. 1982. "Learning in the Context of a Hierarchy of Knowledge-Gaining Processes." In *Learning, Development and Culture: Essays in Evolutionary Epistemology*, ed. H. C. Plotkin. Chichester: Wiley.

Revusky, S. 1985. "The General Process Approach to Animal Learning." In *Issues in the Ecological Study of Learning*, ed. T. D. Johnston and A. T. Pietrewicz. Hillsdale, N.J.: Erlbaum.

Romanes, G. J. 1885. *Mental Evolution in Animals*. London: Kegan Paul–French.

Roper, T. J. 1983. "Learning as a Biological Phenomenon." In *Animal Behavior*, volume 3, ed. T. R. Halliday and P. J. B. Slater. Oxford:Blackwell.

Sage, R. D., P. V. Loiselle, P. Basasibwaki, and A. C. Wilson. 1984. "Molecular versus Morphological Change among Cichlid Species of Lake Victoria." In *Evolution of Fish Species Flocks*, ed. A. A. Echelle and I. Kornfield. Orono: University of Maine Press.

Sasvari, L. 1979. "Observational Learning in Great, Blue and Marsh Tits." *Animal Behavior* 27: 767–771.

Schenkel, R. 1966. "Play, Exploration and Territoriality in Wild Lions." *Symposium of the Zoological Society of London* 18: 11–22.

Shettleworth, S. J. 1983. "Memory in Food-Hoarding Birds." *Scientific American* 248, no. 3: 102–110.

Shettleworth, S. J. 1984. "Learning and Behavioral Ecology." In *Behavioral Ecology*, ed. J. R. Krebs and N. B. Davies. Oxford: Blackwell.

Simon, H. A. 1973. "The Organization of Complex Systems." In *Hierarchy Theory*, ed. H. H. Pattee. New York: Braziller.

Skinner, B. F. 1953. *Science and Human Behavior*. New York: Macmillan.

Sommerhoff, G. 1950. *Analytical Biology*. Oxford University Press.

Sommerhoff, G. 1969. "The Abstract Characteristics of Living Systems." In *Systems Thinking*, ed. F. E. Emery. Harmondsworth: Penguin.

Thorpe, W. H. 1956. *Learning and Instinct in Animals*. London: Methuen.

Tinbergen, N. 1938. "Über der Orientierung des Bienenwolfes (*Philanthus triangulum*)." Reprinted, in translation, in *The Animal in Its World*, volume 1 (Cambridge, Mass.: Harvard University Press, 1973).

Trivers, R. 1985. *Social Evolution*. Menlo Park, Calif.: Cummings.

Vrba, E., and N. Eldridge. 1984. "Individuals, Hierarchies, and Processes: Towards a More Complete Evolutionary Theory." *Paleobiology* 10: 146–171.

Weigl, P. D., and E. V. Hanson. 1980. "Observational Learning and the Feeding Behavior of the Red Squirrel: The Ontogeny of Optimization." *Ecology* 6: 213–218.

Williams, G. C. 1966. *Adaptation and Natural Selection*. Princeton University Press.

Wilson, A. C. 1985. "The Molecular Basis of Evolution." *Scientific American* 253, no. 4: 148–157.

Wilson, E. O. 1975. *Sociobiology*. Cambridge, Mass.: Harvard University Press.

Wyles, J. S., J. G. Kunkel, and A. C. Wilson. 1983. "Birds, Behavior, and Anatomical Evolution." *Proceedings of the National Academy of Sciences* 80: 4394–4397.

Chapter 6

The Evolutionary Implications of Social Behavior

R. I. M. Dunbar

Conventional evolutionary analyses tend to consider a particular problem of survival or reproduction and try to identify the solution that would maximize an animal's chances of contributing to its species' gene pool. The underlying assumption is that an animal's choice of options on what to do is more or less unconstrained, other than by the physical limitations of its anatomy and its physiology. This may well be a perfectly reasonable assumption for most invertebrates, and perhaps for some of the lower vertebrates. But I shall argue here that the kind of sociality that is found in the birds and the mammals imposes its own constraints on what an animal can do: one individual's behavior cannot be seen in isolation from the behaviors of other members of its group.

Let me make it quite clear at the outset that I am not espousing a group-selectionist position. I am not suggesting that we need to look at the behavior of groups of animals in order to find a solution that maximizes some function of group reproduction. Rather, the point I want to make is that an *individual's* options depend in large part on what the other members of its group want to do. And I particularly want to emphasize the constraints that *mutualism* (as defined in Wrangham 1982) impose on a social animal's freedom of movement in strategy choice. (By mutualism I mean the fact that two organisms stand to gain by cooperating because they can solve problems of survival or reproduction more efficiently by working together than either could do on its own). What I have to say is therefore in no way incompatible with Darwinian evolutionary theory as we currently understand it.

I shall begin by briefly summarizing what is involved in the process of evolution. I do not mean to be pedantic in doing this; however, my subsequent argument hangs on an important distinction between the behaviors of individual organisms and the fitness of genetic alleles (or characters), on which evolutionary change depends. I suspect that it is because evolutionary biologists often gloss over this distinction that sociobiologists have experienced so much resistance to their approach.

I shall then outline the role that sociality plays in allowing animals to survive and to reproduce more effectively. With this providing a theoretical framework, I go on to discuss the problems that social living creates for an individual trying to maximize its contribution to the species' gene pool. In the process, I hope to make clear why it is that conventional evolutionary analyses of behavior risk going astray when they are applied to social vertebrates. I shall argue that one of the implications is that optimal solutions will always be context-specific, and that consequently the search for traits that are universal (in the sense of being species-typical) will often be misguided.

Evolutionary Processes

Evolution occurs as a result of the differential survival of genes. Hence, the ultimate objective of an organism, if we can phrase it in these terms, is to contribute as many genes to future generations as it can. In principle, an organism can do this by reproducing itself, or by helping relatives that share the same gene(s) to reproduce more successfully, or by some combination of the two (see Hamilton 1964). Although the process of kin selection adds an important dimension to an organism's reproductive strategies, I shall, for present purposes, ignore it and concentrate on personal reproduction. This will, I hope, make the general thrust of my argument clearer. However, those who wish to integrate kin selection into the same framework will be able to do so easily enough once the general approach has been outlined.

In order to reproduce successfully, an organism has to solve a number of problems relating to survival, mating, and the rearing of offspring to maturity. These in themselves are really clusters or sets of subproblems. Survival, for example, involves two major groups of problems, namely (1) obtaining enough of the right kinds of foods to meet the animal's daily nutritional requirements while (2) avoiding being eaten by anything else (or, if it comes to that, avoiding falling prey to any number of other organic and nonorganic risks of mortality). These problems of survival and reproduction are, to a greater or a lesser extent, mutually incompatible; yet an organism has to solve all of them, inclusively and jointly, within a limited time. Thus, even at the most mundane and crude level, organisms face constraints from their biology that prevent them from solving any one of the problems of survival and reproduction by any means other than optimizing (in the sense of doing the best they can given the restrictions imposed on them). No matter how many potential descendants might be produced if an animal were to devote all its time to mating, such a strategy would in the long run be counterproductive because the animal would run a serious risk of its offspring dying through lack of parental care or of dying itself because it had devoted insufficient time to the business of survival. An animal that has been caught unawares by a predator will obviously not reproduce again. This means that an organism has to arrive at an optimal time-and-energy budget that will allow it to devote at least the minimum amount of effort to each of the essential activities that will permit it to contribute the maximum number of descendants to future generations.

Consider a few examples. Many species have a restricted mating season during which the males devote themselves to the business of mating, almost to the exclusion of everything else. In most of these cases, the males bear a heavy cost for doing so: they are highly susceptible to predation as a result of spending more time isolated on mating territories (e.g. frogs: Wells 1978; antelope: Gosling 1986), or they suffer higher rates of infestation by parasites because they make themselves more conspicuous by giving loud mating calls (e.g. crickets: Cade 1979), and/or they face increased risks of mortality through having spent less time feeding than is necessary to maintain metabolic processes (e.g. frogs: Wells 1978; antelope: Jarman 1979; deer: Mitchell et al. 1976; feral goats: Dunbar et al. 1988). What makes it essential that males incur these costs is the simple fact that, if they do not, other males will monopolize all the females. In other words, the pressure of the competition to mate (generally speaking, the propagation of descendants cannot be achieved without mating) forces males to incur costs in terms of survival. In some cases, the tradeoff between the gains from mating and the costs from reduced survival (and the adverse consequences that these can have for future mating prospects) may be very fine (see Dunbar 1982a; Rubenstein 1980).

The essential point, then, is that tradeoffs and the optimizing of output with respect to constraints imposed by other key factors in a complex biological system are integral parts of the process underlying genetic replication. They are inevitable consequences of the fact that an organism is essentially a coadapted biological system that has evolved to solve a number of radically different problems in order to be able to contribute genes to future generations by producing descendants.

Social Systems as Reproductive Strategies

Given that animals are committed to this kind of problem-solving, the point I want to emphasize in this section is that social behavior and the societies generated by it are part and parcel of organisms' reproductive strategies. Animals are social precisely in order to solve certain key biological problems more efficiently.

Social living can serve a number of different functions. The most important are probably defence against predators (as in many antelopes and primates: see Estes 1974; van Schaik 1983; Dunbar 1987), rearing of offspring (as in many pair-forming birds, where both the male and the female feed the nestlings), and improved foraging efficiency (as in the many social carnivores that can capture much larger prey when hunting cooperatively than they can on their own: see Kruuk 1972; Schaller 1972).

These are essentially reasons for living in groups. Sociality in this crude minimal sense, however, creates or intensifies a number of other problems that tend to negate the advantages of group life. These include problems such as priority of access to whatever resources are essential for reproduction. This applies not only directly in those species that rely on group living to produce the requisite resources (as in the case of cooperative hunters) but also indirectly in species that form groups for other reasons. Thus, many primates and antelopes form groups in order to minimize the risk of predation, but doing so forces individuals into competition for access to the best feeding sites or refuges when these are unevenly or sparsely distributed (as they often are on a micro-habitat scale when a group has to be compact to serve its designated function). Living in groups thus generates competition that would not occur if the animals could disperse over a wider area. In some cases, all members of the group may suffer equally. But whenever asymmetries in power allow some individuals to monopolize the few resource patches that are accessible to a group at any one time, the lower-ranking members of the group are likely to bear a disproportionate share of the costs. Two examples will suffice to illustrate this.

In communally living weaver birds, the risks of being caught by a predator when foraging alone seem to have produced an extreme degree of social cohesion: the birds do everything as a group in a very coordinated way. When food is experimentally restricted so that only one bird can feed at a time, high-ranking individuals are able to monopolize access to the food source. Once they have fed to satiation, they return to the roost. The inherent desire to remain with the flock then forces low-ranking birds to go to the roost as well, even though they have not yet had an opportunity to feed (but could do so if they remained). As a result, low-ranking birds lose weight day by day, whereas high-ranking birds show no change in body weight (Dunbar and Crook 1975). The second example concerns vervet monkeys. Wrangham (1981) showed that when water became a limiting resource during a severe drought, low-ranking females found their access to water (mostly from small holes in trees) restricted by higher-ranking females. As a result, low-ranking individuals had significantly higher mortality rates.

Living in groups in enforced spatial proximity can give rise to additional stresses, both as a result of animals' getting in one another's way (direct costs) and as a by-product of competition for access to resources (indirect costs).

The direct costs of group living come in at least two ways. One is through disruption of feeding bouts. Van Schaik et al. (1983) found that time spent foraging increased with increasing group size in free-ranging macaques. Similarly, Stacey (1986) found that although the members of a large baboon group each acquired the same amount of food in a day as the animals in a small group, they had to spend significantly more time foraging in order to do so. In part, this was a consequence of the fact that their feeding bouts were disturbed more often by the need to keep up with the group as it moved. In addition, low-ranking animals lost a great deal of time and energy locating feeding sites or food items, which high-ranking individuals promptly stole from them. The other direct cost lies in the increased distance the group has to travel each day in order to ensure that each member is able to visit enough food sites (e.g. bushes) to obtain the food it needs that day. A simple linear relationship between the distance traveled in a day and the size of the group has been documented in mangabeys (Waser 1977), baboons (Sharman and Dunbar 1982), capuchin monkeys (de Ruiter 1986), macaques (van Schaik et al. 1983), and chimpanzees (Wrangham and Smuts 1980).

In addition to these direct costs, grouping may give rise to indirect costs that can seriously affect an animal's reproductive performance. The stress created by crowding (or even by low levels of harassment) can have dramatic consequences for a low-ranking animal's reproductive physiology. Bowman et al. (1978) have demonstrated experimentally that the stress of being at the bottom of a hierarchy can so disrupt a female talapoin monkey's reproductive physiology that she becomes temporarily infertile. Socially induced infertility of this kind has been documented in a wide variety of mammalian species, including species as different as wolves (Zimen 1976) and marmosets (Abbott 1984). (For a general review see Wasser and Barash 1983.)

As these costs become more severe, they tend to negate the advantages of living socially. Consequently, in order to be able to benefit from living in groups, animals need to be able to offset these disadvantages (or at least to buffer themselves against the worst effects). Birds and mammals endeavor to do this by forming sets of relationships within the primary grouping pattern. This leads to highly structured groups that consist of subgroupings (or definable sets of more intense relationships between certain individuals). Such cliques generally function as coalitions that keep their members from receiving too much harassment from fellow group members. They may also help to give individuals access to resources that they would have been unable to acquire by acting individually on their own account. Thus, grouping as a solution to one ecological problem can create new problems that did not previously exist; these then have to be neutralized by means of other social strategies. Since these new solutions can generate further problems (nothing is ever cost-free in real life), we can begin to see an animal's social behavior in terms of a nested hierarchy of problems and their associated behavioral solutions.

The interplay between the structuring of social systems and the problems that animals have to solve in order to reproduce may be best illustrated by specific examples. I shall limit myself to just two species, the gelada baboon and the white-fronted bee-eater. These species are by no means unique, however, and to stress this I shall refer in passing to a number of other examples of complex social systems without detailing them. One of the major difficulties in this area is plain ignorance. There has been a general tendency to assume that the social systems of animals are relatively simple and unstructured. But this assumption has been caused (and subsequently reinforced) by the fact that few species have been studied in sufficient detail at the level of known individuals to yield any appreciation of just how complex an animal's relationships with its conspecifics might be. One consequence of this is that rather few examples have been worked out in any detail; doing so requires an immense commitment of time and energy to fieldwork. I emphasize this simply because there has been a tendency to misinterpret an apparent lack of evidence as proof that animals do not possess complex societies.

The gelada baboon occupies a somewhat unusual ecological niche, both as a grazer (it is the only grazing primate) and in its dependence on the massive gorges that dissect its habitat in the highlands of central Ethiopia. Because the best feeding sites (on the flat plateau top) and the safest refuges (on the gorge slopes) are physically separated, the animals cannot exploit both simultaneously. As a result, they have evolved a particularly complex social system, whose fission and fusion properties allow the animals to make the best use of the habitat by adjusting their grouping patterns to the requirements of local habitat conditions (see Dunbar 1986; for more general discussions of this aspect of primate social systems, see Kummer 1971 and Dunbar 1987).

The problems that the gelada baboons face are essentially these: In order to exploit the rich grasslands along the plateau top, they have to form large groups for protection against the predators that occur there in large numbers. Such large groups, however, serve no useful purpose once the animals are back on the safety of the cliffs. Moreover, the rugged broken terrain on the gorge faces makes it difficult to coordinate the movement of large numbers of animals. Consequently, the herds that form on the plateau grasslands inevitably tend to disperse once they move back down onto the cliffs, as individuals move in different directions at different speeds. In addition, the large groups (typically numbering some 200 animals, but occasionally including as many as 600) generate considerable stress as a result of the harassment and repeated displacement that occur when many animals are milling around within a spatially limited area. This creates centrifugal forces that lead to the dispersal of the groups unless they are counterbalanced by the need to maintain a large grouping because of the risk of predation.

Because of the internal stresses generated by the size of the herds formed in the plateau-top feeding areas, gelada baboons form small stable groups centered around clusters of closely related females. These act as coalitions to keep unrelated individuals at a sufficient distance to minimize disruptions of group living without driving them away altogether (and thus losing the benefits of large groups). These groups contain an average of four (but never more than twelve) reproductive females. These small coalitions of related females are themselves, however, large enough to generate a significant amount of strife—so much, in fact, that the lowest-ranking member of a group of ten females can manage to produce only half as many offspring as the top-ranking female (see Dunbar 1984). The females attempt to solve this problem by forming alliances among themselves, primarily between mothers and their daughters. These serve to buffer the individual females against the most immediate sources of harassment, namely the more dominant members of their own social units.

The gelada social system thus consists of a number of sets of relationships among individuals, each of which is designed to solve a specific problem by creating a coalition of a particular size. Kawai et al. (1983) identified six different levels or types of grouping in gelada society, each with its own function.

The example of the gelada baboon highlights rather conveniently the way in which simple solutions to the problems of survival and reproduction are not always possible in complex biological systems. In this case, the animals opt for a solution that reduces the problem of predation sufficiently to allow them to exploit the resources in question, even though in doing so they create a problem: stress from overcrowding. Because of this, their solution to the problem is far from ideal. Forming large groups incurs an unavoidable cost that has to be deducted from the gross reproductive gains obtained by solving the problem of predation. The resulting net gain may often be a great deal less than the maximum they could achieve if they had only the one problem to contend with. In some circumstances (e.g. on the gorge slopes), these costs many exceed the gains; with no pressure to maintain large groups in the face of these costs, the herds disperse. Thus, whether or not a particular population of animals exhibits a given level of grouping may depend on the biological prominence of the problem in question in the particular habitat.

Gelada are far from being unique among the primates in having such a multi-tiered social system. Comparable complexity has been documented in the hamadryas baboon (Kummer 1984). Multi-tiered social systems, albeit with fewer levels, have been found in other primates, including vervet monkeys (Cheney and Seyfarth 1983), tamarins (Garber et al. 1984), and macaques (Caldecott 1986; Robertson 1986). Studies of nonprimate species have suggested that complex social systems may occur in many other groups of mammals. Moss and Poole (1983), for example, were able to identify up to six different levels of clustering defined by patterns of interaction among individual animals in a population of African elephants.

To emphasize that this kind of complexity is not a purely mammalian trait, I take my other example from the birds. Hegner et al. (1982) found considerable structuring of social relationships within colonies of white-fronted bee-eaters in East Africa. Colonies of up to 450 birds use a communal roosting site excavated out of the sandy bank of a riverbed. These large colonies are subdivided into a set of smaller units consisting of up to eleven birds which use and defend a specific burrow system within the colony. These groups (termed *clans*), in turn, consist of several mated pairs, each of which has its own nest chamber within the clan burrow. The subdivisions of the colony also have ecological relevance in that each clan has its own exclusive feeding territory (sometimes as far as 4 miles from the roost). The feeding territory is itself subdivided into a set of feeding areas belonging to individual pairs, though these may overlap considerably with those of other pairs of the same clan.

It is not difficult to see that these groupings probably allow the bee-eaters to solve particular problems so as to make reproduction more effective. Colonies, for example, might allow individuals to gain access to roosting areas when these are sufficiently scarce to pose a problem for any group that failed to monopolize one. In fact, suitable sandy banks do not seem to be very scarce in typical bee-eater habitat, but parasite infestation of recently used nests may make usable nesting areas much less common than they appear to be. Indeed, Hegner et al. (1982) noted that most colonies changed their nesting areas every few years. (An alternative possibility is that bee-eaters live communally not so much because suitable ground in which to excavate burrows is limited but in order to reduce the risk of predation in and around nesting areas.) Within colonies, clans clearly function to preserve access to suitable nest chambers and to prevent harassment of nesting pairs and their nestlings. In addition, temporarily unmated clan members provide a source of help for parents struggling to rear their own offspring. As the basic unit of reproduction, the mated pair functions in the conventional way that pairs do in other species of nidicolous birds (i.e., by producing and incubating eggs and feeding the hatchlings that emerge in due course).

The point I want to emphasize here is the way in which animals use relationships formed with different sets of individuals to solve particular problems of survival and reproduction. Whether these coalitions are formal ones (in the sense that they involve negotiated relationships between two or more individuals) or informal ones (in the sense that they are the inevitable consequence of two animals' being brought up together; see, e.g., Bekoff 1981) is relatively immaterial. The point is that they *function* in the same way as mutual defense alliances against a common "enemy" or for the solution of a common ecological or social problem. With this as a framework, I now want to explore the extent to which this social dimension can both influence and constrain an individual's optimal reproductive strategies, thereby influencing rates of evolutionary change.

Social Constraints on Strategy Choice

Although there are a number of ways in which social considerations affect the reproductive success of individual animals, I intend to concentrate on four:

(1) Coalitions allow individuals to gain access to essential resources when they would be unable to do so on their own.

(2) Demographic structure can limit an individual's choice of social partners.

(3) Competition for access to the best social partners can prevent an individual from forming the alliances that would be most profitable to it.

(4) The need for cooperation can constrain runaway selection for particular behavioral traits.

Social Networks as Alliances

The most conspicuous feature of the social systems of higher mammals is the extent to which individuals use other members of their group to circumvent problems that they face in reproducing. In their most developed form (e.g. in the monkeys and apes), such coalitions form a conspicuous part of society and heavily influence an individual's ability to reproduce. In many cases, coalitions of this kind allow individuals to occupy higher dominance ranks within the group, thereby giving them greater access either to mates or to the resources (e.g. food) that are a prerequisite for successful reproduction. Among gelada baboons, older females who lack coalition partners occupy significantly lower dominance ranks within their groups than do females of the same age who have such partners; as a direct result of this, their fertility is greatly reduced (Dunbar 1984). Similarly, in macaques, individuals that can call on members of a large extended family for support in agonistic contexts receive less harassment than those that cannot (Datta 1983; Kaplan 1978). A particularly instructive case was noted by Smuts (1985), who found that as male baboons aged they made increasing use of coalitions with other males to gain and maintain access to oestrous females. This allowed them to continue mating longer than they would otherwise have been able to do had they been obliged to depend on their own declining physical powers. (For a general review of coalitionary behavior in primates, see Dunbar 1987.)

In some cases, the use of coalitionary support to achieve reproductive aims can become quite sophisticated. De Waal (1982) describes a case in which an old male chimpanzee, Yeroen, was able to manipulate the relationship between the other two males in the group so as to overcome his own natural disadvantages. Yeroen had been the dominant male, but had been deposed by the second-ranking male, Luit. As a result, Yeroen was then denied access to the oestrous females in the group. Some time later, the third-ranking male, the rather younger Nikki, began to challenge Yeroen as well. In due course, Yeroen would have fallen into third rank, but instead of allowing this to happen he capitalized on Nikki's desire to dominate Luit by supporting him against the dominant male. With Yeroen's help, Nikki was ultimately able to depose Luit, even though he was unable to dominate him on his own. Yeroen's status as second-ranking male was then preserved by Nikki's reciprocated support against Luit, who was now forced into third place. Yeroen was able to force Nikki to allow him to have greater access to oestrous females than he would otherwise have been able to have by the simple strategy of supporting Luit against Nikki whenever Nikki tried to prevent him from mating. Nishida (1983) describes an almost identical situation in a wild group of chimpanzees. Riss and Goodall (1977) stress the importance of coalitionary support in the rise to the top dominance rank by successive males in the Gombe community of wild chimpanzees. Kummer (1967) also documents the way in which hamadryas baboons exploit the relationships within their groups to their own advantage by soliciting support from third parties against their opponents during fights.

Although coalitions formed in defense of harems or of mating territories have been described (and their functional significance analyzed) in species as different as lions (Packer and Pusey 1982) and antelope (Wirtz 1982), they are a much less conspicuous feature of the societies of most nonprimate species (Harcourt 1987). Whether this is because they are genuinely rare in these species or whether it is because few of those who have studied these species have been interested in these kinds of questions remains an open question.

Demographic Constraints on Partner Availability
Partner availability necessarily plays a key role in determining just what an animal can do. Hence, the demographic structure of a population emerges as an important factor channeling the strategies adopted by individual

animals. From a given animal's point of view, it is always possible to identify the individual that would make the best social partner. But whether or not the animal can establish such a relationship depends on whether an individual of that particular type is available. Behavior, in short, is always dependent on demography. (See also Dunbar 1979; Altmann and Altmann 1979; Chagnon 1982.)

In some species, females prefer to form alliances with close female relatives. Whether or not they can do so depends primarily on the demographic parameters of the population to which they belong. Populations living in low-quality habitats will have low reproductive rates and high mortality rates. As a result, family sizes will be small. In low-quality habitats, for example, a female Old World monkey can expect to have, on average, only one other adult female in her extended family (i.e. among the descendants of a living matriarch), whereas under more benign conditions the average will be four or five other females (Dunbar 1987). Where female kinship groups are small, females are forced to rely more on their own abilities. As a result, the structure of the social group may differ radically even in different populations of the same species. In the first case, particular families will often be able to dominate a group over extended periods of time, contributing disproportionately to the species' gene pool over many generations (as in the macaque population studied by Sade et al. [1976]), whereas in the second case dominance ranks will be more unstable over time and different families will have more opportunity to contribute equally to the species' gene pool (e.g. in the gelada population studied by Dunbar 1984).

With even the largest family sizes found among primates, the sample size is actually so small that there is a significant probability that a female will, by chance alone, give birth only to sons. Such a female will have no daughters on whom to call for aid in later life when her own physical power is on the wane. Data on gelada show that older females who have no daughters with whom to form an alliance occupy significantly lower dominance ranks than those who have daughters of an appropriate age, and that, as a result, they incur a significant reproductive cost in terms of reduced fertility (Dunbar 1984).

In some cases, a female caught in this situation may be able to offset this cost by forming an alliance with an unrelated individual. In some species (e.g. baboons), a male is by far the most valuable alternative ally because of his large size. Most gelada units, however, contain only a single adult male. Consequently, only one of the females lacking close kin will be able to form an alliance with a male. The others must either seek alliances with unrelated females (generally, not a particularly profitable strategy because of a high risk of desertion) or try to survive as best they can on their own. Either way, these gelada females stand to produce fewer offspring (Dunbar 1984).

There is also evidence suggesting that birth rates among common baboons are influenced by the availability of adult males as alliance partners (Dunbar and Sharman 1983).

Competition for Access to Social Partners

An animal's preference as regards its social partners is not, however, the only factor that determines what animals it interacts with. Its options are also constrained by other individuals' preferences. We need to distinguish two different problems that face an animal in this respect. One is that several other individuals may have the same preference for a particular social partner. This necessarily results in competition for access to the most powerful allies, with the result that the least competitive individuals are inevitably excluded. The other consideration is that even if an animal has uncontested access to its preferred ally, this does not necessarily mean that it will be able to establish the relationship it wants with that individual, for that individual may have no interest in forming such a relationship.

Seyfarth (1977) used simple models to explore the consequences of these two factors for the structure of relationships in small groups of female monkeys. He found that where the time available for servicing relationships was limited and there was marked competition for the most dominant animals (because they make the most powerful allies), the distribution of grooming tended to be such that high-ranking females received a disproportionate share and that the females were arranged into dyads of adjacently ranked individuals that spent most of their time grooming each other. (In primates, grooming is the primary behavioral mechanism used to establish and maintain alliances through time.) The predictions have been confirmed by data on a number of different species (at least for populations in which kinship has not been a relevant variable).

Male gelada baboons face a somewhat analogous problem. A male's tenure as the breeding male in a group of females depends partly on the strength of the relationships that he can maintain with his females (Kummer 1975; Dunbar 1984). However, the females' primary interests lie in forming coalitions with their own close female relatives (mainly mothers and daughters). As the size of the unit grows, the females become increasingly concerned to build and maintain alliances among themselves. Since the male is now a less valuable prospect as an ally, the females tend to respond less enthusiastically to his advances. This, combined with the constraints imposed by his own time budget, forces the male into a situation where, once past a certain threshold size of unit, he is unable to interact with all his females to a sufficient extent to guarantee their loyalty to him. The unfortunate result from his point of view is that the unit becomes susceptible to a takeover by another male, which ends the first male's reproductive career (Dunbar 1984). Thus, the male's reproductive strategy is in effect hostage to the individual females' interests. As a result, it often pays a male to opt for a small unit rather than a large one, since he is able to retain control over a small unit for very much longer. In fact, detailed modeling of the male's reproductive decisions and their consequences for lifetime reproductive output indicate that males can expect to gain approximately the same number of genes contributed to future generations whether they opt for small or large units. Although small units initially produce a lower rate of return (in terms of numbers of oestrous females available per year), the fact that a male can survive longer as a harem-holder cancels this initial disadvantage. Males should, therefore, choose these two options with equal frequency. Data on wild populations confirm that this is precisely what they do (Dunbar 1984). This example, in particular, emphasizes the point that what, on first principles, seems to be the ideal strategy (namely, taking over the unit with the largest possible number of reproductive females) is not necessarily the best strategy in the long run because it runs afoul of other individuals' social and reproductive priorities.

One more example of the way in which other individuals' preferences can constrain the behavior of an animal is provided by Kummer's studies of hamadryas baboons. In this species, the males hold small harems of breeding females. Although males may acquire their females by taking them over from other males, in general they respect one another's hegemony over individual females (Kummer 1967; Kummer et al. 1974). Bachmann and Kummer (1980) found that one of the crucial factors determining whether a rival male would try to wrest control of a female away from her "owner" was the female's expressed preference for her current male, conveyed behaviorally by her willingness to interact with the male and by her readiness to follow him closely around the compound. The results of their experiments suggest that the rival assesses the female's attachment to her current male and takes this into consideration when deciding whether or not to challenge the owner for control of the female. Only if he is physically *very* dominant to the owner will the rival attempt a challenge irrespective of the female's indicated preference.

The importance of the female's preference in this kind of context may well be widespread. Smuts (1985) notes that among common baboons successful attempts to wrest oestrous females away from their male consorts are often preceded by behavioral indications that the female has lost interest in her current male consort (as indicated by a reduced tendency to maintain close physical contact with him). Similarly, Chapais (1983) notes that when a male rhesus macaque attempts to take an oestrous female away from a lower-ranking male, he often does so by soliciting the female with a combination of submissive and invitatory gestures rather than by an outright attack on the male consort. Among gelada, likewise, males attempting to take over reproductive units concentrate on soliciting interactions with the females rather than trying to challenge the incumbent male's hegemony directly (Dunbar 1984). As Chapais points out, such a strategy makes sense because, even if the male is able to defeat and drive off his rival, this in no way guarantees that the females will then transfer their loyalty to him.

The general problem of expressed preferences in a sexual context has important implications for evolutionary processes because it means that low-ranking males may gain fertilizations that they would not be expected to gain on simple "priority-of-access" considerations. On an "all other things being equal" basis, behaviorally dominant males ought to gain a disproportionate share of the matings (and hence of the conceptions) that occur in a given population. Attempts to test the quantitative predictions of "priority-of-access" models with data from primates have, however, shown that even though low-ranking males gain *absolutely* fewer matings than high-ranking individuals, they nonetheless gain many more matings than they ought to (baboons: Hausfater 1975, Strum 1982; macaques: Chapais 1983, Stern and Smith 1984).

Although there are a number of methodological problems that might account for such a poor quantitative fit to prediction, there can be little doubt that in at least some cases the results reflect biological reality. The problem lies in the fact that the theoretical models ignore the effect of female preferences. Studies of several primate species have shown that females often resort to "deceptive" tactics in order to mate with the males of their choice. In a study of captive chimpanzees living in a large wooded enclosure, de Waal (1982) found that females would often go with preferred low-ranking males to secluded parts of the enclosure where they could mate out of sight of the dominant males, who would otherwise attack both the female and the offending male if they caught them associating. Tutin (1979) observed virtually identical behavior in free-living chimpanzees: High-ranking males engaged in promiscuous mating with each and every female as they came into oestrus, but lower-ranking males tended to opt for a longer-lasting consortship with one particular female and to go with her into the forest, where interference by the dominant male(s) was less likely to occur. Similarly, Rasmussen (1985) noted that female baboons who formed consortships with lower-ranking males tended to move with them to the periphery of the troop, where they were less likely to be interrupted by more dominant males.

Social Constraints on Runaway Selection
These particular observations conveniently bring us to the last point I want to discuss, namely the fact that an animal's success in reproducing within these kinds of societies depends on the development of effective social

skills. Its social relationships are necessarily interactive rather than exploi-tative, because social animals are obliged to cooperate if they are to achieve the integrated solutions to the problems of survival and reproduction that social cooperation has to offer.

Communication can be viewed as an attempt to manipulate other con-specifics into behaving in ways that are more beneficial to the communi-cator (Krebs and Dawkins 1984). In socially advanced species, however, an animal's ability to exploit another individual depends in part on that individual's own demands. Thus, success often reduces to the ability to drive a mutually acceptable compromise. A male that cannot persuade a female to mate, for example, will simply fail to reproduce. This is not to say that compromises of this kind do not occur in the normal course of inter-actions among "lower" organisms; it is simply to say that the flexibility of behavior found in birds and mammals (in particular) allows for the evolu-tion of behavior that is both more complex and more subtle. This makes more rapid responses to new developments in behavioral strategy possible, so that the lag between the initiation of a change in gene frequencies and the counterselection against it is likely to be very much shorter. (In some cases, obviously, the response is more or less immediate.) This will clearly tend to stabilize gene frequency distributions in a way that would not normally occur in a purely genetically driven system.

Such behavioral flexibility is, of course, dependent on the existence of highly developed social skills. Anderson and Mason (1978) have shown experimentally that monkeys reared in social isolation are significantly less effective at eliciting coalitionary support in order to gain access to a restricted resource (in this case, a water spout) than animals reared socially. Smuts (1985) compared the behavior and social success of two pairs of male baboons that transferred together into a wild troop. In each case, the more aggressive of the two males tended to scare off the females when he attempted to interact with them; as a result, both of the aggressive males failed to establish any relationships, never succeeded in mating, and even-tually left the troop. In contrast, the more socially adept males succeeded in building up well-meshed relationships with individual females and went on to have successful reproductive careers within the troop. Laboratory studies of macaques (Herbert 1968; Michael et al. 1978) have confirmed that a male's success in mating with females depends on his social finesse because females are hesitant about interacting with overaggressive males. Rather similar results have even been found in studies of lizards (Berry 1974).

Successful meshing of relationships at a behavioral level has been shown repeatedly to be crucial if a relationship is to be productive in terms of reproduction. Kittiwake gull pairs that manage to integrate the timing of egg-brooding duties more closely with each other's foraging needs breed more successfully and tend to remain together for more successive breeding seasons than pairs that are less well integrated (Coulson and Thomas 1983). In the klipspringer (a small monogamous antelope), the male and the female share the task of maintaining watch for predators, usually taking turns while the partner feeds. In newly formed pairs, however, the animals' inexperience results in poor meshing of behavior, with frequent lapses of vigilance when the lookout forgets what it is supposed to be doing and goes off to feed before its partner has finished (Dunbar 1985a). Such poor meshing must inevitably affect the survival (and hence the reproductive prospects) of these individuals. Thus, part of the process of pair bonding is learning to coordinate one's behavior more effectively with that of one's partner.

Runaway selection in favor of certain characteristics that would seem to be reproductively advantageous when viewed in isolation will thus often be counteracted by tendencies for animals that attempt to exploit conspecifics rather than cooperate with them to do less well. In general, animals will be reluctant to risk wasting a reproductive investment that represents a substantial proportion of their potential lifetime reproductive output. A female klipspringer, for example, reproduces for the first time at the age of 2 years and will typically die at age 6. During that time, she will produce one (exceptionally two) offspring each year, so that her expected lifetime reproductive output is only about five. One-third of these animals die before reaching reproductive maturity (R. Dunbar, unpublished data). Thus, a female that loses even one offspring as a result of a wrong decision about the behavioral reliability of a potential mate wastes more than one-fourth of her net contribution to the species' gene pool. So significant a cost to social decisions must surely place a premium on the fine-scale management of relationships. By the same token, no animal can afford to ignore the corresponding requirements of a potential social partner in the pursuit of its own social strategies.

The key point here is that in species as social as most birds and mammals, relationships are *interactive*. These animals are not simply responding to stimuli provided by another object "out there" in the environment; rather, they monitor the behavior of prospective interactees closely in order to ensure that the intended message is being received and understood. A particularly instructive example of this is provided by an experimental study of mating behavior in macaques. In order to study the role that pheromones play in advertising a female's receptivity to a potential male consort, Keverne (1982) blocked males' nasal passages with removable wax plugs that prevented them from receiving olfactory cues. To his surprise, Keverne found that the experimental treatment had almost no effect on the rates of copulation between individual males and females. More detailed observation subsequently revealed that when a male's nasal passages were blocked, he did in fact show significantly less interest in a receptive female. However, when the female became aware that this was the case, she responded by stepping up the rate at which she signaled her receptivity to the male in other ways. In particular, having found that the conventional olfactory signals did not seem to be having the normal effect, she switched channels and made extensive use of other sensory modalities by actively soliciting the male using visual gestures. By adjusting her behavior to the particular context, the female was able to ensure that her message got across to the male.

Some Implications

The theme that I have been developing here has a number of important implications for the way we think about evolutionary processes. The first point to note is that although genes are the correct currency by which to assess the evolutionary significance of a given strategy, they are not necessarily what *causes* evolution to take place. This is simply another way of saying that although it is replicators that get passed on from generation to generation, it is interactors (in Hull's terminology; vehicles in that of Dawkins [1982]) that are responsible for the *patterns* of replication that we see in nature. Because of the constraints operating on organisms (qua interactors), we cannot simply look to see what is best for a given gene and then predict that evolution will inevitably take place in that direction. A gene's likelihood of being replicated depends on how effectively its phenotypic body functions as a unit.

It is the organism that is born, reproduces, and dies, and the frequencies of those events ultimately determine genic evolution, not the gene's own ability to replicate itself. Replication makes it possible for the organism's phenotypic activities to have the evolutionary consequences they have, but it is not what causes those consequences. The theoretical significance of this has been explored by Brandon and Hull in their chapters (see also Dunbar 1982b), so I do not propose to add anything on this score here. The point I do want to make is essentially methodological. It is that if we want to be able to make evolutionary predictions that have more than a random chance of being correct, we need to maintain a clear dichotomy between the gene (or replicator) as the criterion of evolutionary success and the organism (or perhaps more correctly the interactor/vehicle) as the functional element on which selection *acts*.

This problem is compounded when we come to the social vertebrates. Whereas invertebrates might well function in the simple automaton-like way assumed by most evolutionary (and most behavioral) analyses (though I am willing to stand correction on this), the social context in which the higher vertebrates (i.e. birds and mammals) operate introduces an entirely new level of complexity that is completely absent from invertebrate societies so far as we know. No social invertebrate can boast anything that is remotely as complex as the coalitionary behavior found in many higher mammals. This kind of social complexity introduces new constraints that do not exist in any formal sense in invertebrate societies. Of these, the most important is surely the fact that other individuals' preferences can limit the range of options open to an animal: no invertebrate has yet been shown either to have or to express such preferences. This is not to say that we cannot get somewhat (perhaps considerably) closer to understanding the societies of advanced vertebrates by adopting a simplistic genic view of their world. Undoubtedly we can, and such an approach obviously conforms to the best traditions of science in that it proceeds step by step from the simple to the complex. My point is simply that such explanations are only approximations of the first level—heuristic devices (if you like) intended to help us move on more efficiently to the reality beneath the surface. However, to mistake that superficial level for the underlying reality is to have an unnecessarily naive understanding of the nature of biological phenomena.

This raises what is rapidly turning out to be the thorniest issue of the decade in ethology, namely the issue of "cognitive ethology." I have no intention of digressing into a discussion of this issue, however interesting it might be, since it has been explored extensively elsewhere (Griffin 1981, 1982; Dennett 1983). In the present context, I merely want to ask whether the kind of behavioral complexity found among the highest vertebrates is possible if the animals do not themselves do a great deal of their cost-benefit processing on a cognitive plane. This is not, of course, to suggest that they evaluate the evolutionary consequences of their behavior in genic terms (not even humans manage that). But they probably do assess the net gains at a proximate level in terms of indices that are correlated with ultimate genetic fitness. (For a discussion of proximate "rules of thumb" and their relationship to genetic fitness, see McFarland and Houston 1981.) If the answer to my question is Yes (and no one has yet offered convincing evidence for or against it), then we need to bear in mind that this introduces a further causal relationship between genes and behavior that makes the linkage less straightforward than simple one-gene/one-behavior models assume. This issue will not be easily resolved—partly, I suspect, because we are most comfortable when thinking in terms of simple dichotomies (Oyama 1985). The point we need to remember here is that the simple genetic models we use are tools designed to help us ask appropriate questions of nature; they are not intended (or at least they ought not to be intended) as descriptions or even explanations of nature as such.

From an evolutionary point of view, these considerations are most likely to affect the historical process of gene-frequency change by disrupting what would otherwise have been the natural trajectory of a population. I am not at all sure, however, that we can say anything about the *direction* of such disruptions. It seems to me that, in different contexts, such effects could equally well be to slow down the rate of evolution (as when low-ranking animals are able to achieve a higher proportion of conceptions than they would be expected to) *or* to speed it up (because of heightened selection for higher-ranking animals through the reproductive suppression of lower-ranking individuals). Where relatives provide support for one another, the effect will be similar to island effects in that there may be rapid genetic change in favor of those particular genotypes that happen to do well because of accidents of demographic structure in the populations to which they belong. The root of the problem here is that advanced vertebrates generally reproduce rather slowly and live in small population units that are highly structured (at least by comparison with the rather amorphous swarms of most invertebrates). This makes them especially susceptible to statistical sampling effects (Dunbar 1985b). What makes it possible for these species to cope with the uncertainties created by this is their behavioral flexibility at the phenotypic level. And that very flexibility of response will often make it difficult to predict in advance the future evolutionary history of a particular population. Significantly, as Scriven (1959) has pointed out, this does not mean that we cannot arrive at the correct explanation for a past evolutionary change on a postdictive basis.

One particularly important consequence of all this is that it undermines the search for universal traits that has tended to characterize a certain type of sociobiological analysis (e.g. Lumsden and Wilson 1981). Because so much of what higher vertebrates do is context-specific, only the most general rules of thumb will be universal for all members of a given species. These are likely to be limited to a half-dozen rules of thumb (dare one resuscitate the term *drive* once more?) such as "Do whatever is necessary to avoid being hungry, avoid getting hurt, keep warm, and reproduce." Thereafter, the way an organism applies those inherited rules of thumb will be a consequence both of behavioral strategies learned by experience and of the extent to which its cognitive capacities allow it to hypothesize and extrapolate about the future "behavior" of the world in which it lives. This is not to say that genes (as ontogenetic agents) do not have a part to play in the process at all. Clearly they do, though only insofar as they provide the mechanisms necessary for learning by providing a brain of sufficient complexity to perform the necessary calculations. But that does not mean that genes determine behavior in any significant causal sense—or, at least, no more so than it makes sense to claim that the fact that a computer is made out of silicon chips determines the output of its programs. Of course, it may well be that there are genetically inherited propensities to learn particular features of the environment, but there seems to me to be little merit in claiming that such propensities exist when we neither know whether they exist nor need to assume that they do in order to study the evolutionary function of behavior. The extent to which genes are involved in the ontogeny of brains is undoubtedly an interesting question about the evolution of brains. But our interest lies in the adaptive function of behavior, and in these terms it is the evolutionary consequences of behavioral strategies that are of interest rather than their ontogeny.

This in no way obviates the assertion that the replication of genes is what counts in evolution or the assertion that an organism's behavior is geared to genetic evolution. But it does loosen the causal determinacy between genes and future phenotypic behavior. In doing so, it opens the way for a great deal more complexity in the evolutionary process by adding a new link to the equation of biological reproduction. I suspect that we ignore this link at our peril. To be sure, we shall still be able to describe evolutionary changes (as sequences of historical events), but we will often have difficulty trying to explain why these historical sequences took the form they did. If excluding from consideration an organism's behavioral flexibility (and the cognitive processing that this requires) is intended to maintain the objectivity of science, it seems to me that the costs of doing so are so severe as to be counterproductive.

Acknowledgments

I was supported by a University Research Fellowship from the University of Liverpool during the preparation of this chapter. The manuscript greatly benefited from the critical comments of Arthur Cain, Morris Gosling, Henry Plotkin, and Robert Seyfarth.

References

Abbott, D. H. 1984. "Behavioral and Physiological Suppression of Fertility in Subordinate Marmoset Monkeys." *American Journal of Primatology* 6: 169–186.

Altmann, S. A., and J. Altmann. 1979. "Demographic Constraints on Behavior and Social Organization." In *Primate Ecology and Human Origins*, ed. I. Bernstein and E. O. Smith. New York: Garland.

Anderson, C. O., and W. A. Mason. 1978. "Competitive Social Strategies in Groups of Deprived and Experienced Rhesus Monkeys." *Development Psychobiology* 11: 289–299.

Bachmann, C., and H. Kummer. 1980. "Male Assessment of Female Choice in Hamadryas Baboons." *Behavioral Ecology and Sociobiology* 6: 315–321.

Bekoff, M. 1981. "Mammalian Sibling Interactions: Genes, Facilitative Environments, and the Coefficient of Familiarity." In *Parental Care in Mammals*, ed. D. Gubernick and P. Klopfer. New York: Plenum.

Berry, K. H. 1974. "The Ecology and Social Behavior of the Chuckwalla, *Sauromalus obesus obesus* Baird." *University of California Publications on Zoology* 101: 1–60.

Bowman, L. A., S. R. Dilley, and E. B. Keverne. 1978. "Suppression of Oestrogen-Induced

LH Surges by Social Subordination in Talapoin Monkeys." *Nature* 275: 56–58.

Cade, W. 1979. "The Evolution of Alternative Male Reproductive Strategies in Field Crickets." In *Sexual Selection and Reproduction Competition in Insects*, ed. M. S. Blum and N. A. Blum. New York: Academic.

Caldecott, J. O. 1986. *An Ecological and Behavioral Study of the Pig-tailed Macaque*. Basel: Karger.

Chagnon, N. 1982. "Sociodemographic Attributes of Nepotism in Tribal Populations: Man the Rule-Breaker." In *Current Problems in Sociobiology*, ed. King's College Sociobiology Group. Cambridge University Press.

Chapais, B. 1983. "Reproductive Activity in Relation to Male Dominance and the Likelihood of Ovulation in Rhesus Monkeys." *Behavioral Ecology and Sociobiology* 12: 215–228.

Cheney, D., and R. N. Seyfarth. 1983. "Non-Random Dispersal in Free-Ranging Vervet Monkeys: Social and Genetic Consequences." *American Naturalist* 122: 392–412.

Coulson, J. C., and C. Thomas. 1983. "Mate Choice in the Kittiwake Gull." In *Mate Choice*, ed. P. P. G. Bateson. Cambridge University Press.

Datta, S. 1983. "Relative Power and the Maintenance of Dominance." In *Primate Social Relationships*, ed. R. A. Hinde. Oxford: Blackwell.

Dawkins, R. 1982. "Replicators and Vehicles." In *Current Problems in Sociobiology*, ed. King's College Sociobiology Group. Cambridge University Press.

Dennett, D. 1983. "Intentional Systems in Cognitive Ethology. The 'Panglossian Paradigm' Defended." *Behavioral and Brain Sciences* 6: 343–390.

de Ruiter, J. R. 1986. "The Influence of Group Size on Predator Scanning and Foraging Behavior of Wedgecapped Capuchin Monkeys (*Cebus olivaceus*)." *Behavior* 98: 240–258.

de Waal, F. 1982. *Chimpanzee Politics*. London: Allen and Unwin.

Dunbar, R. I. M. 1979. "Population Demography, Social Organization, and Mating Strategies." In *Primate Ecology and Human Origins*, ed. I. Bernstein and E. O. Smith. New York: Garland.

Dunbar, R. I. M. 1982a. "Intraspecific Variations in Mating Strategy." In *Perspectives in Ethology*, volume 5, ed. P. Klopfer and P. Bateson. New York: Plenum.

Dunbar, R. I. M. 1982b. "Adaptation, Fitness, and the Evolutionary Tautology." In *Current Problems in Sociobiology*, ed. King's College Sociobiology Group. Cambridge University Press.

Dunbar, R. I. M. 1984. *Reproductive Decisions: An Economic Analysis of Gelada Baboon Social Strategies*. Princeton University Press.

Dunbar, R. I. M. 1985a. "Monogamy on the Rocks." *Natural History* 94, no. 11: 40–47.

Dunbar, R. I. M. 1985b. "Population Consequences of Social Structure." In *Behavioral Ecology*, ed. R. M. Sibley and R. H. Smith. Oxford: Blackwell.

Dunbar, R. I. M. 1986. "The Social Ecology of Gelada Baboons." In *Ecological Aspects of Social Evolution*, ed. D. Rubenstein and R. W. Wrangham. Princeton University Press.

Dunbar, R. I. M. 1987. *Primate Social Systems*. Ithaca, N.Y.: Cornell University Press.

Dunbar, R. I. M., and J. H. Crook. 1975. "Aggression and Dominance in the Weaver Bird, *Quelea quelea*." *Animal Behavior* 23: 450–459.

Dunbar, R. I. M., and M. Sharman. 1983. "Female Competition for Access to Males Affects Birth Rate in Baboons." *Behavioral Ecology and Sociobiology* 13: 157–159.

Dunbar, R. I. M., D. M. Buckland, and D. Miller. 1988. Mating Strategies of Male Feral Goats. In preparation.

Estes, R. D. 1974. "Social Organisation of the African Bovidae." In *The Behavior of Ungulates and Its Relation to Management*, volume 1, ed. V. Geist and F. R. Walther. Morges, Switzerland: IUCN Publications.

Garber, P. A., L. Moya, and C. Malaga. 1984. "A Preliminary Field Study of the Moustached Tamarin Monkey (*Saguinus mystax*) in Northwestern Peru: Questions Concerned with the Evolution of a Communal Breeding System." *Folia Primatologica* 42: 17–33.

Gosling, L. M. 1986. "The Evolution of Mating Strategies in Male Antelopes." In *Ecological Aspects of Social Evolution*, ed. D. Rubenstein and R. Wrangham. Princeton University Press.

Griffin, D. R. 1981. *The Question of Animal Awareness*. Second edition. Los Altos, Calif.: Kaufmann.

Griffin, D. R., ed. 1982. *Animal Mind—Human Mind*: Springer-Verlag.

Hamilton, W. D. 1964. "The Genetical Evolution of Social Behaviour I, II." *Journal of Theoretical Biology* 7: 1–52.

Harcourt, A. H. 1987. "Social Influences on Competitive Ability." In *Comparative Socioecology of Mammals and Man*, ed. V. Standen and R. Foley. Oxford: Blackwell.

Hausfater, G. 1975. *Dominance and Reproduction in Baboons (Papio cynocephalus)*. Basel: Karger.

Hegner, R. E., S. T. Emlen, and N. J. DeMong. 1982. "Spatial Organisation of the White-Fronted Bee-Eater." *Nature* 298: 264–266.

Herbert, J. 1968. "Sexual Preference in the Rhesus Monkey (*Macaca mulatta*) in the Laboratory." *Animal Behavior* 16: 120–128.

Jarman, M. 1979. *Impala Social Behavior: Territory, Hierarchy, Mating and Use of Space*. Berlin: Parey.

Kaplan, J. R. 1978. "Fight Interference and Altruism in Rhesus Monkeys." *American Journal of Physical Anthropology* 49: 241–250.

Kawai, M., R. I. M. Dunbar, H. Ohsawa, and U. Mori. 1983. "Social Organisation of Gelada Baboons: Social Units and Definitions." *Primates* 24: 1–13.

Keverne, E. B. 1982. "Olfaction and the Reproductive Behaviour of Nonhuman Primates." In *Primate Communication*, ed. C. T. Snowdon, C. H. Brown, and M. R. Petersen. Cambridge University Press.

Kleiman, D. 1977. "Monogamy in Mammals." *Quarterly Review of Biology* 52: 39–69.

Krebs, J. R., and R. Dawkins. 1984. "Animal Signals: Mind-Reading and Manipulation." In *Behavioral Ecology*, ed. J. R. Krebs and N. B. Davies. Second edition. Oxford: Blackwell.

Kruuk, H. 1972. *The Spotted Hyaena*. University of Chicago Press.

Kummer, H. 1967. "Tripartite Relations in Baboons." In *Social Communication among Primates*, ed. S. A. Altmann. University of Chicago Press.

Kummer, H. 1971. *Primate Societies*. Chicago: Aldine.

Kummer, H. 1975. "Rules of Dyad and Group Formation among Captive Gelada Baboons (*Theropithecus gelada*)." In *Proceedings of the Fifth Congress of the International Primatological Society*, ed. S. Kondo, M. Kawai, A. Ehara, and S. Kawamura. Tokyo: Japan Science Press.

Kummer, H. 1984. "From Laboratory to Desert and Back: A Social System of Hamadryas Baboons." *Animal Behavior* 32: 965–971.

Kummer, H., W. Gotz, and W. Angst. 1974. "Triadic Differentiation: An Inhibitory Process Protecting Pair Bonds in Baboons." *Behavior* 40: 62–87.

Lumsden, C. J., and E. O. Wilson. 1981. *Genes, Mind, and Culture: The Coevolutionary Process*. Cambridge, Mass.: Harvard University Press.

McFarland, D. J., and A. I. Houston. 1981. *Quantitative Ethology: State Space Approach*. Oxford: Pitman.

Michael, R. P., R. W. Bonsall, and D. Zumpe. 1978. "Consort Bonding and Operant Behaviour by Female Rhesus Monkeys." *Journal of Comparative Physiology and Psychology* 92: 837–845.

Mitchell, B., D. McCowan, and I. A. Nicholson. 1976. "Annual Cycles of Body Weight and Condition in Scottish Red Deer, *Cervus elaphus*." *Journal of Zoology (London)* 180: 107–127.

Moss, C. J., and J. H. Poole. 1983. "Relationships and Social Structure of African Elephants." In *Primate Social Relationships*, ed. R. A. Hinde. Oxford: Blackwell.

Nishida, T. 1983. "Alpha Status and Agonistic Alliance in Wild Chimpanzees (*Pan troglodytes schweinfurthii*)." *Primates* 24: 318–336.

Oyama, S. 1985. *The Ontogeny of Information*. Cambridge University Press.

Packer, C., and A. E. Pusey. 1982. "Cooperation and Competition within Coalitions of Male Lions: Kin Selection or Game Theory?" *Nature* 296: 740–742.

Rasmussen, K. R. L. 1985. "Changes in the Activity Budgets of Yellow Baboons (*Papio cynocephalus*) during Sexual Consortships." *Behavioral Ecology and Sociobiology* 17: 161–170.

Riss, D., and J. Goodall. 1977. "The Recent Rise to the Alpha-Rank in a Population of Free-Living Chimpanzees." *Folia Primatologica* 27: 134–151.

Robertson, J. M. Y. 1986. On the Evolution of Pig-tailed Macaque Societies. Ph.D. thesis, Cambridge University.

Rubenstein, D. I. 1980. "On the Evolution of Alternative Mating Strategies." In *Limits to Action: The Allocation of Individual Behavior*, ed. J. E. R. Staddon. New York: Academic.

Sade, D., K. Cushing P. Cushing, J. Donald, A. Figueroa, J. Kaplan, C. Lauer, D. Rhodes, and J. Schneider. 1976. "Population Dynamics in Relation to Social Structure on Cayo Santiago." *Yearbook of Physical Anthropology* 20: 253–262.

Schaller, G. B. 1972. *The Serengeti Lion*. University of Chicago Press.

Scriven, M. 1959. "Explanation and Prediction in Evolutionary Theory." *Science* 130: 477–482.

Seyfarth, R. N. 1977. "A Model of Social Grooming among Adult Female Monkeys." *Journal of Theoretical Biology* 65: 671–698.

Sharman, M., and R. I. M. Dunbar. 1982. "Observer Bias in Selection of Study Group Size in Baboon Field Studies." *Primates* 23: 567–573.

Smuts, B. B. 1985. *Sex and Friendship in Baboons*. New York: Aldine.

Stacey, P. B. 1986. "Group Size and Foraging Efficiency in Yellow Baboons." *Behavioral Ecology and Sociobiology* 18: 175–187.

Stern, B. R., and D. G. Smith. 1984. "Sexual Behavior and Paternity in Three Captive Groups of Rhesus Monkeys (*Macaca mulatta*)." *Animal Behavior* 32: 23–32.

Strum, S. C. 1982. "Agonistic Dominance in Male Baboons: An Alternative View." *International Journal of Primatology* 3: 175–202.

Tutin, C. E. G. 1979. "Mating Patterns and Reproductive Strategies in a Community of Wild Chimpanzees." *Behavioral Ecology and Sociobiology* 6: 29–38.

van Schaik, C. P. 1983. "Why Are Diurnal Primates Living in Groups?" *Behaviour* 87: 120–144.

van Schaik, C. P., M. A. van Noordwijk, R. J. de Boer, and I. den Tonkelaar. 1983. "The Effects of Group Size on Time Budgets and Social Behaviour in Wild Long-Tailed Macaques (*Macaca fascicularis*)." *Behavioral Ecology and Sociobiology* 13: 173–181.

Waser, P. M. 1977. "Feeding, Ranging and Group Size in the Mangabey, *Cercocebus albigena*." In *Primate Ecology*, ed. T. H. Clutton-Brock. London: Academic.

Wasser, S. K., and D. P. Barash. 1983. "Reproductive Suppression among Female Mammals: Implications for Biomedicine and Sexual Selection Theory." *Quarterly Review of Biology* 58: 513–538.

Wells, K. D. 1978. "Territoriality in the Green Frog (*Rana clamitans*): Vocalisations and Agonistic Behavior." *Animal Behavior* 26: 1051–1063.

Wirtz, P. 1982. "Territory Holders, Satellite Males and Bachelor Males in a High-Density

Population of Waterbuck (*Kobus ellipsiprymnus*) and Their Associations with Conspecifics." *Zeitschrift für Tierpsychologie* 58: 277–300.

Wrangham, R. W. 1981. "Drinking Competition in Vervet Monkeys." *Animal Behavior* 29: 904–910.

Wrangham, R. W. 1982. "Mutualism, Kinship and Social Evolution." In *Current Problems in Sociobiology*, ed. King's College Sociobiology Group. Cambridge University Press.

Wrangham, R. W., and B. B. Smuts. 1980. "Sex Differences in the Behavioural Ecology of Chimpanzees in the Gombe National Park, Tanzania." *Journal of Reproductive Fertility* suppl. 28: 13–31.

Zimen, E. 1976. "On the Regulation of Pack Size in Wolves." *Zeitschrift für Tierpsychologie* 40: 300–341.

Contributors

Robert N. Brandon
Department of Philosophy, Duke University

R. I. M. Dunbar
Department of Anthropology, University College London

David L. Hull
Department of Philosophy, Northwestern University

F. J. Odling-Smee
Department of Applied Biology, Brunel University

H. C. Plotkin
Department of Psychology, University College London

Name Index

Subject Index